THE ELEGANT OAKEY

This steel engraving, made from a photograph of A. Oakey Hall by Sarony, shows him shortly before he became Mayor of New York City. It presents him at his elegant best. His troubles were yet to come.

The Elegant OAKEY

by

Croswell Bowen

New York
Oxford University Press
1956

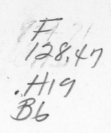

© 1956 by Croswell Bowen

Library of Congress Catalogue Card Number: 56-10456

Printed in the United States of America

This Book Is Dedicated to

My Brother

William Dougherty Bowen

A Rather Elegant Gentleman Himself

CONTENTS

1. The Burdell Murder Case   3
2. Young Man in a Hurry   17
3. Mayor Hall and Mr. Tweed   37
4. 'The Elegant Oakey'   70
5. The Tweed Ring Exposure   87
6. First Grand Jury Testimony   118
7. The Riot of the Aldermen   144
8. Indictment and First Trial   155
9. The Second Trial   171
10. The Third Trial   188
11. Hall Goes on the Stage   198
12. The Disappearance of Oakey Hall   211
13. Oakey Hall in London   227
14. The Suit Against Bryce   249
15. The Long Decline   264
Acknowledgments and Bibliography   279
Index   287

THE ELEGANT OAKEY

1

THE BURDELL MURDER CASE

I

In its 167-year-old history Tammany Hall has had as candidates for Mayor of New York a fair number of eminently respectable men, some of them possessing marked administrative ability. It has also won and lost with a good many run-of-the-mill party hacks, some dolts, and several first-class zanies. According to a present-day district leader its ideal is somewhat intricate, without being subtle. 'The Hall,' he declared, 'is always looking for a candidate who is respectable, entertaining to the public, and politically reliable.' The last two of these qualifications have not been hard to come by. It is contemplation of the first — in combination with the others — that has often filled Tammany council rooms with stale smoke.

In the fall of 1868, Tammany chose as its candidate — a procedure it has often followed — the District Attorney of New York County, an amiable, easy-going, compliant man named A. Oakey Hall, a graduate of New York University who had attended Harvard Law School and was well read without being scholarly. He wrote dreadful plays and execrable poetry, and contributed to many newspapers and

3

magazines. He was a member of nine New York clubs, including what the *Times* referred to as 'all the higher clubs,' and was often referred to as the best-dressed man in town. He was undoubtedly the best-dressed chief magistrate the town has ever had. Jimmy Walker, the last of the sartorially resplendent mayors, being complimented one day by reporters at City Hall — he had just appeared in a new suit with slanted pockets in the jacket, his own idea — waved all praise away. 'I don't even compare,' he declared with feeling, 'to the way the Elegant Oakey used to dress.'

'The Elegant Oakey,' — such was the title by which Hall was known to his contemporaries; with reason, as will amply appear. He was a slim, blue-eyed man with a high-bridged, generous nose, a well-waved head of plentiful black hair, a General Grant beard, and wore pince-nez from which a black ribbon dropped like a plummet through the leaves of a luxuriant bow-tie, to be lost in the dazzling depths of a stiff shirt. He had the look of a professor — benign, knowledgeable, and full of jokes which, in his case, were chiefly puns.

Politically, Hall was handicapped, at first, by the fact that some of his ancestors were English — an almost fatal blemish in the eyes of the Irish voters, who predominated. But he had a trump card. He claimed descent, on his mother's side, from Colonel John Okey, one of the regicides of Charles I, who was later hanged and quartered at Tyburn under Charles II. Hall saw to it that this noteworthy item in his background was frequently included in newspaper stories about him. Colonel Okey's existence in the family tree provided him with both ancient lineage and a thoroughly democratic background. The Irish community, on its side, looked with considerable favor on a man who could point to an ancestor who had helped to judge and execute an English king. When Hall was elected Mayor, Okey's portrait was installed in his City Hall office.

4

Another handicap had been that he was one of those whom the New York *World* termed 'the respectabilities.' He was not only socially acceptable himself, but he was married to a socially prominent woman, the former Katherine Louise Barnes. Hall and his wife lived in a brownstone house on Forty-second Street between Fifth and Sixth Avenues, opposite the reservoir that later became the site of the Public Library and Bryant Park. They spent their summers on a pleasant estate called Valley View in what is now Short Hills, New Jersey. They had six children. The family was included in the forerunner of the *Social Register,* 'The List.'

Hall's public career came close to being entirely destroyed in 1857 as a result of the Burdell murder case and its fantastic sequel. In one of his many well-filled scrapbooks he wrote above the first clipping dealing with this case: 'I was made a victim to popular passion' — i.e. he was not re-elected District Attorney for the following term. In 1862, when he ran again, people had forgotten all about the Burdell case, and he won. It might have been better for him had his public career stopped there. The Burdell case found him facing, as prosecutor, an opponent of great skill, Henry Lauren Clinton. who was later to prosecute him for his alleged part in the Tweed Ring plunders.

II

The facts in the Burdell murder case read like an overwritten Victorian melodrama. On the morning of 31 January 1857, Mary Donohue, a housemaid at Mrs. Cunningham's 'Select Boarding House for Gentlemen' at 31 Bond Street, rushed screaming into the dining room to announce in an Irish brogue edged with hysteria that Dr. Burdell had been 'murdered something terrible.' He had. His office boy had just found him 'surrounded with blood'; it was later ascertained that there were fifteen wounds, any of which would have been fatal. All had been inflicted by 'a dirk or sharp instrument.' Burdell's office was in the house, which he owned, and it was considered very remarkable that no one had heard the slightest sound even though it was apparent that a fierce struggle must have take place between the victim and his slayer in the dead of night. In addition to Mrs. Emma Augusta Cunningham and her two daughters, Augusta, 18, and Helen, 16, the inmates were: George V. Snodgrass, 20, son of a noted clergyman; Daniel Ullmann, a lawyer; John J. Eckel, a permanent lodger; and two servant girls.

As soon as Mrs. Cunningham heard the news, she set up a wail. 'Poor, darling Harvey!' she exclaimed. 'He is dead, and once more I am a widow.' This news came as a surprise to everybody, especially the doctor's relatives, who knew them as mortal enemies. She had complained to a number of people that he had brought females into the house 'for improper purposes.' He had told his relatives that her lease on his house was up on 1 May, and out she was going on that date. In fact, the dentist hated Mrs. Cunningham so much that he refused to eat her meals, going instead to a Broadway hotel. The servants reported that their quarrels had been loud and abusive. They had sued and counter-sued each other in the courts.

At the coroner's inquest, Mrs. Cunningham said that she and Dr. Burdell had been married on 28 October 1856 at the home of the Rev. Uriah Marvin, minister of the Dutch Reformed Church on Bleecker Street. The minister, while admitting that he had married Mrs. Cunningham, a widow, said he couldn't remember much about the man who had been with her. The condition of Dr. Burdell's body, when Marvin was taken to the morgue to view it, made identification by him impossible.

The coroner, after learning this disheartening piece of

news, took another tack in his questioning and asked him how the bride looked at her wedding. The minister was puzzled and the coroner said, 'Did she have any virgin, angel blushes? Was she like a virtuous woman, or a woman of easy virtue?'

'You must remember,' the minister replied, 'that she described herself as a widow.'

Mary Donohue, the hysterical housemaid, told the coroner that Mrs. Cunningham had said 'it was time he [Dr. Burdell] was out of this world, for he was not fit to live in it, or something like that. Her eldest daughter, Augusta, said the same; she said he was a bad man.' The coroner took a dim view of Mary's testimony and told her, 'I knew, Mary, I knew that you carried your tail behind you, by gracious.'

With the case occupying most of the columns of the newspapers, Mrs. Cunningham applied through her counsel, Henry Lauren Clinton, for a widow's share of Dr. Burdell's estate. Samuel J. Tilden, representing the dentist's relatives, opposed this move. He, too, was to play an important role in Hall's career. The coroner's jury brought in a verdict that Mrs. Cunningham and John J. Eckel, lodger, 'were principals in the commission of said murder,' and it was up to Hall, as District Attorney, to prosecute the case.

'It was assumed,' according to Clinton's own account, 'that she (Mrs. Cunningham) procured someone to simulate Dr. Burdell at the marriage ceremony; that she was guilty of cold-blooded . . . deliberate, long-premeditated, fiendish murder, in order to gratify an insatiate greed for money. The coroner appeared to imbibe the same belief . . .'

III

The trial opened on Monday, 4 May 1857, in the Court of Oyer and Terminer of the City and County of New York. The Hon. Henry E. Davies, Supreme Court judge, presided.

Mrs. Cunningham was dressed in black bombazine and sat between her two pretty daughters. Clinton, her counsel, was a distinguished looking, sharp-eyed lawyer whose beard was trimmed like that of President Harrison. Hall, the prosecutor, reveled in his role of best-dressed District Attorney, and appeared to be enjoying the attention the case was receiving. There was only one thing to mar his pleasure. The newspapers, which had been clamoring for the indictment of Mrs. Cunningham, were now sympathetic to the 'poor widow.' In his opening to the jury, Hall took account of this. He soared, oratorically. He warned that Mrs. Cunningham was 'demanding by her looks the sympathy which belongs, not to a murderess, but to a woman.'

'We shall mince no words before you, gentlemen,' he declared. 'Crime has no sex. . . . You are not here to judge the woman but the crime . . . When we remember the mother of our prayers, when we remember the sister of our household adoration, when we remember the wife of our life until death, when we remember the children who are to be future women of the world, that sit upon our knee, and we feel as we look upon young girlhood and growing maidenhood, we say, can it ever be that this being, upon whom God Almighty has put his own seal of purity, should ever live to be the perpetrator of crime, the midnight assassin, to cherish hate and revenge and jealousy? And yet, when we open the book of history we are forced to come to the conviction that crime knows no sex.' He now drew upon his reading: 'The name of Messalina has become an historical word; and Fulvia, when the head of Cicero was brought to her, she spat upon it, drew from her bosom, which had nourished children, a bodkin, and drove it through the tongue until it quivered; and the same dramatist who speaks about the wife of William Tell will speak of her who foreswore the very maidenhood purity of her name — Agnes, Queen of Hungary, who bathed her feet in the blood of sixty-three knights, and said, "It seems as if I were wading in May dew." '

He touched on the relationship between the accused woman and the dead man: 'She had known him three years, and she said he was the father of a child who never saw the light. She was his mistress, though she claimed to be his wife.' He mentioned their quarrels: 'The domestics will tell you how she hunted and haunted him. Police officers we shall bring to you, that came from the street at his bidding to settle the quarrels that clustered around him. A police officer who came there in September and saw this woman strike him; other officers who came in later, who heard her asserverate that she was his wife by every tie on earth — morally perhaps she was, and morally perhaps she is. . . . And there came to the house one day he who sits in Court — a man that neither you nor I would quarrel with. The greedy, lustful eyes of this woman-fiend were fastened upon him, and by the evidence in this case — irresistible, and not to be confuted — he became, in one story, the counterpart of him who had been her paramour on the story below. And she did love him — she did love him, this man Eckel; and she, the mother of daughters who were themselves candidates for marriage, fastened her greedy, lustful eyes upon him. I have nothing now to say of him. Let him be taken care of hereafter. But this we must not forget in this case, as step by step there is progression, that whether she was the wife of the murdered man or his former mistress, in either case she was alike guilty of the grossest infidelity in her conduct with him who occupied the apartment adjoining her own. He had made up his mind that life to him was useless so long as he had this shadow at his side, and he had made up his mind to let that house, of which she was the tenant and he the landlord, to another person. And she heard of it. She saw that which was going on, and, gentle-

9

men, on the very night before the murder, the very respectable lady who was to have become the tenant of that house for the year commencing last Friday was going through the house, meeting the servants, and, seeing her going out, she still, though he was absent, pursuing him, comes down before one of these domestics and says: "Hannah" (which was the name of the cook), "what was that woman doing here?"

‘ "Why, madam, she was looking through the house."

‘ "Is she going to take this house?"

‘ "Yes; they've been looking all around in the kitchen."

‘ "Is Dr. Burdell going to let this house to her?"

‘ "Yes; it looks so."

'Then she said — and the woman of the world would not have said what fell from her lips — "Before tomorrow morning he shall be a corpse," or "He may be a corpse" . . . on that very night the deed was done.'

Hall told the jury that she had asked Mr. Ullmann, when he was going out, what time he would return; he replied 'about midnight.' Young Snodgrass was asleep. One domestic had gone; the other, the cook, had deposed that Mrs. Cunningham, with Eckel present, had ordered her to bed — 'a thing she had seldom done before.' He came now to the victim: 'He comes in alone; his apartments are entirely secluded and locked up; she has the pass-key, and she alone, to the front room where his bedroom was . . . every particle of mortal injury which was done to that man was done in the briefest possible space of time. Wherever struck, which is for you to find out hereafter from the testimony, whether in a sitting posture by the fire, taking off his shoes, whether in throwing off his shawl, by someone who met him at the door, who had a pass-key, and who had entrance, and who could wait for him; but whether struck there or here, this one damning fact will come out, that whoever struck that [first] blow was probably a left-handed woman; and she, left-handed, carefully watched in the prison to see it, and the domestics of the family swearing so . . . he fought, no doubt, with the desperation of a whole army; and he fought with the whole army of miserable, festering hates which cluster in a woman's heart.

Heaven hath no rage like love to hatred turned.
And hell no fury like a woman scorned.

Scorned she had been — scorned to her acquaintances, scorned to her face, scorned to her domestics.'

Hall had a great deal to say about Mrs. Cunningham's behavior on the morning of 31 January: 'Word is brought to her by the inmates of the house and the neighbors that Dr. Burdell is dead. He is dead; they tell her so. What, gentlemen, is the instinct of the man or the woman, not to say the wife or relative, or even the friend? There is one of two things — either the fainting and the unconsciousness at the dreadful news, or the rushing to see if it be true. She was ready to act her own part. She does not go down; she has her great apparent agitation, but no redness of the eyes of any consequence; and when Dr. Main comes in and says, "Dr. Burdell is dead," she says, "Oh! I am so glad to hear that . . . for I thought he was murdered," and almost instantly, "I have a dreadful secret to tell you," she says to this one and that one, and out comes the marriage certificate; "my name is Emma Augusta Burdell; I was married to the doctor; here is my certificate." No going down yet to see whether he were dead or murdered, but moving about the room, spasmodical in one corner, calm in the next, theatrically tearing her hair in another place — the same feelings in her breast that were there on that night when the coroner sent up to examine her as a witness, and she said, "I won't come unless I have counsel." Why, what has this woman to do with counsel?'

11

IV

What Mrs. Cunningham had to do with counsel was shortly made abundantly clear. In counsel, whether she was innocent or guilty, lay her refuge, and in Henry Lauren Clinton lay her deliverance. She had chosen wisely. Clinton had served in many capital cases; he deprecated Hall's oratory, and read aloud the laws of evidence. Where Hall had aroused the jury — and, indeed, the city — against his client, Clinton now began to turn the tide. He struck at official brutality, always a good gambit in a court of law. His audience was electrified — and shocked. Mrs. Cunningham had been examined for scratches. 'In defiance of law — in defiance of humanity — in defiance of common decency,' Clinton thundered, 'her person was examined! Yes, there were men, under the control of the coroner, at 31 Bond Street, who perpetrated this foul outrage! Suspected as she was, had the examination been conducted with decency, and by *her own sex*, we never would have expressed the first word of complaint.' The court rocked. 'The result is such,' Clinton continued, 'that we are bound to introduce it here, as showing her innocence.' As for the absence of noise the night of the murder, he told the jury that he himself had stood in the murder room and screamed 'Murder!' at the top of his lungs, without being heard by an assistant upstairs. As for the door and the pass-key, he had a locksmith testify that Burdell's door would open on a push, without a key, whether locked or unlocked. As for motive, Burdell had plenty of enemies in the outraged husbands and brothers of the victims of his amorous propensities. When Clinton, however, tried to make something of the fact that Mrs. Cunningham and her two daughters had sung a hymn on the morning following the murder, the words of which began,

> God moves in a mysterious way
> His wonders to perform,

Hall immediately made this testimony the excuse to recite a hymn which, he said, was 'an appropriate one for the other side and their witnesses.' Mercifully, it was short:

> Hark from the Tombs a doleful sound,
> Thine ears attend the cry;
> Ye living men, come view the ground
> Where ye must shortly lie.

As the trial neared its close, Clinton asked the prosecution to list the principal points of law on which the conviction of Mrs. Cunningham rested. Hall turned over this phase of the trial to Charles Edwards, who was acting for the Attorney General of the State of New York. Edwards felt called upon to try his hand at versifying by changing the words of the hymn Mrs. Cunningham and her daughters had sung. 'That was not the hymn she sang,' Edwards said. 'It was to the same tune; but the words must have been:

> Woman moves in a mysterious way
> Her wonders to perform.'

Judge Davies' charge to the jury was fair and dispassionate. But after reviewing the evidence, he said: 'To your decision I now commit the fate of this unfortunate woman, and the future of herself and her family. While you deal justly by her, it is your privilege also to deal mercifully; for, as I have before remarked, if you have any reasonable doubt of her guilt, that doubt is to be cast into the scale in her favor, and entitles her to your verdict of acquittal. If, on the contrary, on a review of the whole case, you deem the charge contained in the indictment proven, it is your duty to your country and your God to say so, though it be with anguish of heart, and may cause deep shame and sorrow to others. But if, in this final reviewing, you are not satisfied of her guilt, pronounce a verdict of acquittal, and let the accused go free.' It was a mandate. The jury retired, and returned in a few minutes with a verdict of 'Not guilty.' The prosecution of Eckel was abandoned. In his own account of the trial, Clinton asserts his complete faith in Mrs. Cunningham's innocence.

V

The sequel proved stranger than the trial itself. Mrs. Cunningham may not have been a murderess, but she had no scruples about fraud. In attempting to perpetrate it she raised the curtain on a fatal flaw in the character of Hall as a public man: his love of drama and his lack of restraint.

Mrs. Cunningham and her two daughters moved back into 31 Bond Street. As the summer wore on, Mrs. Cunningham appeared about to have a baby. In July, she had a series of talks with Dr. David Uhl about her coming accouchement which, she told him, would result in the birth of Dr. Burdell's child. Dr. Uhl easily ascertained that she was not going to have a baby, Dr. Burdell's or anyone else's, and went to see Hall about it. Hall told him to string her along. Finally, she got around to suggesting to Dr. Uhl that if he would provide her with a child and say it was hers, she would give him a thousand dollars. Dr. Uhl was really frightened now but Hall reassured him, getting one of his raffish friends, the same Dr. John de la Montagnie, of Fishkill, for whom he had named his first child, to make arrangements for the fake accouchement.

Hall stopped all his other work to enter into this new dramatic production. He was anxious to justify his prosecution of Mrs. Cunningham. He provided 'a cart load of olla podrida furniture' for the room at 190 Elm Street to which Mrs. Cunningham was to come for her 'newly born' child. Dr. Uhl had told her that a California lady would be willing to give her a child she was about to have as a result of having been indiscreet while her husband was prospecting for gold.

Mrs. Cunningham was delighted with the plan. One of the props for this phase of the production was a suitcase Hall provided which belonged to his wife. Because it bore the initials K.L.H., Hall arranged for Dr. de la Montagnie to take the name Karl L. Herwig. On the appointed day Dr. de la Montagnie went to Bellevue Hospital and borrowed a baby girl of 'a poor woman' named Mrs. Elizabeth Ann Anderson. He took the baby to the room on Elm Street, where a messenger from Mrs. Cunningham picked it up in a basket Hall had provided and took it to Mrs. Cunningham's house at 31 Bond Street. There, Dr. Uhl and another medico, a Dr. Catlin of Brooklyn, assisted at a fake accouchement. Dr. Catlin, who was apparently interested only in accepting a thousand dollars, was promptly arrested as he left the house. Hall and Police Inspector Dilks then walked into Mrs. Cunningham's room, and Dilks took the baby out of her arms. 'Don't touch my baby,' she shouted and then said: 'This is the child of Harvey Burdell.' She was immediately arrested under a statute making it a felony to pretend to have a child who would be entitled to inherit property. But the charge did not stick, and the case was not prosecuted.

Hall was criticized in the papers for having staged the circumstances which made it possible for her to break the law, acting in a sense as an *agent provocateur*. Clinton, again defending Mrs. Cunningham, was furious. He later wrote that he gave up the case because she 'sank herself so deeply in moral degradation that it was beyond the power of her counsel and friends to resurrect her had they been so disposed . . . The public career of Mrs. Cunningham Burdell began with the most startling and thrilling tragedy; it ended in thoroughly disgusting low comedy.'

Nothing daunted, Hall wrote a farce called *The Coroner's Inquest,* which was a burlesque of what had taken place at the inquest of Dr. Burdell. It was played as a curtain-raiser on a benefit night at Burton's New Theatre, Broadway 'opposite Bond Street,' and was subsequently published in Samuel French's 'Minor Drama' series.

The enormous labors involved in the Burdell case, plus those which Hall gratuitously assumed, kept him from home a great deal, as several letters from his children show. Cara wrote, in penciled block letters, in January 1857: 'My dear Papa I love you very much and I am very glad you are coming home and I, wish you would, come soon, for I, want to, see you. [The commas are hers.] Alice sends her love to you Your Cara.' Maria Theresa wrote at the same time: 'My dear Papa I wish I could see you I send you my love and I think I would like to have you come home your little Theresa.'

They sounded dictated.

2

YOUNG MAN IN A HURRY

I

ABRAHAM OAKEY HALL WAS BORN 26 July 1826 in Albany, New York. His father was Morgan James Hall, son of William Hall, a carpenter from Hampshire, England, and Mary Morgan, of Wales, who had emigrated to America 'for political reasons' and settled in New York City. His mother was Elsie Lansing Oakey, the daughter of Abraham Oakey, Deputy Treasurer of the State of New York for twenty-five years, and Alicia d'Assignie Oakey, a refugee Huguenot countess. A strong attachment to his mother is evident throughout the life and career of Abraham Oakey Hall. Elsie Lansing Hall was a woman of strong character combining, it was said, the charm of her aristocratic French mother and the somewhat sterner heritage of her English Puritan forebears. A genealogical note by a member of the Oakey family states that she and her husband were in New Orleans when the time of her confinement drew near, and in order to have her children — twins — born under her father's roof she made the long journey to Albany, alone, in midsummer. There, in her father's house on State Street, was born the

17

future Mayor of New York; his twin, a girl, died shortly after birth. Years later, during his political campaigns, Oakey Hall forestalled taunts about his not being 'a native New Yorker, born and raised,' by telling his audiences: 'I was born in transit, but barring the accident, as Samuel Lever says about St. Patrick, I think I am entitled to be called a New York boy.'

Mrs. Hall, with her son, now rejoined her husband in New Orleans, where he had set up a wholesale grocery business under the firm name of Hall and Kemp. He had been enabled to do this through the assistance of Mrs. Hall's brother, Samuel Oakey, who about the year 1819, before his twenty-first birthday, had emigrated to the Crescent City to make his fortune. It is just possible that Morgan James Hall met his future bride through Samuel Oakey, for both had been employed by the New York firm of Chandler Starr & Co., dry goods merchants. Samuel had prospered, and was fast becoming a man of wealth and power in cotton. He was to become an officer of the New Orleans Chamber of Commerce and president of the Exchange. A Southern contemporary has described him as 'a man of courtly and knightly bearing with a love of the drama and a taste for military display' — attributes which were not to be lost on his young nephew. Generous and eccentric, Samuel became famous in the Crescent City for having killed an English cotton buyer named Wright who had written articles in the Vicksburg *Sentinel* accusing the cotton factors of unfair business practices. Samuel Oakey took it on himself to become the champion of all the New Orleans factors. He challenged Wright to a duel. The challenge was accepted — a gentleman could do no less in those days. Wright had some skill with the rifle, and chose it as his weapon. Oakey, who had never handled any sort of firearm, was undaunted. The duelists faced each other at a distance of sixty yards. Oakey's second handed him a yager, afterwards known as the Mississippi rifle, and showed him how to manipulate the bolt. When the signal was given, Wright fired hurriedly and, as it proved, wildly. Samuel, however, calmly raised his rifle, took deliberate aim, and shot the cotton buyer through the heart. The duel colored the rest of his life. He assumed the title of 'Colonel,' had an elaborate uniform made up for himself, and claimed command of a non-existent regiment, 'The Bloody Forty-ninth.' When celebrities visited New Orleans, he was often on hand to greet them, dressed in full military regalia, on behalf of himself and his 'regiment.' Nobody in New Orleans seemed to mind, but it sometimes puzzled the celebrities.

In the summer of 1830, while traveling North on business, Morgan James Hall was removed from his ship at Charleston, South Carolina, a dying man. Unknown to himself, he had contracted yellow fever in one of the recurrent epidemics New Orleans was subject to. He died in Charleston. To escape the epidemic, his wife had removed to the country above New Orleans; there she gave birth to a second child, Marcia d'Assignie Hall. After the burial of her husband in New Orleans, she took her two children to New York, where her husband's parents still lived. As she was left with little or no property, she did what apparently all New York City widows did at the time to provide for themselves — she took in boarders. She was ambitious for her children and managed, according to Hall, to send him 'to the best schools in the city.' He, in turn, followed the pattern of many bright young men brought up by widowed and ambitious mothers and became a young man in a hurry. Throughout his early life he seemed urgently driven to become a successful lawyer and to achieve fame as a writer, and to do both as rapidly as possible. His mother, to whom he remained a dutiful and devoted son, lived to see him achieve great success, and also disgrace.

II

One of Hall's uncles on his mother's side was an alderman in the Fourth Ward and he often used to take his
nephew on visits to City Hall and the courts. In later years
Hall claimed that these excursions were the genesis of his
interest in government and the law. 'The first man outside
of my family circle,' Hall wrote, 'of whom I have a lively
remembrance was Mayor Aaron Clark. My uncle took me —
an urchin — to a City Hall reception. Was I awed by the
dignity of the man? I think not. I was struck by the splendor
of his patent leather "pumps." The Democrats nicknamed
him "the dancing Mayor." The Whigs were called a "silk
stocking" party. Clearly he embodied that idea. I then and
there made up my mind one day to be a Mayor and to wear
patent leather pumps. There was a little entertainment at
the tea . . . where the aldermen who then were unsalaried
had their metaphorical "tea and toast." Here the Mayor
gave me a half dollar, which my pious mother deprived me
of because it was, she said, the proceeds of a lottery. The
Mayor, who had been an Albany politician, and six times
Clerk of the Assembly, had made a fortune in the lottery
business before it was made illegal.

'Not long afterwards I was taken to the Court of General
Sessions in the Tombs (it was removed thence in 1852), of
which court an alderman was then a side judge, or, as the
lawyers called it, a puisne judge (I lay no stress on the pro-
nunciation). There the remembrance of the Mayor and his
"pumps" faded before a determination to become one of
the men who stood at the table below and held conversation
with the judges.'

That Hall as a child had fancied himself as Mayor and
also as District Attorney, two offices he was later to fill, may
have been a fancy that grew in retrospect. But there is no
doubt that he was precocious. When he was only fourteen, in

the fall of 1840, he matriculated at New York University. According to material he later supplied a friendly biographer of the New York *Herald,* this was the scene that took place shortly before he was enrolled:

'I want to go to college,' he said one day to his mother.

'I am too poor, my son, to send you to college,' she answered sorrowfully, 'though I would sacrifice anything to do so.'

'You board me and I'll pay the college bills,' he answered with eager impetuosity.

'How will you get the money?'

'Work for it.'

'Work at what?'

'Head work. I'll manage it some way.'

'And young Oakey did enter college,' the *Herald* biography, published in 1868 — the year Hall ran for Mayor — continued. 'He was examined and found fully prepared. He entered in 1840 New York University. It was a happy day for him. The temple of knowledge was to him sacred. Through its portals he saw in the dim distance avenues leading to goals of highest ambition. He appreciated his opportunities too highly to waste his time. An indefatigable student, always prompt and almost always perfect in the recitation room, his studies were not wholly confined to the prescribed text books.'

From a slightly more impartial source — a classmate — is this description of Hall as a student: 'A sharp black-haired young man quick, ready, and always in the foreground.'

Hall's 'head work' proved to be working for newspapers. While at New York University he wrote for the *Evening Signal* and *Tatler,* the *Aurora,* and the *Evening Mirror.* His pieces included, according to his *Herald* biographer, 'light essays on literary topics, exhaustive treatises on grave questions of government, finance, political economy and reform, book reviews, dramatic criticisms, police reports, dead and live topics — anything that had an interest, pointed a moral or adorned a tale.'

Once, while he was an undergraduate, he was stopped at the door of the Park Theatre on an opening night. The manager, Edward Simpson, found it difficult to believe that what appeared to be a young boy was a bona fide drama critic for a New York newspaper. To establish his right to be there, Hall showed the manager copies of several reviews he had written and happened to have in his pocket. 'You can pass,' Simpson growled at Hall after looking over the reviews, 'but draw your criticism milder next time, if you please.'

Hall was graduated from New York University, 2 July 1844, with the degree of Bachelor of Arts. At the Commencement exercises held on that date in the old Church of the Messiah, he and another student recited 'A Colloquial Poem' in two parts — 'Shade of the Future' and 'Shade of the Past.' Both parts, fortunately, appear to be lost. Hall, solus, also recited an original sonnet, 'Written Beneath a Portrait of Keats.' It began: 'I weep while gazing on thy placid face.' Among the thirty-nine students on whom the chancellor conferred degrees were a number bearing the names of famous New York families and who were themselves to become distinguished members of the community. Three college mates were to reappear in Hall's life — Timothy Jarvis Carter, who became a minister and officiated at the marriage of his friend five years later; Aaron J. Vanderpoel, who was to become Hall's law partner; and John de la Montagnie, who became a doctor and was to figure in a fantastic and somewhat sordid episode co-operating with Hall when the latter was District Attorney.

Hall entered Harvard Law School in the fall of 1844 as a result of receiving financial help from his New Orleans uncle. Harvard's Law School had just reached its ascendancy under the brilliant guidance of the then aging former United States Supreme Court Justice, Joseph Story, who occupied the chair of Dane Professor of Law. The chair had been created for him in 1828. The distinguished Story had expressed anti-slavery views as early as 1808, when he had become a member of Congress. Two years before Hall came to Cambridge, Judge Story had drawn up the rules of equity practice for the United States Supreme Court. He was a member of the Board of Overseers of Harvard College and a Fellow of the Harvard Corporation. He died in 1845 at the age of sixty-six. Hall, who had become a disciple of Story, wrote a poem commemorating his death and, later, articles recalling his greatness.

'It was our privilege,' he later wrote in the *International Magazine,* 'to have spent days of pleasure in his presence. In the sunshine of his intellect our mind has sunned itself. To his gray-haired teaching we have paid personal reverence and we unaffectedly hope to have caught from his society and intercourse a spark of that professional enthusiasm which is the only true guiding star of the plodding lawyer.' Hall also became a disciple of Simon Greenleaf, who was Royall Professor of Law, 'a deliberate, slow, impressive man who was a good tutor.' Greenleaf was probably the leading authority on evidence, and formed with Story a team of legal brains that was the forerunner of many such to which Harvard's Law School was to give birth.

But Hall was homesick for New York. He wrote his mother that an 'obliging friend, George H. Moore, sends me several *Mirrows* (a evening) and am not "poor" off for news.' Hall mentioned a New York friend, who was then in New Orleans and who thought of 'home' much and longed for a drink of iced 'Croton.'

Hall's principal difficulty at Harvard seems to have been keeping warm. 'Booh! Booh!' he wrote his mother. 'How cold it is. I stuck myself out of door this morning in slippers and was glad to return to boot and cloak — I have just completed my household arrangements — which are when returning from breakfast — to make my fire, take up ashes, sweep the hearth, clear the room and get ready for action. It took me just 2 minutes this morning to get my stove red hot and set the tea kettle on top singing 91/1 right merrily.' He liked the law, or what he had learned of it, and especially savored the prospect of receiving the high fees that, as he had learned, often went with its practice:

'I shan't be able to write a very long letter this morning,' he told his mother, 'because there is a cause in equity to be argued before Judge Story this morning at the law library — Senator Choate and Prof. Greenleaf with Loring the Abolitionist are against Hon. Dick Bosworth of N.Y. City — Hon. Mr. Fletcher etc., etc. It is the case of a man who purchased 20,000 acres of land in Maine on false pretense — Motion now made to set aside the sale on the ground of fraud — The case has been in chancery since 1835 — And the papers, evidence etc. occupy 3 large *printed* vols of 200 pages each — And this Judge Story tells us is a small case — Choate's fee is $1000 — Hurrah for the law! I'm quite in love with my profession and so bet I get hold of a clear law book don't care a cent for all the girls in the world — All that I'm afraid of is that the cords of my heart will contract and in time I become a perfect 'Ralph Nidelby' — but you are wound in those cords and if they do contract it will bring you nearer to me — so all right — Clear the track for lawyer Hall!'

Two of Hall's classmates were George Hoadley, who became Governor of Ohio, and Rutherford Birchard Hayes, who became President of the United States. Hayes, Hall later remembered, was 'a swell,' and he had the impression that Hayes' money came from the Birchard family. Hall's career at Harvard, according to his *Herald* biographer, 'was brief but brilliant. He attended faithfully the lectures, in the "mock trials" he bore off the palm, for sagacity in sifting evidence and adroit and eloquent summing up he was un-

equalled, and at a supper party, given by some of the fledgling
lawyers on the completion of a new law building, gave swing
to his poetic proclivity in a lively epigram, the two closing
lines of which ran thus:

> How fittingly fame's laurel climbs
> Its Green-leaf to one Story height.'

When Story died less than a year later, Hall wrote the following poetic tribute:

The Death of Judge Story

The conq'ror now has won a noble prey!
— The lamp of wisdom which illumed the soul
Of one — a scholar and a patriot sage —
Which dimmed the sight of all who saw its ray,
    At last is oilless and beyond control —
Leaving to deeper darkness a degen'rate age!
    Mourn, oh my country! for thy loss is great,
    Crumbled, has one more pillar of thy state.
Yet is there left to thee a legacy
    Which few can leave, and none may dare refuse;
— The legacy of learning and integrity —
    That — least of all should freedom's children lose
His mem'ry knows no blot! True greatness filled
The temple which a God alone could build.

It is a fair sample of his poetic ability, and was probably
written with feeling.

Hall left Harvard on 17 January 1845, at the end of one
term, according to the official University records. He told his
Herald biographer that he left because he 'found it slow business.' For several months Hall read law at the offices of
Charles W. Sanford in New York. He then went to New
Orleans to live with Samuel Oakey and read law in the office
of John Slidell. (Slidell later achieved some fame for his

part in the 'Trent Affair.' With James M. Mason, Slidell boarded the British mail steamer *Trent* at Havana, bound for England and France to seek aid for the Southern cause. But officers of the U.S.S. *San Jacinto,* under the command of Captain Charles Wilkes, boarded the *Trent* and took Slidell and Mason into custody. They were imprisoned at Fort Warren in Boston Harbor. The British immediately protested. President Lincoln, in instructing Secretary Seward to release them, commented: 'We fought Great Britain in 1812 for insisting on the right to do precisely what Captain Wilkes had done.' The two men continued their journey and at last arrived in England. But their mission accomplished nothing.)

III

In 1846, Hall was admitted to the Louisiana Bar. One of his examiners was Judah P. Benjamin, later to become Attorney General and Secretary of State under the Confederacy. The son of English Jews, born and raised in the West Indies, educated at Yale, Benjamin came to be known as 'the brains of the Confederacy.' Hall made him his friend and kept up the friendship for more than half a century, even being present at Benjamin's deathbed when he died in Paris in 1884. By 1852, both Slidell and Benjamin had been admitted to the exclusive Union Club in New York. They were probably instrumental in getting Hall into this social fortress in 1861.

During his stay in New Orleans, Hall helped to support himself by writing for both the New Orleans *Delta* and the New Orleans *Commercial Bulletin* and also 'wrote for and partially edited' the *Literary World.* Most of his pieces for the latter were titled 'The Manhattaner In New Orleans.' In one of them he said the *Delta* 'Like a spoiled child, had

its own way with everybody.' The *Commercial Bulletin,* he
said, was like the New York *Journal of Commerce* and 'its
editorials aim rather at the solidity of dignified comment
than at the piquancy of gossip.' His *Literary World* pieces
were published in 1851 by J. S. Redfield, New York and
New Orleans, in a book called *The Manhattaner in New
Orleans.* It was dedicated to Samuel W. Oakey, Esq. In it
Hall revealed his love of New Orleans, calling it the 'Cal-
cutta of America.' He said that it was a great place to make
money in but few stayed to make it their home.

'Thwarted enterprise,' he wrote, 'baffled endeavor, youthful hope, desperate plannings, all emigrate to its precincts
to battle with fate, or to court fortune; to amass wealth, and
if living after the "gold hunt is over" to return home to
spend it. . . . Except among the Creoles — the aborigines
of the place — a man of leisure is a wonder.' One of his more
memorable passages concerns his dawn vigil in the dome
of the St. Charles Hotel. It is a fair sample of the prose of
his day, particularly his own: 'A dusky cloud,' he wrote,
'swung to and fro like a dropsical balloon above the swamp
on my right; and the slightest possible fog was rising from
the Mississippi that, far as my eye could reach "went on in
its winding way" like a huge slimy serpent creeping upon
the face of the earth. I was above the entire city with a very
extensive drop of the eye upon chimneys and roofs. . . . A
tow-boat in the river, some miles below the city, was puffing
its way to the city, hugging in its monster grasp a brace of
thousand-tonned ships. Above, one of the crack Louisville
packet-steamers came by the groves of ghostly cypresses as
proud and imperious in bearing as a mettled racehorse upon
the turf which his hoofs had successfully known time and
again.

'The sun was next beheld hovering over the Gulf, maturing
an audacious dash at the many eastward windows of the

27

city. A faint hum began to be heard; the groans of the city for the coming of another day of trial; increasing every minute:

> From field surburban rolled the early cart,
> As slept the revel so awoke the mart.

First the rattle of the milk wagons. Next the dashing cabs from the early mail-boat that was taking its morning smoke behind the swamp. Now and then the clatter of hoofs upon the pavement told that some shoulder-bent book-keeper was taking his morning equestrian exercise, and, sportsmanlike, thinking of the race the "ledger" daily gave him. The ponderous dray shook the houses as it thundered toward the Levee, drowning even the stentorian voice of its driver "boy" improvising upon "Mary Blaine" or "the Rose of Alabama" . . . The hum soon became a roar. The caldron of New Orleans commerce was again upon the boil, and as I looked around I could scarcely keep from moralizing and extemporizing an essay upon the eternal American theme of the country's destiny.'

IV

In the fall of 1848, Hall returned to New York, where he saw 'a wider field for his ambition and the more assured prospect of a successful career in his profession,' as he told his *Herald* biographer. Within a few months he was admitted to the New York State Bar. He claimed that he went through 'the usual starvation process' at the beginning of his practice of law, but the record shows that he moved ahead rapidly within the next two years. Apparently he was even entertaining his youthful dream of becoming a judge, because he wrote his mother and sister, who were visiting Samuel Oakey in New Orleans, that 'you must make up your minds to read some very scratchy legal penmanship such as

I hope to puzzle lawyers with some day when I come to write opinions.'

That first winter in New York proved to be a memorable period in his life, the law apart. He wrote his mother in February 1849: 'Never mind your fine weather — we had the mercury at 15 above zero last night. Going through Whitehall Street to supper was a freezing operation.' Presumably he had decided that the lack of heat in New York was compensated for by the warmth of his love for the girl he was going to marry, Katherine Louise Barnes, whose father was Joseph Nye Barnes, alderman of the Eighth Ward, owner of Vermont marble quarries, and a man of wealth and power. It was important to Hall that Kate, as he called his fiancée, and his mother be congenial. In one of his letters to his mother that winter he apologized for Kate's not having written, explaining that she had been 'quite indisposed with an affection of the throat and had not felt like writing you. . . . She will write next week. She appears very fond of hearing me speak of you. But people have said she was a coquette of no years' standing and there is no knowing what a coquette will do!!'

Hall continued to write for his two New Orleans papers, the *Commercial Bulletin* and the *Delta,* sending them New York correspondence under the names of 'Croton' and 'Hans Yorkel.' He also began writing for the *International Magazine,* which was then edited by Rufus W. Griswold, and for the *Home Journal,* edited by his friend, General George Pope Morris, author of 'Woodman, Spare That Tree.' Hall was so devoted to the General, who came by his title via the National Guard, that he dedicated one of his books, *Old Whitey's Christmas Trot,* to him.

Even after he began practicing law, Hall seems to have been ready to give his full time to newspaper work. In fact, one of his favorite anecdotes concerned his attempt to get a job on the editorial staff of the New York *Commercial.* He liked to tell the story to reporters who came to interview him as an illustration of the part chance plays. The editor of the *Commercial* interviewed Hall, looked over his clippings, and said he could have the job if the man to whom he'd promised it did not turn up for work — apparently, he had some doubts about it. The man, Theophilus C. Cailicot, did turn up, worked for several years as a reporter and city editor, and then got into some sort of trouble that resulted in his being sent to prison. After Hall became District Attorney he always ended his telling of the story by pointing out that, but for the strange workings of the Goddess of Chance, he might be wearing prison stripes instead of prosecuting criminals.

Hall's activities in the fields of writing and law did not prevent his having an active social life. 'This week,' he wrote his mother on 10 February 1849, 'has been a sort of carnival in my winter experience — for during it I have been "out" the only two nights since my return from N.O. I mean to a ball. 3 nights ago I went to the 50th Anniversary of the Euterpean Society — Concert by the members — after which floor cleared (at the Apollo) for an impromptu hop — Dodworth's cornet band being the "sweet little cherub not sat up aloft" and discoursing most capital music I went with Kate and Mary and Bro Ned — Supper at 12 home at 3. The company very select and agreeable. Last night I was at White W. Lizzie and Elsie gave a party and done the thing up brown — 70 or 80 present — very agreeable party — Minck the band leader discoursed most excellent music brought up for the occasion — for a sample as I told him. Oh your acquaintances, the Landfords were there, and the grandest folks, and Mr. and Miss Marsh, James and Violetta as of course — no old folks. Uncle John and Aunt Eliza led off the first quadrille! being in the breast pocket of my coat. The only figure they appeared pat in was doze-a-doze. Afterwards they surveyed the festivities from the mantelpiece and

went down to supper. The latter was spread out in the basement — fine table — oysters with cream and Charlotte Russe
— confectionery — cakes — wine Champagne etc etc as of
old. The dancing was kept up until 2 a.m. Uncle Wm arrived
from Albany in the evening to be present at a military presentation of plate from which he returned about 10 p.m. bringing in some of his staff whose gay uniforms made the place
quite the thing. Uncle Wm was in the undress uniform of a
Brigadier General and looked very much like Gen. Taylor.
Very kind enquiries were made after you by many.'

V

In 1849, Hall was associated as junior counsel in a case
with the distinguished lawyer, Nathaniel Bowditch Blunt.
Blunt liked the ambitious young lawyer and persuaded him
to set up a law partnership with two of his former law colleagues, Augustus L. Brown and Aaron J. Vanderpoel. Brown
was a conservative man, quiet, grave and very businesslike.
Vanderpoel, a native of Kinderhook, New York, the Van
Buren country, had a solid Hudson Valley Dutch background. Blunt was connected with the firm in an 'elder
statesman' role. Vanderpoel was married to a sister of John
Lloyd Stephens, the famous explorer of Central America
who, on Kroger's Island in the Hudson River, set up a
replica of an entire Mayan city in ruins. Vanderpoel
looked like a Dutch sea captain, the result of the way he
trimmed his beard. He also was said to resemble Charles
Dickens. A great orator and trial lawyer, he was called by
ex-Mayor Philip Hone, 'the Kinderhook roarer.' Hall had
known Vanderpoel slightly at New York University.

The firm got off to a good start largely because Vanderpoel
was able to bring in such clients as Jay Gould, who was then
paving the way for the plunder of the Erie Railroad, and
Samuel J. Tilden, who was to become in a few years an

avenging angel to the Tweed Ring and, as a result of his role as a reformer, one of New York State's most dynamic governors. The firm acquired a diversified clientele. It represented sheriffs, coroners, boards of police commissioners, the commissioner of charities and correction, and various railroads. Hall's contribution was probably his political connections — always a useful asset in a law firm. He had acquired the friendship of Thurlow Weed, then an editor and Republican leader in Albany, and William H. Seward, a senator in the Albany legislature. Hall acted, as he put it, as counsel to various legislative commissions in Albany. Later, his critics were to refer to this phase of his career as lobbying.

Hall's *Herald* biographer, who tended to look at his subject in a worshipful light, wrote of Hall's legal ability: 'In the first place, he is unquestionably, for his years, one of the best read lawyers at the New York Bar. On occasions his argument is close and rigid, a compact network of steel impressions to assault. Generally, however, his legal arguments abound in coruscations of vivacious fancy. He has a faculty of breathing into the dullest topics material and imparting animation to the dryest topics. Conceiving his arguments strongly and clothing his thought with the choicest phraseology he beguiles his audience of weariness by his combined logic and wit. . . . His style of speaking is mainly colloquial. Like Minerva glittering from the brow of Jove, his thoughts come forth mature and splendid. There is nothing of patchwork in his ideas and nothing of labor in his manner and gestures . . . never in his private practice a suit he advised bringing.'

By the fall of 1849, Hall and his fiancée had set a date for their wedding. The ceremony was performed at 99 Grand Street, the home of the bride's parents, by the Rev. Timothy Jarvis Carter, deacon of Calvary Church, at a quarter past eleven in the morning. For St. Valentine's Day, 1850, Hall surprised his wife with the following poem:

My wife! my darling cherished wife
   A song for thee to-day
I offer with the fondest vows
   A *husband's* heart can pay.

As I glance back to hours gone
   When hope & faith were mine
I think of many when my pen
   Bent o'er *thy* Valentine;

When thou wert in thy girlish prime
   When many a song was brought
As offerings to thy cherished love
   So many a suitor sought.

And shall I *now* that time prepares
   No seasons such as those
For thee to blossom as the maid
   To whom all hearts propose;

Now that the lover's *name* is lost
   (Tho' still his heart remains)
Shall I omit the season's song
   Which custom's law ordains?

Take then a husband to thy heart
   — *He* is thy Valentine —
Thy heart where e'en ambition kneels
   As to a sacred shrine.

It is not all clear, except the feeling.

The Halls' first child, Cara de la Montagnie Hall, so named after his doctor friend who had been his classmate, was born 1 October 1850 in their house at 149 Hudson Street, corner of Hubert Street. Like most first-born children, Cara was Hall's favorite, and she was to have almost as exciting and varied a life as her father.

At the time of Hall's marriage, Blunt was elected District

Attorney of New York County, and he appointed Hall as an assistant District Attorney. Hall held this job for three and a half years, until Blunt's death, when Governor Seymour appointed Lorenzo B. Shepard to Blunt's post. Hall thereupon resigned 'to resume,' he said, 'his private practice and literary labors.' But Hall had acquired political ambitions and, six months later, he ran against Shepard for the office of District Attorney and won — a post he was to hold for fourteen years. Except for a three-year period when he was not returned to office, he was District Attorney of New York County for the next fourteen years — until 1869, when he took office as Mayor. He remained a semi-active partner in his law firm. An elegantly printed communication which he addressed 'To the Police Justices of the City and County of New York' while District Attorney is not without interest. Dated 10 May 1855, it read:

'Gentlemen:

'I notice that a large number of arrests have been made, charging persons with selling liquor without license.

'I beg leave to call your attention to the recent decision of the Court of Special Sessions, adjudging that by a defect in the existing statute this act is not punishable.

'There being no process of appealing from a judgment of this character, it is final.

'I therefore submit the same to your respectful consideration and action.

> 'With great respect,
> 'Your ob'dt ser'nt.,
> 'A. Oakey Hall.'

He also recommended to Mayor Fernando Wood a startling reform in the administration of justice.

'Dear Sir,' he wrote the Mayor on 22 November 1855. 'From recent investigations into criminal matters, I am officially convinced that the cause of public justice in this city, will be subserved and the rights and privileges of citizens best protected by general removal of all those policemen (without any invidious distinctions as to persons or party) who are in any wise detailed to special duty at the various Criminal Courts and Offices of this City, to make place for new ones fresh from routine duty: and I respectfully recommend that this change occur every half year.

'The association of policemen (perfectly necessary in the due discharge of their functions in searching for culprits, for witnesses and making arrest upon warrants) for any long period of time with the lower order of criminal lawyers so eager to give per centage on fees from clients recommended through the officer; or their association with the harpies who infest Police Courts, in almost every state and county as bail masters or as arrangers of complaints, as brokers in felony, as agents for influencing and deterring witnesses, who may be ignorant or weak-minded, cannot but exert an injurious effect upon such official action as they take under the direction of their magistracy, and much embarrass the intentions of the latter.'

Five days later, Mayor Wood proclaimed: 'In pursuance of the recommendation of A. Oakey Hall, Esq., District Attorney for this County . . . I shall detail an entire new Police force for the several Courts every six months.'

During the 1850's Hall moved into a new home every time he and his wife had a baby. As the city expanded uptown, the only direction in which it could, Hall moved with it. His second child, Maria Theresa, was born at 109 West Twenty-eighth Street. His third child, Alice d'Assignie, was born at 45 East Twenty-eighth Street. His next three children — Josephine Barnes, Louise Oakey, and Augustus Oakey Vanderpoel — were all born at 107 Madison Avenue. All five were baptized on Christmas Day, 1859, by the Rev. H. E. Montgomery, at the Church of the Incarnation, Madison Avenue and Twenty-eighth Street. Augustus Oakey Vanderpoel Hall died in 1861. Hall's seventh and last child, Herbert Oakey Hall, was born on 29 April 1862 at 13 West Forty-second Street. It was at this address that he raised his children and spent the happiest years of his life.

3

MAYOR HALL AND MR. TWEED

I

HALL'S ULTIMATE POLITICAL DESTINY was shaped in the fall of 1861 when, after three years of being out of office, he ran again for District Attorney of New York County. He received the nominations of the Republicans and of Mozart Hall, a dissident wing of Tammany Hall, as well as endorsements from several other groups. His principal opponent was Nelson J. Waterbury, the regular Tammany candidate. A third candidate, Abraham R. Lawrence, a reformer, had the endorsements of the People's Union and the Parlor Conventions as well as support from the city's German groups who were beginning to assert themselves in the face of the strong political power of the Irish. Hall defeated Waterbury by 967 votes, polling 21,715 votes. Lawrence polled only 13,510 votes.

The political situation in New York during the fall of 1861 was especially complicated, if not confused. The Civil War and the issues of slavery and states' rights cut through local party lines. Tammany Hall naturally tended to go along with the views of the Democrats on national issues. To add to the confusion, the reign of Fernando Wood, who had been twice elected Mayor, in 1855 and again in 1860, was drawing to a close. Wood, whom one historian has called 'the first really dominating corruptionist in New York City,' had controlled the Democratic party with his own organization, called Mozart Hall, eclipsing for the moment Tammany Hall. His Board of Aldermen was so corrupt that it came to be known as the 'Forty Thieves.' One of its members was a rising young politician named William Marcy Tweed whose name was to become a synonym, to future historians, for big-city corruption.

But today's concept of Tweed as an illiterate oaf does not jibe with the picture he presented to his contemporaries. Matthew P. Breen, a distinguished lawyer and former member of the New York state legislature who disapproved of Tweed's political morality, wrote that 'Tweed was a man of rather commanding presence, standing fully five feet eleven inches in height, and weighing nearly if not quite three hundred pounds. His complexion was slightly florid, his features large, and there was always a merry twinkle in his eye when in the company of those he knew to be his friends; and a heartiness in the grasp of his hand, which were reassuring to those properly introduced to him . . . he scarcely ever partook of more than a sip of wine when extending hospitalities, and never permitted strong drink to get the best of him; neither did he have the tobacco habit. He was scrupulously careful concerning his attire, while never striving to make a show of dress. He was always suave and polite in manner.'

In the fall of 1861, Tweed's political fortunes were accumulating for him the power that was to give him control of Tammany Hall and terminate Fernando Wood's leadership of the Democratic party. Hall had been a friend of Wood's and was a Republican, but he allowed his desire to hold office to dictate his political direction. Although Tweed and Hall were not personal friends, in fact didn't like each other, they complemented each other very well. Tweed had an enormous appetite for money and preferred to operate politically behind the scenes. Hall was indifferent to money — he could have made plenty in his own law firm — and loved to hold public office and receive the attention of the people. His desire for approval was as inordinate as Tweed's desire for money.

Although, at the start of the Civil War, Hall had expressed himself as loyal to the cause of the Union, it was not too difficult to be sympathetic to the Confederacy in the New York of his day. Many businessmen, particularly those in cotton and shipping, were having difficulties as a result of the blockade. And Hall had ties with the South. He was chided by the editor Theodore Tilton for favoring the cause of slavery. Hall replied that he was not anti-Negro, writing on 22 January 1862: 'As a politician and a public man I must look at expediency and the greatest good of the greatest number.' As the war continued, Hall opposed what he called 'military arrests in states not included in hostile lines by the government.' He definitely lined up with the Tammany Union Democracy and was made secretary of the Democratic State Committee. He signed the registration book of the Tammany Society on 1 February 1864, just nine months after Tweed became Grand Sachem.

Received at last in the sanctum sanctorum of the New York County Democratic party — the Tammany Society or Columbian Order, founded in 1789 in opposition to the aristocratic Society of the Cincinnati, composed of officers in the Revolutionary army — Hall signed in with a flourish, writing in the membership book before the assembled Sachems:

> Whilst Council fires hold out to burn,
> The vilest sinner may return.

> OK.

The following July Fourth, at a Tammany Society picnic, he made a speech in which he said he had 'sought in the

Democratic Ark a refuge from fanaticism which threatened
to engulf the Union.' Hall concluded that 'all that was worth
saving was in the keeping of the Democratic Ark.' In a
lighter vein, he declared that he had left the Republican
party because it had again nominated such an uncouth fellow
as Abraham Lincoln.

II

In the fall, he took an active part in the Lincoln-McClellan
campaign and, according to the *Herald*, 'accused [Lincoln]
of all the crimes in the decalogue.' The speech 'was reported
by a government stenographer, with a view . . . to proceed
against him for incendiary and violent language.' The government didn't proceed against Hall and the Democrats used
the speech as campaign material. Despite his new political
position, the record shows that in the draft riots of July,
1863, Hall was not deterred from performing his duties as
District Attorney and prosecuting the most flagrant offenders.
One newspaper said he was 'doing a righteous work — one
in which every law-abiding citizen will sustain, and with
gratitude remember him.'

As the Civil War ended and the post-bellum period in the
city's history began, Tweed and two other Democratic politicians gained complete control of Tammany Hall and the
Democratic party and, by the simple method of bribing its
leaders, made inroads toward controlling the Republican
party, which in turn controlled the upstate vote. Tweed's
co-conspirators were an unctuous, Uriah Heep type bookkeeper named Richard B. Connolly and Peter B. Sweeny, a
lawyer of great native shrewdness. Sweeny was a bachelor
who lived with his sister and brother-in-law, State Senator
John Bradley, in rather sumptuous style. It was said that
Bradley was nothing without the wealth and power of his
brother-in-law. Sweeny was a completely cynical man to

whom exercising the arts of politics came as naturally as breathing. He admired Hall's ability as a lawyer and recognized that Hall's ambitions to hold public office and his popularity with people could be turned to political advantage. Hall became his protégé.

Sweeny was a member of the Union Club but prided himself on never visiting the clubhouse. He had a rather sinister look, the result of his dark, unruly hair and black piercing eyes too small for his rather large face. His walrus mustache was jet black. A reporter for the *World* described him as a man 'of medium height, solidly built with a good shaped head liberally covered with thick black hair . . . a bright clear sallow complexion bronzed to a healthy ruddiness by the sun . . . an expressive mouth capable of forming itself into a peculiarly pleasant smile or into one of cynical bitterness.'

In preparing a slate of candidates for the 1868 elections, Tweed, Sweeny, and Connolly agreed on Horatio Seymour, Governor of New York, for President. Recorder John T. Hoffman, a Tammany party reliable, would run for Governor, and A. Oakey Hall, with a long and successful career as District Attorney behind him, would run for Mayor. It was reported that Tweed and his fellows were so confident of the success of the political formula they had developed — bribing all the party leaders — that they planned to move on to Washington and put Hall or Hoffman into the Presidency.

Many years later, in the mellow days of his retirement, Sweeny described to a reporter for the *World* the circumstances leading to the conferring on Hall of the nomination for Mayor. 'It became necessary,' Sweeny said, 'to nominate the strongest man in the organization. Mr. A. Oakey Hall was the man. He then held the office of District Attorney. He had held it for several terms. He was a vigorous, prompt, and successful public prosecutor, as is well known. He was a graphic writer and a graceful, witty, and eloquent speaker, the star of all public occasions. He was universally held in the highest regard. It would be difficult to conceive a position more popularly enriched or more satisfactory to the pride and ambition of man than that which Mr. Hall then held in the community. When he was asked to accept the nomination he declined it without hesitancy. It was not in the line of the profession to which he was devoted and neither his inclination or his fortune would allow him to abandon his career. He finally yielded to persistent importunity.'

III

During the years Hall acted as a public prosecutor he kept up his partnership in his private law firm. He also wrote a great deal, both for the New York stage and for newspapers, and managed as well to be a first-nighter and man-about-town. Beneath his veneer of frivolity there was a serious vein. He found time to express enlightened and constructive views on the treatment of criminals, the result of his observations as an official. Writing about New York's Tombs prison, he said it was 'most appropriately known as The Tombs. This was built upon piles over a swamp. It cramps those whom the law presumes to be innocent with confinement more impure and irksome than is meted out to convicted criminals. The young girl imprisoned for the theft of urgent temptation is compelled to hear the blasphemies of the criminal crone. Oliver Twist and Fagin meet within conversational distance. Foul air, fouler association and absolute lack of exercise unite to make the Tombs the High School of Crime as the State Prison is its University.'

In his extensive library at his home on Forty-second Street he had what was probably the city's finest collection of books on crime — transcripts of great murder trials in England

and the United States, books on prisons, on the behavior of criminals, everything that would tend to give a prosecutor a broader view of his work. His interests in this direction were similar to those of another writer who was to serve as an assistant District Attorney in New York — the late Arthur Train. Once, Hall gave a lecture before a group of lawyers in which he touched on his interest in the field of criminology and told amusing incidents about his work in the District Attorney's office and the criminal courts. He was so successful that he was called upon to give the same talk before groups in Albany and in other cities. This lecture was titled 'A Night in Crimeland.' Soon he was lecturing on marriage and divorce; on literature and the drama; on politics; on New York history; and on topics of the day.

According to the *Herald*, Hall's lectures 'were always delightful literary treats. His recent lecture before the Young Men's Catholic Association of Brooklyn on "The Modern Drama" was of surpassing interest. His soul was in the theme, and he wove into it a spirit and life drunk from Shakespeare, the great master of the passions. It is in his speeches on grand public occasions, such as the recent unveiling of the Vanderbilt bronze statue, at great political gatherings and at public dinners that his power as an orator is fully developed. His style of sentences is of the order of Wendell Phillips, Victor Hugo and Carlyle — suggestive, sententious and pointed. He indulges in no stereotyped rehash of worn-out platitudes. He plumes his feathers and lets grow his wings. His speeches are full of masculine force, fire, humor, pathos — whose words haunt us as eagles haunt the mountain air.'

For the theater, Hall confined himself largely, during these years, to the writing of short skits and burlesques for Mrs. John Wook at the Olympic Theatre. Some of the titles of his skits were: *Loyalina, Brigadier General Fortunio and His Seven Gifted Aides-de-Camp*, an extravaganza; *Humpty*

Dumpty, a burletta; and *Let Me Kiss Him For His Mother,* another of the same. With Park Benjamin he wrote a comedy, *Fiscal Agency.*

For his many roles, he was sometimes under attack. In addition, as a District Attorney he had acquired the enmity of some of those he had prosecuted. One of them turned out to be a writer who signed himself 'Civis.' In his paper, *Red Flag,* he wrote of Hall: 'In contemplating Oakey Hall we are inclined to believe in progressive development and that he is the next stage above the ourangoutang. The fellow's mouth is so frightfully large that when he once went to have a tooth pulled out the dentist said, "Excuse me sir, I should prefer remaining on the outside." Surely there is no Mrs. Oakey Hall in existence? A Special Act of the Legislature should be brought in to prevent the perpetuation of such a breed. Naturally, the hideous-looking hound was designed to herd geese upon a common but might be advantageously employed as a scarecrow. In literary matters he makes no difference between *meum* and *tuum* or his neighbors' property and his own, but whatever he touches he contrives to defile.'

Hall pasted the clipping in his scrapbook and noted beside it: 'From a scurrilous paper called the Red Flag by a man named Idsen whom I had hitched into as District Attorney in 1858.' A month later, Hall was able to paste up a long and favorable article about himself from the New York *Leader,* which said: 'A. Oakey Hall is a scion of good stock. He is well posted in matters literary and political; has good oratorical ability, and talks well and easily on almost any subject. He is still young, not over thirty-five years of age. In person he is tall and slim, has good taste and wears spectacles. He is a family man; domestic in his habits and as might be expected, from one of his reading accomplishments, elegant in his tastes and distinguished for social ability. He lives well — works hard; has strong feelings and opinions, and expresses and acts on them with boldness and consistency.'

Hall was indeed 'distinguished for social ability.' Added to all his other talents was this special one for knowing people, of high and low degree, and some in between. He wanted to be accepted by all — and was.

IV

It can be said that 2 January 1861, the date Hall was admitted to membership in the Union Club, marked his arrival socially, as distinct from mere popularity, in New York. He could drink and dine, if he wished, with a Schermerhorn, a Schuyler, a Van Buren, a Stuyvesant, one of four Van Rensselaers, or one of seven Livingstons.

The Union was founded in 1836 by what the elder James Gordon Bennett called 'all the aristocratic names of New York.' Some of the more well-known founding members were Philip Hone, Beverly Robinson, and J. de Peyster Ogden, as well as such 'aristocratic names,' according to the elder Bennett, as 'the Kings, the Jays, the Hamiltons, the Livingstons, the Hoffmans, the Laights, the Wilkeses, the Maxwells, the Lynches, and the Saltonstalls.' Not without reason did the Union Club come to name itself 'the mother of clubs.' The Knickerbocker Club was formed by impatient young men who felt they had waited too long to be admitted to the Union, the Brook Club by impetuous young members of the Union, one of whom had joined in the placing of a fried egg on the head of a distinguished elderly officer of the club who was dozing in an easy chair in the club's living room. In 1863, the Union League Club was founded by Union Club members whose patriotism led them to insist that Judah B. Benjamin, Secretary of State under the Confederacy, be expelled. A Democratic newspaper commented, at the time, that the Union League consisted 'of able-bodied gentlemen, whose purpose is to induce other able-bodied men to enlist.' The Democratic gentlemen matched the Union League by forming *their* club — the Manhattan. One club, the Calumet, which lasted for a number of years, was set up with the express purpose of occupying the time of young gentlemen waiting for old members of the Union to die so that they could finally be admitted. During Hall's time, the Union was described as 'a citadel of the *jeunesse dorée,*' and one observer of the mores of the day remarked that the Union Club's special appeal to the gentry lay in the fact that it was 'both wild and respectable and open all night.'

When Hall was admitted in 1861, the officers of the Union included John A. King, Anthony Lispenard Robertson, and Robert S. Hone. Four years later J. P. Morgan, the elder, was admitted. The younger James Gordon Bennett was tardily admitted ten years after Hall. Young Bennett wanted to be a member, whereas his father, when asked to be a founding member in 1836, had written tirades in the *Herald* against the club, denouncing it as an attempt to create 'a London society.' Young Bennett, however, was so loyal to his fellow members of the Union Club that he left standing orders at the *Herald* that any difficulties or scrapes members of the club got into were to be ignored. His editor, William C. Reich, commented to one of his drinking companions: 'How in hell can I be expected to carry the names of all the members of the Union Club in my mind?'

Just who sponsored Hall's application for membership in the Union the record does not reveal, but he had three old friends who had been members for more than ten years before he was admitted. They were August Belmont, the great financier, admitted in 1848; Judah P. Benjamin, admitted in 1852; and Charles O'Conor, the fiery lawyer, later to achieve fame as a prosecutor of the Tweed Ring, admitted in 1853.

Belmont was one of the Board of Governor's of the Union and Hall may have become friendly with him as a result of having worked, in New Orleans, for the Slidell brothers, who were relatives of Belmont's wife, the former Caroline Slidell Perry. She was the daughter of Commodore Matthew Calbraith Perry, who had 'opened up' Japan. George Templeton Strong, the lawyer, noted in his diaries Belmont's intense loyalty to 'his friend Oakey Hall.' Belmont, one of the great bankers of his day, carried an aura of European splendor about him. He was a power in the Democratic party on a national level, and locally a Sachem of Tammany Hall.

In 1864, Hall had occasion to come vigorously to the defense of Belmont. On 6 October the New York *Post* printed an editorial commenting on the Democratic Convention of that year. 'Prominent among the intriguers,' the *Post* said, 'who sought to shape the policy of the Convention, was Mr. August Belmont, chairman of the Douglas National Committee, a reputed son and accredited agent of the Rothschilds, the great bankers of European monarchs. Going about the city in his sumptuous carriage, he seemed a fitting representative of those minions of the royal and aristocratic classes of the old world. It was understood and one prominent Democrat asserted that he paid the expenses of the Convention, particularly when the use of his wealth was likely to enable him to obtain his influence and co-operation in carrying out his plans.'

Five days later Hall wrote the *Post* as follows:
'Gentlemen:

'The personal friends of August Belmont Esq. insist upon a criminal prosecution of the author of the editorial in the Evening *Post* of last Thursday Oct. 6, 1864: speaking of him as a "reputed son etc etc" as and for a libel.

'It is not for me to prejudge the case at this juncture; but I have deemed it my duty to lay the complaint forthwith before the proper tribunal.

'I understand the proprietors to be the Messers W. C. Bryant, Parke Godwin and Isaac Henderson.

'Prima facie, it is they against whom I must proceed. However, I desire to obtain the exact name of the writer that I may proceed against him alone. Can you furnish it to me before 10 a.m. of Wednesday?

'I do not believe Mr. Bryant wrote it because I do not think a gentleman of his refined instincts would ever engage in personalities and hazard a world-wide reputation. I am loath to suppose it to be Mr. Godwin for other reasons. I am almost sure it is not Mr. Henderson because he has suffered such injustice at other hands that he would not himself speak lightly of another's standing.

'Therefore I ask very respectfully that the responsible "writer" be named quite as much to save some of you, as the public, trouble.

'With assurances of my desire to do justice both to yourselves and Mr. Belmont's friends

'I am Gentlemen
'Your Obt. Ser't
'A. Oakey Hall.'

Belmont also filed a civil suit against the *Post,* but neither the criminal nor civil cases ever came to trial. Belmont was not so much interested in obtaining financial redress as he was in scotching a rumor that carried with it the implication that he was an illegitimate son of a Rothschild. The truth was that he came of a wealthy and landed family named Schoenberg — in English, Belmont — in the Rhine Palatinate. From the age of fourteen he had worked for the Rothschild banking firm, first in Frankfurt-am-Main, then in Naples, and later at the Papal Court in Rome, where he negotiated for them. When he learned of the financial panic of 1837 in the United States he came here immediately, and later set up on his own what was to become one of the great banking firms of its time, August Belmont & Co.

Belmont was undoubtedly instrumental in bringing Hall into the 'Democratic Ark,' as Hall was to refer to the Democratic party when he came to join it. When the Tweed Ring scandals came about, Belmont, despite his being a Sachem of Tammany, went unscathed. For a time he remained loyal to Hall but, in the end, Hall was left to fend for himself.

V

The summer of 1868, the Democratic National Convention, the first since 1860 that had been fully attended on account of the war, was held at Tammany Hall's new headquarters uptown on Fourteenth Street. Tweed was responsible for the new edifice, the cornerstone of which had been laid just a year before. Tweed's candidate for the Presidency, Governor Seymour of New York, received the nomination, and later that month Hall was designated to run as the Democratic nominee for the office of Mayor. Hall's acceptance speech was greeted with 'prolonged cheering and merriment.' It was not remarkable for its high political morality.

'I would not take the office,' he said, 'if I did not take it as the trustee of the Democracy, and be able to do in the new office what I always did in the old — to take care of my friends, and to ask my friends to take care of me. . . . But somehow or other the press of business in my office has been so great that I have never yet found time to prosecute a man for taking a drink after 12 o'clock at night.' As a result of this speech, a number of newspapers printed pious editorials deploring the fact that a public official had boasted of his having failed to enforce the law, in fact, had virtually invited people to disobey it. Hall knew perfectly well what he was doing. Laws restricting a man's right to drink whisky were no more popular among New Yorkers in 1868 than they were in 1919, half a century later.

Hall worked hard to get his ticket elected. It was reported that he sent telegrams to the upstate New York Democratic party leaders, signing Samuel J. Tilden's name, asking them to wire to New York estimates of the upstate results before the polls closed. The purpose of this maneuver was to adjust the New York City Democratic vote to offset the heavy upstate Republican vote. The Republicans had done the same thing, in reverse, a year before. Tilden, who was a Democratic leader on a national level, was furious when he learned about it.

Tweed and his colleagues actually violated one of the rules of local politics during the 1868 election — they carried on a dishonest election despite the fact that it was also a Presidential year. A few years later, that celebrated politician and articulator of New York City political verities, Peter J. MacGuinness, explained that he wouldn't cheat in a Presidential election year because it was a Federal offense and 'I might be brought before a Federal judge I didn't know, and then where would I be?'

Hall's Republican opponent was Colonel F. A. Conkling, whom he defeated by 75,054 out of 96,054 votes cast. The *North American Review* later estimated that 8 per cent more votes were cast than the entire voting population of the city. The election was so corrupt that the House of Representatives in Washington appointed a committee to investigate. Tweed was called and admitted that the election inspectors had lumped the votes together, without counting them, and declared the outcome. Tammany had printed up, for the occasion, 105,000 applications for citizenship and 69,000 certificates of naturalization. The Republicans did the same thing but used different colored paper. The *Tribune* said that citizens were made 'at the rate of a thousand a day with no more solemnity than . . . the converting of swine into pork in a Cincinnati packing house.' For fourteen days, a Tweed judge, George G. Barnard, remained in his office from six until midnight naturalizing 10,093 men. Repeaters received an average of five dollars a vote and managed to vote an average of nine times. Hall claimed, later, that he didn't know what was going on, and it was never suggested that he had any part in the fraud.

He accounted for his large majority on the grounds that he had been sympathetic to the Irish and German voters. In fact, some newspapers had nicknamed him Mayor von O'Hall. As District Attorney he had not vigorously prosecuted laws which made difficulties for the then popular German 'beer vaults.' He was sympathetic to the problems of the ill-fed, uneducated Irish immigrants. He refused to prosecute liquor dealers who failed to pay the Federal excise taxes on whisky, maintaining it was not the job of his office to do so. It was said that although he had prosecuted some 12,000 cases during his years as District Attorney, he had pigeon-holed 10,000. These latter were, as might be expected, cases in which his legal or humane judgment, as well his political judgment, told him it was not expedient to prosecute.

When a friend congratulated him on his election, Hall said: 'Few persons have so many tried friends as I have — and *tried* friends are always magnanimous.' His puns were to become one of the trademarks of his administration as Mayor.

VI

Hall was only forty-two when he ran for Mayor. A good deal of his appeal to the voters was based on his being a character. Some historians have assumed that Hall made a fool of himself in order to act as a front man for Tweed, his political boss. It would appear otherwise. Hall liked to dress up and make amusing speeches, and the fact that it helped him politically he considered all to the good. Here is a picture of him as he was about to become Mayor, as seen through the eyes of the New York correspondent of the Pittsburgh *Chronicle,* who wrote: "[Hall] is a compactly built man of about medium height; of slight frame but well knit; and has a look of agility very suggestive of grand and lofty tumbling. Black hair, black beard and mustache slightly tinged with gray, pleasant blue eyes, a prominent nose, a well-balanced but not large head, with perceptive "bumps" fully developed and the whole face illuminated by a bright, wide-awake intellectual look . . . He is an active little man . . . not quite an orator but seldom fails to command the attention of his audience . . . He is a man of conviction . . . His changing of his politics, it is said, was not so much a change of heart but a change of base . . . He is a genial companion full of the play and sparkle of wit and, when he chooses to be, a clever writer . . . It is easy enough to like the man . . . even when we cannot like the politician.'

There is ample documentation of the fact that his contemporaries thought of Hall as both a wit and a humorist. Although he relied heavily on puns to get laughs, some of his remarks can still bring a smile. Once, when he was lecturing before the law students at New York University, the gas-lighted chandeliers began to flicker and grow dim. 'There seems to be,' said Hall with a dead pan, 'a conflict between one gas and another.' There is reason to believe that Hall was one of the earliest users of the dead pan. 'Much of his wit,' a contemporary wrote of him, 'is due to the extraordinary imperturbability of [his] face and manner.' At a funeral for a city employee which Hall attended while he was mayor, he was buttonholed while leaving the church by an eager job-seeker. Hall listened gravely to the man's pleadings to be allowed to fill the new vacancy and then, with a complete dead pan, said: 'My dear boy, I have no power over his place. You must see the sexton for it.' (Another version of the story, as reported by the *Tribune,* is that the dead man was an Alderman Hartt and that an ambitious politician tried to approach Hall at the funeral and Hall at first refused to meet him. Finally the man was told he could have 'only a word.' 'Mr. Mayor,' he said, 'to be plain with you I would like to take Hartt's place.' 'I'm willing,' Hall said, according to the *Tribune;* 'just apply to the undertaker.')

One of Hall's most useful anecdotes concerned the unfortunate daughter of an indigent family who further added to her family's difficulties by producing a baby out of wedlock. Hall would let himself be reminded of the story in connection with a point he was making and then play down his punch line: 'But then, as the mild-mannered lassie said excusingly to the irate overseer of the poor, "Indeed, Sir, it is such a little one, I ought to be forgiven." '

According to Stephen Fiske, a distinguished New York editor and writer of the late nineteenth century, Hall attended a breakfast at Wyndham House in New York for Oscar Wilde and turned out to be the life of the party while Wilde was something of a frost. The visitor had perhaps exhausted his humor when he landed and was asked by a customs officer if he had anything to declare. 'I have nothing to declare,' Wilde replied, 'but my genius.' According to Fiske, 'Hall kept his end of the breakfast table in roars of laughter. There were no speeches and when Hall left the dining room he thanked Manager Palmer, remarking, "You have removed one of the terrors of breakfasting in public. Eloquence is not a bird of early flight." '

An intense though eclectic reader, Hall's favorite book was Hamilton's *Logic.* He regarded a certain passage from the Bible as the best writing in the world. 'There is no poem,' he wrote, 'in any language more filled with true imagery than the concluding chapter [of Ecclesiastes]. Then, to hear it chanted in the original Hebrew, by a sweet-voiced rabbi, is to appreciate that the rhythm is as fine as the imagery.' The New York *Herald,* speaking of Hall's reading habits at college, said: 'Discontented thoroughly with all of Euclid and the conic sections and the differential and integral calculus laid down in the college course he was not content with the limitation to the ancient classics. Virgil, Horace, Cicero and Seneca were his favorite Latin authors and there was a time when he could repeat half the odes of old Quintus Horatius Flaccus. He read all their works with avidity.' A New York playwright said that Hall's 'knowledge of men, events and books was inexhaustible. . . . His wit was as ready as his logic or his law.'

VII

In Hall's day, New York was as intimate as a small town. Eccentric men like Horace Greeley and the elder James Gordon Bennett aired their eccentricities in their newspaper columns. There were many witty men whose remarks were broadcast by word of mouth in restaurants and clubs and on the street. One of the town's best wits was Henry Clapp, Jr., the drama critic on Hall's paper, *The Leader,* who once said: 'I only work in my leisure hours.' Of Horace Greeley, he said: 'This is a self-made man who worships his creator.' One night at a bar, Artemus Ward, the writer, who was having great success as a lecturer, showed Clapp a telegram he had received from a San Francisco theatrical manager named Macguire. The telegram read: 'What will you take for one hundred nights?' Clapp persuaded Ward to let him dictate the reply — 'Brandy and water.' Clapp's wit was sharper than Hall's because it was generally at somebody else's expense. Hall liked people too much to wound their feelings. He was often humorous at his own expense. And when he quarreled with Greeley, it was only politically. He wrote a pamphlet called, 'Horace Greeley, Decently Dissected,' which proved mainly that Greeley was inconsistent, which he was. But Greeley liked Hall, as he told friends. The elder James Gordon Bennett liked Hall so much that he gave him an extraordinary amount of highly favorable publicity in the columns of the *Herald*. When Hall became Mayor, Bennett published this comment on him:

'It will be a refreshing novelty to have for Mayor of New York a strictly upright, honorable, capable man, and at the same time one who writes a drama or a farce with equal success, acts a part as well as most professionals on the stage, conducts the most difficult cases on the calendar, sings a good song, composes poetry by the yard, makes an effective stump-speech, responds to a toast with remarkable eloquence and taste, mixes a lobster salad as well as Delmonico's head cook, smokes the best cigar in New York, respects old age, and admires youth, as poets and orators invariably do.' In calling Hall a poet 'by the yard,' the *Herald* was not exaggerating. At New York University and at Harvard he had filled many notebooks with his verse. Much of it, as might be expected, was dedicated to the fair sex. He wrote poems to his wife on her birthday and on Valentine's Day, and poems to his friends. He also wrote an 'Epithalamium' on the marriage of General Morris's daughter.

Hall's verse was published in many newspapers and magazines. He also wrote a number of books: a children's book entitled *Old Whitey's Christmas Trot;* a satire on a Congressman, *The Happy Lobbyist's Holiday;* and a book about New Orleans, *A Manhattaner in New Orleans.* He actually helped pay his way through college, and added to his income in his early years as a lawyer, by writing for various publications. He was most proud of his pieces in *International Magazine,* but he also wrote for *Harper's Monthly.* He gained particular distinction for an article he wrote for the latter called 'A Dinner At The Mayor's,' describing an affair he had attended at the residence of Mayor Fernando

Wood in 1855. The guests included General Winfield Scott, ex-President Martin van Buren and his son, 'Prince John,' Commodore Matthew Calbraith Perry, Washington Irving, Horatio Seymour, Governor of New York State, Ogden Hoffman, Attorney General of New York State, and George Bancroft, the historian. Hall caught the best of the conversation with all its nuances so well that the piece reads as if it had been written yesterday.

Such was the man who, in the fall of 1868, stood forth as one of the most successful and promising political figures in the country. Although only forty-two, he had behind him a twelve-year reputation as District Attorney — always a great political asset. Despite his cultural proclivities, he was an immensely popular figure. He knew how to be urbane, charming, and witty without antagonizing the electorate. Not only his political friends, but a number of newspapers predicted that he would eventually go to the White House. 'Nothing seemed impossible to his ambitions,' said the New York *Sun*. 'At the height of his popularity it was confidently predicted by friends and foes that he would yet be Governor of the State of New York and President of the United States.'

Hall was to spend four full years as Mayor of New York City, three of them in the decade which Denis Tilden Lynch, the New York political historian, likes to call 'the Wild Seventies.' Hall was Mayor while the city's treasury was robbed by the Tweed Ring of a sum which one authority places as high as $200,000,000. He became one of four city officials to whom Thomas Nast, the cartoonist for *Harper's Weekly*, was to give a certain immortality in what is generally believed to be the finest and most effective political cartooning ever done in the United States. The others were Tweed, Sweeny, and Connolly.

Hall's association with the Tweed Ring, which destroyed his career, was the result of a law then in effect which required the Mayor of the Corporation of the City of New York to countersign vouchers authorizing payment of funds out of the city's treasury. It has never been proved one way or another whether he received any of the 'boddle,' as graft was called then, or if he ever knew what was going on. The courts acquitted him, but the public did not. Well aware of this, he went to the length of writing a play about an innocent man falsely accused and took the leading role himself. It lasted three weeks on Broadway. He was to go to his grave, thirty colorful and exciting years later, still proclaiming his complete innocence of any wrongdoing.

VIII

When Hall became Mayor in January, 1869, the job paid $7,500 a year. As District Attorney he had received $5,000 a year. He kept his partnership in his law firm but didn't have to work too hard at it. His value to the other members lay in his political connections and the prestige, such as it was, of having as a partner the Mayor of the city.

Early that January, the *New York Times* took note of Hall as a writer, devoting an editorial to a piece the Mayor had just published in *Galaxy Magazine* called 'Our Crimeland Excursion.' The piece was an imitation of Bunyan's famous allegory. The excursion was conducted by 'Mr. Clergyman, Mr. Detective, and Mr. District Attorney, the latter being,' according to the *Times,* 'our inchoate Mayor.'

'Crimeland's territory is boundless,' Hall had written, 'and appertains to moral and physical geography.' He then went on to visit 'Misdemeanorshire, Assault and Batteryville, Good Law, Forgery Dale and Embezzlement.' The *Times* added that 'Embezzlement we trust does not mean for the future of City Hall. . . . Let us hope the obliging guide [Hall] has himself emerged from these queer surroundings . . . and that his new surroundings in City Hall will illustrate that pure, simple, innocent and Arcadian "Good Law" of which he pleasantly sings.' At the end of March, Hall saw fit to issue 'a caution against New York Circulars, tickets, shares, prospectuses in co-operative syndicates, gift enterprises and dollar stores . . . Every such advertised scheme is necessarily a swindle.'

He attended the funerals of the leading citizens of the town. He was present, along with other distinguished New Yorkers, at the funeral of ex-Mayor James Harper, the 'first adherent of total abstinence,' and a partner in the publishing firm of Harper and Brothers. In the middle of June, he acted as a bearer at the funeral of Henry Jarvis Raymond, the great *New York Times* editor. Other bearers were Horace Greeley, Admiral Farragut, General John A. Dix, and A. T. Stewart, the department store head. Henry Ward Beecher preached the funeral sermon. Both the *Times* and *Harper's Weekly* were soon to play crucial parts in Hall's life.

In the spring, the newspapers complained that the city was 'over-run with dogs' and the *Telegram* began a minor crusade to have dogs licensed. Hall was well aware of the political dangers of offending dog lovers and ignored the suggestion. The *Telegram* said: 'Mayor Hall does not intend incurring even the displeasure of the dogs.' For several days the *Telegram* printed barbs directed at the Mayor. 'Going to the dogs — The Health Board by direction of Mayor Hall.' 'It is neither fair nor true that the Mayor is a blockhead because he is Oakey.'

Hall replied in the *Leader*, which he had begun to edit — it was owned by Tammany leaders — that 'criticisms like these from opponents will enable any politician to sell his political birthright for a pot of message.'

'A. Oakey Hall, our eccentric but talented Mayor,' the *World* retorted, 'says and writes more bright things and commits more stupid blunders than any politician we know of.'

In handling the matter of a rotted tree which his Street

Commissioner, George W. McLean, proposed to cut down, Hall decided to risk the displeasure of tree lovers and wrote and made public the following letter to the Commissioner:

'I am told that many sentimental appeals have been made to you in behalf of the grand old tree fronting Broadway, just above the St. James Hotel, and which (the tree not the hotel) was once a sapling upon the Varian farm; all "once upon a time" when there existed a morass where now stands the bronze statue of Vanderbilt. Most people have forgotten the song of "Woodman, Spare That Tree," but they have not forgotten General Morris, its author, nor Henry Russell, who so generously sung it thirty years ago. Let us also forget the sentiment implied in that lyric, and cut the tree down. Age has withered it, and custom has staled its infinite variety of "interviewing" with busy Broadway. A very excellent arborist informs me, as some of the neighbors fear, that the tree is in danger of unexpectedly falling over upon the adjoining buildings, or into the crowded thoroughfare during the "wild chilly blasts of December."

'I shall hope to meet you at the dinner of the St. Nicholas Society, and hear you or Richard Mount discourse upon the association connected with or sprung from the aforesaid tree, which has already been embalmed in David Valentine's *Manual*. But meanwhile, I cry aloud to you, Inspector of Street Incumbrances, and spare not.

'Very truly, your obedient servant
'A. Oakey Hall.'

IX

That spring of 1869, in Albany, the groundwork was laid for the public scandal which was to have a devastating effect not only on Hall's life but on the entire City of New York. By bribing Republican members of the Legislature, Boss

Tweed, who was now a State Senator, President of New York's Board of Aldermen, and the holder of some forty-odd other city jobs, arranged passage of a new charter for New York City. Later known as the Tweed charter, it was carefully drawn so that it would expedite the diverting of monies from the city's treasury and at the same time assure Tweed's retaining control of the city's government. Among other provisions, it abolished the election of the twelve members of the city's school board and specified that the Mayor would appoint them. It marked the beginning of a long record of political hacks, appointed on a political basis, on the school board. To get the charter passed, Tweed had bribed five Republican senators at $40,000 apiece. Democratic senators were, of course, to be counted on, and didn't have to be paid. Tweed later testified that, in order to get the bill passed, he also had to 'subsidize' the Albany *Argus* and the Albany *Evening Journal*. Asked to explain, he said he paid the publishers 'sometimes $5,000, sometimes $1,000, sometimes $500. It was a general dribble all the time. . . .'

The charter, said to have been written by Peter Sweeny, was so well drawn and arguments in its favor so well presented that even Horace Greeley hailed it as a reform measure. Reformers in New York paid little attention to its passage. The only real opposition came from a group who called themselves the Young Democracy. One of its leaders was Henry W. Genet, known as 'Prince Hal, the Modern Monte Cristo,' because of his high living. Genet was the grandson of Citizen Genet, French ambassador of Revolutionary fame, who had married a daughter of George Clinton. Genet was the only Democrat in the Legislature who voted against the charter.

Although Tweed later testified that passage of the charter cost him hundreds of thousands of dollars and that Oakey Hall contributed $25,000 toward a fund for getting it passed, the record does not show that Hall was a member of Tweed's inner circle. In fact, there is even an indication that Tweed and Hall were not friendly. Tweed was reported to have said: 'Hall's all right, all he needs is ballast. If Oakey had had ballast enough to hold him down in the District Attorney's chair, he would have become a great man in time. Now he won't. Politics are too deep for him. They are for me and I can wade long after Oakey has to float. He's lightheaded.'

Only one letter from Tweed to Hall has survived in the Hall papers, and it concerns a minor political matter. Dated 3 December 1869, it reads 'My dear OK — Your note of last Saturday relative to the appointment for Morrissey I sent to the School office of 7 Ward with a request to do *it* — I had however prior to that seen Mr. Mahar Morrissey's nephew and explained to him the fact that there were sisters of two of our most prominent Democrats in this Ward who had been serving as floating teachers in the Ward who would first have to be provided — after their cases are disposed of our friends on the Board will comply with your desire with pleasure. Your frd W M Tweed.' The letter was on the stationery of Tweed's office at 237 Broadway.

There is no doubt that the Tweed charter vested a large amount of power in the hands of Hall, and it is likely that Tweed arranged this, believing that he could count on Hall to do his bidding. According to M. R. Werner, author of the distinguished work, *Tammany Hall,* who studied the charter, 'Mayor A. Oakey Hall was given the absolute and unlimited power to appoint every important city official without the approval of anyone. The officials of the courts were to be appointed by the Comptroller whose own appointment, as we have just seen, was also controlled by the Mayor. The heads of departments were to report to the Mayor alone and only at his request, so that no one except the Mayor could know the condition of the City's affairs. The Mayor and the Comptroller were also authorized to fix the amount

WM. M. TWEED,
No. 237 BROADWAY,
NEW YORK CITY.

3 Dec 1869

My dear OK

Your note
of last Saturday relative
to appointment for
Morrissey. I sent to the
School Officer of 7 Ward
with a request to do
it = I had however
prior to that seen
Mr Mahar Morrissey
nephew and had
explained to him the

This letter from Boss Tweed to Mayor Hall shows (1) his handwriting was literate; (2) he called Hall by a nickname; (3) he didn't need a secretary to get off a letter.

of the salaries of all civil judges and all court attendants at any sum they might see fit, not exceeding $10,000 a year. The Ring guarded against the exercise of these vast powers by anyone except their own A. Oakey Hall, by providing in their charter that these powers were conferred only on the then incumbent of the Mayor's office, and in case of his removal by death, disability or resignation, the same powers were to be exercised by the Comptroller, who would succeed him in office.

'The charter also created a Board of Audit consisting of the Mayor, A. Oakey Hall, the Comptroller, Richard B. Connolly, the Commissioner of Public Works, William M. Tweed, and the President of the Board of Parks, Peter B. Sweeny. This board was to audit all claims against the City and by this right it controlled all municipal expenditures. At its first meeting, the Board passed $6,312,000 worth of bills against the City, of which sum, it was subsequently discovered, 10 per cent were legitimate. It was said that $15,-750,000 worth of fraudulent bills were approved by this omnipotent board of directors.'

There was no doubt that the city administration was spending a great deal of money in 1869. The new white granite County Court House building, now the City Court, was going up in back of City Hall. The sums of money being spent to plaster and paint its walls, carpet its floors, and provide it with lighting fixtures and furniture were astronomical enough, it was said, to build the houses of Parliament in London.

X

In September, 1869, there appeared in *Harper's Weekly* a cartoon by a comparatively unknown artist named Thomas Nast. It was called 'The Democratic Scapegoat,' and showed Hall's friend, August Belmont, with horns growing out of his head and with the body of a goat, carrying five full bags on his back marked 'Sins of the Democrats — Defeat in 1864 — McClellan — Defeat in 1868 — Seymour & Blair.' Tweed, drawn for the first time by Nast, was standing on a dais and his chair was marked: 'Reserved for Mr. Tweed — Democratic National Emergency Committee.' Next to this was a sign headed, 'Tweed Association — A. Belmont is an Inefficient, Undevoted, Unsuccessful, and Unpopular Chairman — Furthermore that his Dearth of Capacity, Lack of Purpose, Indifference as to Results and Want of Acceptability Were the Chief Cause of our Defeats.' Irishmen with plug hats and faces like baboons were kicking Belmont. The words on the sign referred to Tweed's attempt to get control of the machinery of the national Democratic organization.

XI

Hall continued to make little jokes for the newspapers. In October, for example, he had a tiff with the New York *Sun* — the result of his having received from the business manager of that paper a request for payment of a bill for legal advertising for the city. The *Sun's* business manager had pleaded, 'We are hard pressed for funds.' Hall returned the letter to the *Sun*, asking that it be printed. The *Sun* complied and sent Hall a bill for $60. Hall then made a great deal, in talk and in print, of the fact that the *Sun* 'charged money for printing news.'

Hall's contempt for the town's newspapers was justified. The *North American Review* estimated that fifty-four dailies and twenty-six weeklies in and around New York were receiving subsidies in the form of legal advertising at a dollar a line in return for not attacking the administration. Some newspaper writers received stipends of $2,400 a year from

Tammany. On the other hand, the *Leader,* of which Hall was unofficially the editor, was said to be subsidized by Sweeny and other members of the Tweed group. It was, of course, a vigorous defender of the Tammany or Tweed administration.

Hall got on well with working newspapermen. Often, when Tammany was under attack, he went unscathed. Once he claimed that the *Herald* had not 'done justice' to Tammany Hall. The editor, using Hall's favorite form of humor, replied, 'We trust we have always done that [justice] to Tammany, Mozart, Oakey, and every other Hall.' On 28 November 1869, the *Herald* made full amends to Hall by publishing a half-page biography of him. It was headed simply, 'A. Oakey Hall,' and the subtitle said: 'Brilliant Type of Young America — and Long Chapter of Brilliant Successes — College Studies and Early Journalistic Career and Struggles — Ten Years as District Attorney — Career as Private Lawyer, Politician, Mayor, Orator, and Literateur — His Personal Life.'

It was the kind of story often seen in New York newspapers and known as a 'front office story.' Hall was a personal friend of the elder Bennett, the publisher, and had done legal work for him. Its value lies in the fact that the reporter who wrote it probably worked closely with Hall, so that we seem to get a pen-portrait of the Mayor at his desk.

'His election was a splendid triumph,' the article said, 'a triumph more of personal popularity than party power. The public, irrespective of party, are well satisfied with the result. Everybody knows the conscientious zeal and fidelity with which he has discharged his duties as Mayor.' Hall was not only a literary man, but was also very practical, the article said. 'His messages are models of conciseness and elegance. His first message as Mayor, in point of perspicuity and attractiveness, might have been written by Thackeray. His mind acts intuitively and rapidly, yet methodically. Although for recreation he dabbles in poetry, philosophy, and belles lettres, he is eminently practical. His words, acts, thoughts, are all practical.'

Passages describing the daily routine in the Mayor's office at City Hall are probably more reliable: 'At the inside iron gate stands as sentry Jim Golden, an ex-detective. Marshal Tooker, at the head of the license bureau, is regulating the hacks, trucks, and Peter Funks. Colonel Johns, a brother-in-law of the Governor [John T. Hoffman], is attending to the auction licenses, and communicating with other departments. Major Hart is acting as aide-de-camp to the Marshal. Edward J. Hall [the Mayor's cousin] is computing merciless columns of figures. Gus D. Cardoza, a brother of the Judge and the gentleman par excellence of all clerks, is arranging marriage statistics. Dr. Harris has a long list of all newly arrived emigrants before him. Major Hoey, like Mrs. Gump, "the hardworkingest of creatures," is distributing the mail. Two other officers are waiting for orders. In the ante-room messengers from the treasury and the law departments and from the newspapers are waiting.

'In the sanctum sanctorum sits the Mayor. Everything about the office . . . is an exponent of the man. Paintings, pictures, photographs of friends and statuettes adorn the walls and mantles; the ceiling is richly frescoed, capacious armchairs softly cushioned invite guests to comfortable seats; the desks are of the most elegant description, and casting a genial glow over the warm bright carpet is a blazing fire of cannel coal in the cozy grate . . . Beside [Hall] his private clerk, J. C. Goldsmith, pen in hand, [is] dashing off the shortest of shorthand notes into a hundred various memorandums, as they come quick and fresh from the lips of the superior.

'An hour later messengers go in all directions with these messages and documents. And then the tide of visitation pours in, Mayors of other cities, reporters, editors, beggars,

66

Although exposure of the Ring scandals had begun in the summer of 1871, Oakey Hall went about performing the traditional Mayoralty duties. He laid the cornerstone of Turners' Hall on 17 July. The woodcut is from *Leslie's Weekly*.

politicians, generals, colonels, merchants, aldermen, and officials. Politeness to every visitor, the humble and lowly as well as the proud and rich, is a marked and most pleasing feature in [Hall's] character. He transacts his routine business with dispatch, and examines resolutions and bills with a keen and all-seeing eye.'

'The Mayor,' Hall himself later wrote, 'had pleasantly ornamental duties. He was an entertainer of foreign and tourist guests; and the recipient of a dozen dinner invitations per week; and was the traditional toastmaster at public banquets. He laid cornerstones at public buildings and thereby accumulated a set of silver trowels . . . The Mayor was frequently importuned to perform the marriage ceremony. . . . If the bride was young or winning, the Mayor had the perquisite of osculation; or if she were elderly or plain, the ingenious task of excusing himself.'

In June, 1869, Hall officiated at the marriage of a young French refugee who had been teaching at a fashionable girls' boarding school in New Haven. The bride, Mary Plummer, had been a pupil of the teacher, Georges Clemenceau — later to become Prime Minister of France during World War I. Hall often injected into his performance of the ceremony the phrase, 'until death or the divorce court do thee part.' He explained that he did not wish 'to become an accessory before the fact to the marital perjury . . . when the couple might afterward meditate divorce.' In the case of Clemenceau and his bride he was right, as they were divorced in France in 1892.

XII

Not everyone was charmed by Hall. *Every Saturday,* for example, published a piece on him which said that 'His Honor . . . for twenty years has maintained a quasi or direct connection with the press. He is not lacking in the culture of desultory reading, and when he chooses to do so can bear himself like a gentleman. Of such a thing as dignity of character, he appears to have but a faint conception. Pedantry is more to him than profundity, and to tickle the ear of the town with a cheap witticism he deems a greater thing than to command it with a forcible presentation of grave issues. . . . He is a harlequin with the literary ambition of a Richelieu. . . . He can write clearly and concisely when he will, but he prefers to provoke with odd quips and far-fetched conceits. He patronizes journalists and magazine writers with a sort of grotesque familiarity, and readily makes himself at home among the Bohemians of Literature.'

Hall ended his first year in office on a slightly tipsy note. Asked to address New York's venerable New England Society, he gave a scholarly, somewhat oratorical speech studded with Latin quotations. He concluded by saying, 'especially do we admire the taste you have displayed in quitting that part of the United States, where, as we Knickerbockers believe, New Englanders continue to prosecute each other for opinion's sake. Here you enjoy extensive freedom — freedom in newspaper abuse; freedom to gamble in Wall Street; freedom in marriage; freedom in divorce; free lager; free fights; free love!'

In the *Tribune,* Horace Greeley commented that, 'New York must be delivered from the thralldom of the Hall family. It is wearied of Tammany Hall, Mozart Hall, all the political halls, Oakey Hall, and alcohol.'

The storm clouds were gathering.

4

'THE ELEGANT OAKEY'

I

IT WAS DURING HALL'S second year as Mayor that his reputation for elegance in attire really blossomed. It was perhaps unfortunate for him that this was so, for a time was rapidly approaching when conspicuity in the outward man, if that man were connected with the city administration, was something less than an asset. But some weakness in Hall, springing perhaps from insecurity, drove him to pay an extraordinary amount of attention to dress. Often in company with the town's 'swells,' he was not content with the dignity of his position, but chose rather to out-Herod Herod, so that even the 'swells' were forced to emulate some of his innovations. Freize coats with velvet collars, made to order by the town's most fashionable tailors; shirts of the finest quality linen; fancy vests of many colors and materials, some of them embroidered by his wife; ties of the finest silk — these were now articles of everyday wear. His beard was trimmed frequently, and he kept his hair just long enough to show a wave.

Fine jewelry also exerted a fascination for him; but his was not the ostentatious display that led Tweed and other Tammany bigwigs to wear huge diamond shirt studs on festive occasions. Instead, he liked to drop in at Tiffany's and work out his own design for a piece of jewelry, particularly for his wife. One piece was a gold deer on which a diamond studded 'U' was imposed. For his own use he designed elaborate cuff links, a dazzling collection of which fell to his descendants. His stationery was embossed with a personally designed monogram consisting of an 'O' enclosing two perpendicular awls, and crossed by a key to form an 'H.' Some of it also carried the Oakey family crest whose motto was 'Fortuna Juvat Audentes' — Fortune Favors the Bold.

Nevertheless, although he had a lot of style, Hall was not pretentious. Soon after becoming Mayor he abolished, while he held the office, the salutation of 'Your Honor.' He also refused to accept from the city the traditional pair of Mayor's lamps for his residence. He explained his refusal to accede to this Manhattan-Dutch tradition by writing that he 'didn't want my family to be annoyed by callers, who in passing by and seeing two lamps, would fancy the house a hotel or restaurant or something more improper.

'Moreover, I did not believe in the useless expense to the city treasury of maintaining lamps which, however useful or distinguishing in an early metropolitan era, had in progressive times lost their significance of display. In my official case these traditional lamps came only under the Latin sarcastic maxim of "Lux e non lucendo." '

Although he had access to the most exclusive social circles in town, he preferred the company of writers, artists, and newspapermen. 'I've been called The King of the Bohemians,' he said, 'and I'm jolly proud of the title.' When he took office he announced that he considered being the editor of a great newspaper like the New York *World* a greater honor than being Mayor. The *World* immediately replied that the job was waiting for him. Hall did edit, before and while he was Mayor, a small weekly New York paper called *The*

Leader. One of his fellow editors wrote that 'After the paper was out, we went to supper, generally to his house in Forty-second Street. There was a chafing-dish ready on the table, with oysters, a bird, or a joint of venison, and Mrs. Hall to peep over the banisters to see that everything was prepared so that Mr. Hall could cook while he talked. Never was his talk more brilliant than at two o'clock in the morning, with Mr. Hall as insensible to fatigue, as if he had not done the work of five clever men during the long day.'

Before 1870, the newspapers had carried only short paragraphs about his elegance in dress. The *Herald,* for example, had stated that 'Oakey Hall is the best dressed man in the annals of Mayordom; he wears a different necktie every day. Oakey Hall is inclined to fancies; he sports a different pair of sleeve buttons every day.' But this was nothing to what was to come.

Hall followed the tradition of holding open house at City Hall on New Year's Day. 'The Knickerbocker custom,' he later wrote, 'was then in vogue and each official . . . spread a refection of viands and liquids . . . by noontide the office and City Hall became thronged with callers, while a large room in the basement of the City Hall was encumbered with casks of lemonade, urns of coffee, kegs of lager beer, tureens of pickled oysters and trays of sandwiches.' On New Year's Day, 1870, Hall was in especially good form. A German newspaper commented the next day on his performance as a host: 'The Mayor wore the colors of the Nord German Bund, a ribbon of green Erin and gaiters à la Knickerbocker, thus uniting the mightiest elements governing this mighty metropolis. In acknowledging the victory [of Lager Beer] the brewers of New York ought to provide the Mayor for life with free Lager.'

At a patriotic parade some months before, a newspaper had carried a small item which said: 'Oakey Hall's get-up at

the parade yesterday was gorgeous. His blue suit represented the cause of the Union; his gray overcoat that of the
Rebs; his be-e-eautiful necktie the bright Heavens above
us, and his polished boots the culture so pre-eminently his
own.'

A week later, at the Annual Ball of the Americus Club
held at the Academy of Music on Fourteenth Street, Hall,
according to a newspaper report, 'was faultlessly attired in
a bottle-green fly-tail coat, with half sovereigns of pure guinea
gold for buttons and a green velvet collar and lapels, a waistcoat and a light unwhisperable of the same material and color
and a new satin necktie of large dimensions. His kids were
also green; his shirt front was embroidered with shamrocks
in green floss silk, and immense emeralds winked in his but-
ton holes. He wore a pair of eye glasses with rims of Irish
bog-oak and attached to a green silk cord.'

There were other aspects to his showmanship. Hall usually
left his office around one or two in the afternoon to go to
Delmonico's where he dined every day (dinner was an afternoon repast in those days). 'He always arrived in a carriage
or sleigh,' a friend who also frequented Delmonico's has
recorded, 'carried about $500 in cash with him, and was
princely in his expenditures.'

Hall should have taken political stock of himself for that
month. For the second time within a few weeks, Nast had
included him in cartoons in *Harper's Weekly* attacking
Tweed and other members of his group. In the first, he had
been shown in the robes of a cardinal, holding a staff and
wearing a cardinal's hat labeled 'City Hall-O.K. Ha?l,' standing in attendance at a mock Papal Court while Swiss guards
(Irish immigrants with baboon faces) opened boxes marked
TAX PAYERS AND TENANTS' HARD CASH, as Tweed, Sweeny,
and Hoffman greedily watched. In the second, Nast drew
fourteen panels showing the things that were corrupt in

New York — Elections, 'The City of Dust,' The Water Board, The Schools, The Street 'Cleaners,' The Fire Department, The Board of Health, and Saloons. In a panel directed at 'Central Park Under The Tammany Commissioners,' 'O.K. Ha?l' was shown with Tweed, Sweeny, and Connolly as statues in the park. This cartoon, called 'Shadows of Forthcoming Events,' was a remarkable instance of prophecy because all the corruptions illustrated in the panels were exposed eighteen months later. In both the cartoons, Nast blurred the second 'l' in Hall's name. Later, he regularly spelled his name 'Haul.' Although Hall appeared to be unconcerned about these broad hints impugning his honesty, there is no doubt that he noticed them. Meeting Nast on the street one day, he stopped and said, "I have not seen your "handwriting on the wall" of late.' Nast looked at him without smiling and said, 'You will see more of it, presently,' then walked on.

II

During February, Hall was busy helping to found the Lotos Club. According to the official club history Hall 'pressed the literary gentlemen of his time' into forming a club 'along the lines of the Garrick and Savage Club of London' where 'members of the literary, art, musical and dramatic world and such merchants or nonprofessional gentlemen whose tastes and inclinations led them to a regard for fostering of these professions' could meet. Hall felt that 'a more suitable place than the Chamber of Commerce should be established to entertain such foreign notables as Thackeray and Dickens.' De Witt Van Buren, George Hows, and four other like-minded gentlemen met at the offices of the *Leader,* the paper of which Hall was editor, and founded the club. The Lotos took as its motto the lines from Tennyson's poem, 'The Lotos-Eaters':

In the afternoon they came unto a land
In which it seemed always afternoon.

Hall afterwards introduced a resolution which made it
possible for the club to accept works of art from artists in
lieu of their initiation fee.

Inasmuch as Hall already belonged to so many clubs, it
seems strange that he should have been interested in forming
still another. He was not, apparently, using the swank Union
Club much at this time, meeting his political friends at the
Manhattan Club, of which he was a governor. The prominent Democrats who frequented the Manhattan were regarded as the respectable or reform wing of their party,
as opposed to the Tammany wing, headed by Tweed.

One possible explanation of Hall's desire to participate in
so many phases of New York life is that he wanted to be
three people — Hall, the gentleman, member of the Manhattan and Union Clubs; Hall, the writer, poet, and scholar
who liked 'the company of literary gentlemen'; and the Hall
who was ready with a witty speech at the tap of a gavel and
who therefore attended affairs of political clubs like the
Tweed-dominated Americus and Blossom. In the winter
of 1870, he made himself conspicuous at the 'Brennan Ball.'
Sheriff Matthew T. Brennan was a Tammany district leader
who was to go down in history as the official designated to
arrest Tweed. Hall attended the Brennan Ball in company
with Billy Florence, the actor.

'Mayor Hall smiled at everybody,' the *Sun* reporter wrote,
'and shook hands twice all round. At midnight he was invited into the committee room, where wine and food were
given him. He passed on the beets, on the cold beef, on the
sandwiches, and the pickled olives, but he boarded a plate
of boned turkey covered with jelly, and did not leave it until it had been nearly demolished. The hungry politicians
surrounding the table were compelled to go without any

boned turkey, owing to the Mayor's royal appetite. One of the politicians gave vent to his indignation thus: "Well, this Mayor's style is all well enough outside the committee room, but here he don't give a decent feller a show." '

A few days later a friend of Hall's sent him a clipping of the *Sun* story. 'Brother Oakie,' the friend wrote, 'I know that in old times you were a good feeder. But I had no idea you had become as terrible a gourmand.'

When St. Patrick's Day came around on 17 March 1870, Hall contributed further to the legend of his elegance in dress. He waited until the great parade arrived at City Hall and, according to the New York *Illustrated News,* 'came out of his office wearing a green suit.' The late John A. Hennessy, a *Times* reporter, recalling the event years later, commented: 'In those days, the Irish didn't amount to much in the city. They were mostly immigrants and day laborers. Naturally, the St. Patrick's Day Parade was not the great thing it is today. It began at Cooper Union and ended at City Hall. The reviewing stand was in front of City Hall. In 1870, when the great day came, there was a terrible snow storm. It was an Irish snow storm, flakes as big as your fist. Well, the elegant Oakey stood on the reviewing stand dressed in a green suit, a green hat, a green tie, everything green, even green spats. He stayed all through the parade despite the inclement weather. Naturally, it made a great hit with the Irish. Hall himself was of English descent, I believe, but after that people took to calling him Mayor O'Hall.'

The late Matthew Breen, who witnessed the incident, wrote that in March, 1870, Hall reviewed the parade 'dressed in the regalia of an Irish prince with not only a sprig of shamrock in his buttonhole but a green tie and a green tailcoat. He repeated the performance in 1871.' Breen went on to say that Hall was regarded in his day as the apostle of the Irish societies and that the New York Irish were called the 'Exiles of Erin.' Breen wrote that this was a mistake, as the real Irish exiles were in Ireland because 'all the Irish were in New York.'

Hall was well aware that it was woe to any New York politician who failed to please the Irish. In his speeches to Irish groups, he could always get a big hand by stating that his initials, A.O.H., stood for the 'Ancient Order of Hibernians.'

The day after the parade, the *Sun* commented that 'Mayor O'Hall is said to have solemnly assured a committee of Germans that if the French get beaten during the present war, he will come out immediately in a full suit of Prussian blue. Meanwhile, he is having a tri-colored suit made, in case of another contingency. As for the famous green suit, with the shamrock buttons, it is laid for the present on the shelf.'

In later years, a legend grew up that Hall's dressing in green for the St. Patrick's Day parades was forced on him by Tweed, who wanted to maintain the popularity of the administration with the Irish voters. In the telling and retelling of the legend of the Elegant Oakey, it was said that Tweed had made a fool of a member of New York society by forcing this indignity on him. Hall needed no urging to dress in green for the occasion. He was a born dresser — perhaps a born actor.

Although Hall seemed to be carrying on in his office as Mayor with a good deal of gaiety, there are indications that he was becoming anxious. In a note he left in June, 1870, for one of his City Hall factotums, he wrote: 'We are so d—d popular around the circle that I begin to fear inexplicable tornadoes etc., etc. In a great calm reef the sails.'

What circle was he alluding to? What inexplicable tornadoes had he begun to fear? The note mentioned other matters at City Hall. He said he would 'increase Refferts' salary. But he is about as useful as a pen sponge on your desk.' It was 'all right' as to Patterson, but as for taking care of Field he would write Hugh Scott to see if 'he can go on Docks. Neither Tweed nor I can place him.' A large part of politics has always been getting jobs for incompetents.

A month later, however, Hall was the leading spirit at Tammany Hall's Fourth of July celebration. He collected and presented to the Tammany Society examples of Indian dress and fighting equipment. Andrew J. Garvey, a plastering contractor to whom Nast was to give the names 'Prince of Plasterers' and 'Handy Andy,' provided 'every conceivable kind of patriotic decoration.' Tweed made one of the few speeches of his career. 'We consider,' he said, 'this bright auspicious day as a forerunner for another when the great Democratic party, through which alone this great country can be properly reconstructed, shall again resume sway, and place us in the condition of constitutional prosperity we were in before the late civil war. . . . Brothers, as there will be much good talk by the warriors and braves, I will spare you the infliction of a speech from me, except these welcoming words to the Wigwam.' 'Patriotic airs' were provided by Grafulla's Band, which was to perform a year later at the fabulous wedding of Tweed's daughter.

III

In the fall of 1870, the rumors of City Hall graft and corruption grew more frequent. Many of the rumors concerned the building of the new County Court House (now the City Court), which was still under construction. It was also reported that the city's books, if examined, would show great irregularities. The *Times* was the only paper admitting the truth of the rumors, but as yet spoke only in generalities. In one *Times* editorial the people of the city were called upon 'to shake off the rule of the dozen sordid men of selfish hearts and narrow brains who have plundered millions yearly, obstructed our material growth, made our markets, our wharves and piers and streets, mere monuments of their rapacity, our elections a farce, and now have put up judges in our Courthouse to sell injustice for a price.' On 3 October, the *Times* said: 'We think it quite as true now as when old President Dwight [of Yale University] said it, that although every Democrat is not a horse-thief, it is quite certain that every horse-thief is a Democrat.'

Inasmuch as an election was coming up, Connolly, the City Comptroller, and Hall appointed a committee of distinguished citizens to examine the books. Nast immediately attacked the committee, which consisted of John Jacob Astor, Moses Taylor, Marshall O. Roberts, George K. Sistaire, E. D. Brown, and Edward Schell. He drew Astor, Roberts, and Taylor with the bodies of mice, running in different directions. Hovering over them was a snake marked PRESTIGE being cut in two by a sword marked SHARP EDITORIALS. The caption of the cartoon was 'Three Blind Mice! See How They Run!'

The committee members approved the city's books, reporting that they had 'come to the conclusion, and certify, that the financial affairs of the city, under the controller, are administered in a correct and faithful manner,' and commented that the city's debt would be wiped out in twelve years. Later, the names of the members of the committee appeared as directors and large stockholders in connection with the building of the viaduct railway. Tammany historian M. R. Werner wrote that the committee members were threatened with having the assessments raised on their real estate holdings unless they brought in a favorable report.

Regardless of the mounting disrepute of Tammany and the Tweed group, the Hall held a gigantic political rally on 27 October which overflowed into the streets for blocks. On the platform, besides Tweed, Sweeny, Connolly, and Hall, were Horatio Seymour, former Governor of New York and a candidate for President of the United States in opposition to General Grant; the Governor of New York, John T. Hoffman; Samuel J. Tilden; and James Fisk, Jr. Colonel Fisk, who held a reserve commission in the National Guard's 69th Regiment, and who had suddenly become enthusiastic about New York politics, gave a speech in which he said: 'I never yet voted the Democratic ticket but now I will vote for it on account of my friend, Tweed; yes, vote for it, if I can, three times a day, and I will bring with me the 25,000 men under me.' As he sat down, he was cheered.

Nast drew several cartoons in connection with the fall campaign, directing them at the 'Tammany Ring-Dom.' Tweed was pictured as a Falstaff, 'The Power Behind the Throne,' on which Governor John T. Hoffman sat. Hall was either omitted or shown, in the background, in the costume of a court jester.

IV

Although Hall was re-elected in the November elections, Nast's cartoons and the rumors linking him with Tweed had had their effect. On 9 November, the distinguished lawyer and trustee of Columbia College, George Templeton Strong, wrote in his diary: 'Oakey Hall runs far behind his ticket "which do please me mightily" to quote Pepys.' The major portion of the public disapproval of Hall was stemming from his own group — the 'respectabilities.'

Hall was again ignored in Nast's post-election cartoon, printed in January, 1871, in which Tweed was shown with Sweeny robbing a safe marked the PUBLIC TREASURY. Protruding from Tweed's stomach was his huge diamond stickpin; it was labeled '$15,000.' This barb, directed at Tweed's vulgar taste in jewelry, particularly incensed the Boss. 'That's the last straw!' he is reported to have said, 'I'll show them damned publishers a new trick!' His new trick was to reject all Harper bids for schoolbooks and to destroy $50,000 worth of Harper books the city already had on hand. They were replaced by books from the New York Printing Company, a corporation owned by the Tweed Ring. The firm of Harper's was ready to throw in the sponge, but Fletcher Harper was for continuing the fight. At a meeting of the firm's executives, he walked out after saying, 'Gentlemen, you know where I live. When you are ready to continue the fight against these scoundrels, send for me. Meantime, I shall find a way to continue it alone.' Fletcher Harper's view prevailed, but after some delay, so that Nast's answer to the textbook ban did not appear until 13 May. This cartoon showed Tweed cuffing a child, who was sitting at his school desk, with his left hand, while his right hand knocked a Wilson 'Reader,' published by Harper's, off the child's desk. Sweeny was shown throwing Harper's textbooks out the window. In the background, Hall, as the teacher, was pointing to a blackboard on which was written:

HOFFMAN WILL BE OUR NEXT PRESIDENT

TWEED IS AN HONEST MAN

SWEENY IS AN ANGEL

HALL IS A FRIEND OF THE POOR.

The titles of the new Tammany textbooks were shown —

HONEST GOVERNMENT BY TWEED AND
ARITHMETIC BY CONNOLLY

To try and stop Nast, Tweed even went to the length of referring to him in a bill presented in Albany regarding a school-tax levy. The bill mentioned 'an artist encouraged to send forth, in a paper that calls itself a "Journal of Civilization," pictures vulgar and blasphemous, for the purpose of arousing the prejudices of the community against a wrong which exists only in their imaginations.' Tweed had a strong ally in the Irish Catholic voters who hated Nast for the anti-Romanist views expressed in his cartoons. In his paper, *The Leader,* Hall referred to Nast as the 'Nast-y artist of Harper's Hell Weekly — a Journal of Devilization.'

The *Times* became more definite in its attack on the administration, saying editorially that 'There is absolutely nothing — nothing in the city which is beyond the reach of the insatiable gang who have obtained possession of it. They can get a grand jury dismissed at any time, and, as we have seen, the Legislature is completely at their disposal.'

In March, Nast again included Hall in a cartoon entitled 'Gross Irregularity not Fraudulent.' It showed Tweed and Sweeny sitting at a table looking over a map of Broadway. Tweed was saying to Sweeny, 'To make this look straight is the hardest job I ever had. What made Watson go sleigh riding?' In the background, Hall was shown sweeping up with a large broom. A carpenter's square was hanging on the wall but was labeled NOT USED IN THIS OFFICE. Nast's cartoons, at this time, were full of such symbols. Hall's sweeping was the cleaning up that he, as one of the few gentlemen in politics, was supposed to be doing for Tweed and Sweeny. Watson was the County Auditor under Tweed whose death in a sleighing accident had interrupted his buying up, for Tweed, certain rights of way in connection with a plan to widen and straighten Broadway. The cartoon may also have referred to the fact that after Watson's death a bookkeeper named William S. Copeland had been employed in the County Auditor's office and had copied down the entries from a certain ledger which contained data regarding the monumental graft being perpetrated by Tweed. Copeland had turned over his information to his friend Sheriff James O'Brien, who had been unsuccessful in an attempt to shake Tweed down for more graft in connection with his official prerogatives as sheriff. O'Brien shopped around among the newspapers offering this information, but found no takers.

V

Hall again decked himself out in green for the 1871 St. Patrick's Day parade. The *Times* reported that Hall, 'who so loves Ireland and the suffrageration thereof, rode in a barouche at the head of the parade.' At City Hall he got out and reviewed it, dressed, according to another newspaper, 'in a new suit of green and black cassimere. He wore a green necktie from which shone a brilliant horseshoe; his gloves were the color of the shamrock and in his buttonhole was an immense bouquet.'

At the end of May, 1871, there was another big Tammany social event, news of which was cabled all over the world. Tweed gave in marriage his eldest daughter, Mary Amelia, to Arthur Ambrose Maginnis of New Orleans. They were married in Trinity Chapel by the Rev. Dr. Joseph H. Price, who had married Tweed and his wife. Delmonico's catered. What made the wedding fabulous was the array of wedding presents which, James Gordon Bennett said in the *Herald*, cost $700,000. Lord & Taylor gave the bride a $5,000 parasol. Peter Sweeny gave her jewelry which the *Times* said cost $40,000. Hall, apparently, gave nothing, but his law partner, Augustus Brown, gave a silver pitcher, fruit dish, and bowl costing $250. There is some indication that Hall did not have any social relations with Tweed or his family. Mrs. Hall, according to descendants of the family, refused 'to have Tweed or any of those Tammany politicians in the house.' The newspapers compared the gifts to the crown jewels of England. Long lists of the presents were cabled abroad. One London editor asked, in the columns of his newspaper, if all the presents arriving at the bride's home bore price tags.

That summer Hall got off one of the worst puns of his career. The question of passing the Chinese Exclusion Act was being debated throughout the country. Hall told an audience that 'on such a hot night as this, it is well to consider the coolie question.' He and his family spent the summer, as was their custom, at his estate at Valley View, in New Jersey. Meanwhile, in New York City, on an especially hot night in July, ex-Sheriff James O'Brien appeared at the office of the *Times* editor, Louis John Jennings, and what transpired within the next few minutes made possible the exposure of the greatest piece of municipal corruption in the history of New York. It not only destroyed the Tweed Ring, but carried Hall into political oblivion and obloquy.

Jennings related, some years later, the exact conversation which took place. O'Brien began the conversation by saying it was a hot night.

'Yes, hot,' Jennings agreed.

'You and Nast have had a hard fight,' continued O'Brien.

'Have still.' Jennings nodded rather wearily.

'I said you *have had* it,' O'Brien repeated, and he pulled a roll of papers from an inner pocket. 'Here are the proofs of all your charges — exact transcriptions from Dick Connolly's books. The boys will likely try to murder you when they know you've got 'em, just as they've tried to murder me.' After O'Brien had left, Jennings sat up until daylight studying the documents.

Tweed must have learned almost immediately that the *Times* had the documents because its publisher, George Jones, was called to the office of a lawyer who was a tenant in the Times Building. When Jones arrived at the office he found Connolly waiting to see him. Connolly then offered Jones $5,000,000 not to publish the documents.

'I don't think the devil will ever make a higher bid for me than that,' Jones said, in one of his rare humorous moments. Connolly pointed out that 'with that sum you can go to Europe and live like a prince.'

'Yes,' Jones said, according to his account of the conversation, 'but I should know that I was a rascal. I cannot consider your offer or any offer not to publish the facts in my possession.'

The *Times* began its exposure of the Tweed Ring frauds on the morning of 8 July 1871. 'We lay before our readers this morning,' Jennings said on the editorial page, 'a chapter of municipal rascality which in any other city but New York would bring down upon the heads of its authors such a storm of indignation as would force them to a speedy accountability before the bar of a criminal court, or compel them to take refuge in flight and perpetual exile.

'We apprehend that no one will complain of a lack of facts and specifications in the articles to which we now call the reader's attention; and that not even *The Tribune* or any other of the eighteen daily and weekly papers that have been gagged by Ring patronage will be able to find an excuse for ignoring the startling record presented here, on the ground that it is not sufficiently definite.'

In a companion editorial, John Foord wrote: 'Who are responsible for these frauds? First, Mayor Hall and Controller Connolly, who pass upon these claims and sign checks for their payment — knowing them to be fraudulent. Second, William M. Tweed and Peter B. Sweeny, who pocket their share of the proceeds — knowing them to have been fraudulently obtained.'

Jennings took special aim at Hall in his editorial 'If Mayor Hall,' he wrote, 'and Controller Connolly object to being branded as thieves and swindlers, as we once more brand them now, they can sue us for libel, and we will prove our charges to be true by means of Controller Connolly's own books. It will not do for Hall to try and sneak out by saying that he is "used to newspaper attack." We do not attack him now on political grounds, or in wild language — but we call him a thief because we can prove him to be one.'

Two months later, Hall answered the taunt by doing exactly what Jennings had suggested — he sued the *Times* for libel. Meanwhile, however, another municipal crisis had arrived to plague him. But serious as it was, compared with the gloom which was fast encompassing him around, the new crisis was in the nature of a respite.

5

THE TWEED RING EXPOSURE

I

HALL HAD RECEIVED WARNING early in July that there was likely to be trouble in connection with the annual parade of members of the Orange Societies of the city. New York's Orangemen, immigrants from Ulster County in the north of Ireland, were Protestants who bitterly resented the power of New York's Irish Catholics, who greatly outnumbered them. The parade was held on 12 July each year in honor of Orange Day, the anniversary of the Battle of the Boyne when, in 1690, the Protestant King, William of Nassau, met and defeated the Catholic King, James II of England. The battle took place near Drogheda in the vales of Maeth through which the weedy River Boyne flows. As the old song went:

> Twas bright July's first morning clear,
>   Of unforgotten glory
> That made this stream through ages dear,
>   Renowned in song and story.

(The discrepancy in dates is due to the change which took place in 1752 at which time eleven days were dropped from the English calendar.)

There had been trouble in connection with the Orange Day parade in 1870. About 2,500 Orangemen dressed in full orange regalia, and carrying the flags of Ulster, Nassau, and Orange, had marched up Eighth Avenue to Nineteenth Street singing 'Boyne Water,' 'Derry,' and other songs, the hearing of which brought murderous thoughts into the hearts of all Irishmen from counties south of Ulster. Two hundred loafers, probably Irish, followed the procession, calling out curses and threats. Just before the parade arrived at its picnic grounds, Elm Park, at Nineteenth Street, the 'rabble,' as a contemporary writer called them, stopped to persuade another group of about three hundred Irish laborers, who were fixing the street, to join them. After the Orangemen had opened up their picnic baskets and begun the day's festivities, designed principally for the entertainment of the women and children, the newly augmented Irish mob arrived and let loose a hail of stones they had brought with them — materials meant for paving the street.

The ensuing battle was fought in two parts — the park where the women and children were attacked, and down Eighth Avenue where a group of Orangemen assembled to take the battle away from the womenfolk. At first only two policemen arrived and they 'could do nothing but stand and look on the murderous conflict.' Finally, about fifty police arrived. Some of the Orangemen tried to take refuge in the Eighth Avenue cars, but the Irish hurled stones through the windows. At seven o'clock that night, Police Superintendent John Jourdan inspected three bloody corpses in the basement of the 31st Precinct. He learned that hundreds were wounded. By morning, two more persons died as a result of the riot. The town's Irish population was intensely excited. Although things quieted down after a day or two, the police predicted that extremely serious trouble was likely to develop at future Orange Day parades. Hall and his administration were not criticized for what had taken place. It was conceded that the police had done the best they could under difficult circumstances. There was some talk that Hall had arranged that the Irish rioteers, who were arrested, be let off with merely a warning to behave in the future. The newspapers treated the affair as a joke. The New York *Star,* for example, printed a couplet —

> Oakey Pokey Tammany Fum!
> Smell the blood of an Orangeman.

Another paper provided a pun for Hall by saying that the Orange Day parade was a 'Boyne of Contention.'

Now, in July, 1871, with the Orange Societies asking that arrangements be set up by the city for their parade, Hall was faced with the decision whether to risk another outbreak of disorder. (The city was still paying judgments rendered against it in connection with the Draft Riots of 1863.) It was being said that the Orangemen were unpatriotic in that their loyalty to their societies was higher than that which they held for the United States. The most alarming report was that the Irish Catholics had resolved during the past year to prevent, by force if necessary, the Orangemen from parading again. The head of the Gideon Lodge of the Orange Society, realizing that Hall was hesitating about granting the necessary permits to parade, wrote a letter to the *Times* in which he complained that Irish Catholics were trying to prevent the Orange Day parade. The Catholic clergy deplored the injection of a religious issue into the matter and urged their parishioners to make no disturbance.

Hall and his advisers were placed in a difficult dilemma. As one contemporary writer, J. T. Headley, put it, 'If they allowed the procession to take place, they would be compelled to protect it, and shoot down the men whose vote helped largely to place them in power. If they forbade it, they feared the public indignation that would be aroused against such a truckling, unjust course.'

Tweed and Connolly prevailed on Hall that the best course would be not to permit the Orange Day Parade. Connolly, especially, took the view that there being more Catholic voters than Protestant voters the only right thing to do was to bow to the rule of the majority. It was, therefore, arranged that Police Superintendent James J. Kelso issue the order forbidding the Orangemen to parade. Hall and Tweed must have felt a certain uneasiness in finding themselves on the Catholic side of a Catholic-Protestant battle. Both their families faithfully attended Trinity Chapel.

Known as General Order No. 57, Superintendent Kelso's statement began by speaking of the inadvisability of such a demonstration as the Orangemen contemplated 'in perpetuation of foreign feuds' and concluded: 'You are ordered to prevent the formation or progression of the public street procession of the 12th instant, and of all processions under pretense of target practice. You will also on that day impartially keep all the streets cleared from groups and assemblages of every class of citizens whether sympathizing with or against the proposed procession, or whether they are lawlessly disposed or otherwise.'

Headley commented that, 'This ludicrous attempt on the part of the Mayor to shift the responsibility from his own shoulders, awakened only scorn, and the appearance of the order was followed by a storm of indignation that was appalling. The leading papers, without regard to politics, opened up on him and his advisers, with such a torrent of denunciations that they quailed before it. Processions of all kinds and nationalities were allowed on the streets, and to forbid only one, and that because it was Protestant, was an insult to every American citizen. Even Wall Street forgot its usual excitement, and leading men were heard violently denouncing this cowardly surrender of Mayor Hall to the threats of a mob.'

An impromptu meeting was held at the Produce Exchange

and a petition was presented asking the president to call a formal meeting. Excited men stood in line two hours waiting to affix their signatures to the petition. A committee was appointed to call on Mayor Hall and remonstrate with him. Hall called a meeting of the City Council, meanwhile, to discuss revoking the order. The Catholic hierarchy decided to take a position on the matter and both Archbishop McClosky and Bishop Jeremiah O'Donovan Rossa issued statements opposing the banning of the parade.

Governor Hoffman hurried to New York from Albany to confer with Hall, Tweed, and Connolly. Hoffman, whose fame will probably rest solely on the fact that he was the author of the phrase, 'Save me from my friends,' decided to issue an order permitting the parade. He had, after all, his national reputation to consider; he was being groomed for the Presidency by Tweed. According to George Templeton Strong, Hoffman had concurred with Hall in forbidding the parade, but when 'he saw that it was raising a storm of popular indignation,' he issued 'a masculine proclamation.'

Hall now rescinded General Order No. 57.

On Thursday morning, 12 July, the people of the city awoke to see in their morning papers a proclamation by the Governor of New York State warning 'all persons to abstain from interference with any such assembly or procession [of the Orangemen] except by authority from me; and I give notice that all the powers at my command, civil and military, will be used to preserve the public peace, and put down at all hazards, every attempt at disturbances; and I call upon all citizens of every race and religion, to unite with me and the local authorities in this determination to preserve the peace and honor of the city and State.'

The Orange Day parade was definitely on — come what may. Strong noted in his diary that 'any peaceable and orderly people who wish to solace themselves in this infernal weather are at liberty to do so and shall be protected in the enjoyment of that right.' Throughout the city, one could feel the tensions mounting. To add to the general anxiety, the police found a secret circular showing that the Irish groups opposing the Orangemen had made elaborate plans to disrupt the parade. They had established watchwords and signals, and designated at what points along the line of march the parade was to be attacked.

II

In accordance with Hoffman's orders, the New York State militia was alerted and posted throughout the city, under the command of General Shaler. Federal troops were on hand under the command of General Pleasanton. Shaler, from police headquarters on Mulberry Street, arranged for the posting of armed guards at all the town's armories beginning at seven in the morning. Early reports pouring into headquarters told of groups of women assembled uptown in the various Irish quarters who were 'gesticulating and talking wildly.' Groups of Irishmen were walking about the city, many of them carrying rifles. In the upper part of the city a body of Irishmen moved south, stopping whenever they found any Irish day laborers at work and 'compelling' them to leave work and join them. A few groups attempted to break into the armories to obtain arms.

At nine o'clock, the quarrymen at Central Park quit work in a body and gathered in excited groups, swearing 'that God Himself could not make it possible for the Orangemen to parade.' Shortly thereafter came a report that the Harper Building at Franklin Square housing the publishing firm which edited and printed *Harper's Monthly, Harper's Weekly,* and Harper books was about to be attacked. Fifty policemen were despatched to protect it.

At ten o'clock the Orangemen, dressed in brilliant orange colors, and with massed banners, assembled at their headquarters at Eighth Avenue and Twenty-ninth Street. Five hundred police were stationed around the Orangemen's hall.

At noon, the Irish attacked the armory at 19 Avenue A, where there were 138 stands of arms. One hundred police arrived in time to drive the rioters off with clubs. Shortly thereafter word came that Hibernia Hall, where the Irish were passing out arms, had been seized by Drill Captain Copeland and five companies of soldiers. In this instance, the men rioters resisted largely with curses. Captain Copeland reported that women rioters hurled stones. At one o'clock a group of rioters rushed down Eighth Avenue, cheering and shouting, led by a man waving a sword cane. They were dispersed by police, and Eighth Avenue was cleared from Thirtieth Street to Twenty-eighth.

At two o'clock the parade began. At its head the Orangemen carried a huge banner bearing the inscription:

Americans! Freemen!! Fall In!!!

Few of the thousands of bystanders joined the procession.

The marchers were only ninety in number. John Johnson, head of the Gideon Lodge of the Orangemen, mounted on a spirited horse, rode at the head. As the parade moved down Eighth Avenue, Headley afterwards wrote, 'the bayonets of the military force designed to act as an escort could be seen flashing in the sun, as the troops with measured tread moved steadily forward. Crowds followed them on the sidewalks, or hung from windows and house-tops, while low curses could be heard on every side, especially when the Twenty-second Regiment deliberately loaded their pieces with ball and cartridge. The Ninth Regiment and then the Sixth came into view, as the Orangemen flung their banners to the breeze.' Then came the Twenty-second and Eighty-fourth Regiments. Just as the parade reached Twenty-eighth Street, the Orangemen's band struck up a martial air and a shot rang out. At the next block another shot was fired and a volley of stones was hurled at the paraders. At Twenty-fourth Street, the parade halted a moment.

Again a shot was fired. It blew off the top of the head of a private in Company K, killing him instantly. The men of the Eighty-fourth pointed their rifles at the second-floor corner window from where the shot had apparently come. No orders had been given, but at that moment one of the soldiers fired. The shot was followed by volleys from the Sixth and Ninth Regiments. The Seventh, made up of veterans of the Civil War, kept its poise. One of the volleys hit a platoon of police at the corner of Twenty-sixth and Eighth Avenue. Colonel Jim Fisk was on horseback and become so terrified that he dismounted, fled to a saloon, escaped through a rear door, scaled several back fences, changed his uniform at his office on Twenty-third Street, took a cab to the North River, boarded an Erie tug, and found refuge in Long Branch, New Jersey.

Fisk's fellow officers who stayed at their posts rushed among the men, ordering them to cease firing. When the smoke cleared, a terrible scene of confusion presented itself. 'Men, women and children,' Headley wrote, 'screaming in wild terror, were fleeing in every direction; the strong trampling down the weak, while eleven corpses lay stretched on the sidewalk, some piled across each other. . . . Here a dead woman lay across a dead man; there a man streaming with blood was creeping painfully up a doorstep, while crouching, bleeding forms appeared in every direction.'

General Varian, furious with the Eighty-fourth for firing without orders, banished the proud old Regiment to the rear. The parade was resumed, and when it reached the Fifth Avenue Hotel at Twenty-third Street there were greetings of applause and welcome for the first time. There, some 3,000 people cheered the ninety marchers with wild enthusiasm.

Meanwhile, at Bellevue Hospital, horse-drawn ambulances

were driven to the receiving entrance to discharge the
wounded. 'Groans of distress and shrieks of pain filled the
air,' an eyewitness noted. Inside, long rows of cots were filled
with wounded men, women, and children. Hospital attendants held down wounded men on tables while the surgeons
dressed their wounds. A similar scene was taking place at
Mount Sinai Hospital.

By nightfall it was known that one soldier and one policeman were dead whereas thirty-one citizens had been killed,
none of whom were Orangemen. Twenty-four soldiers and
police and sixty-seven citizens were wounded. Many of the
citizens killed or wounded were not rioters but bystanders.
As dusk fell over the city, Headley noted, 'a pile of dead
men's hats stood on the corner of Eighth Avenue and
Twenty-fifth Street untouched, and pale faces stooped over
pools of blood on the pavement.'

The next day a newspaper suggested that 'there should
be written on the tombstone of Wednesday's victims:
MURDERED BY THE CRIMINAL MANAGEMENT OF MAYOR A.
OAKEY HALL.'

III

Thomas Nast, who was beginning to warm up in his attacks on Hall's administration, published a double-spread
cartoon in the 29 July issue of *Harper's Weekly*. It was entitled 'Something That Will Not Blow Over: July 11 and
July 12, 1871.' It consisted of six panels of drawings and two
pieces of verse on the subject of the Orange Riots. The center
panel showed a riotous mob of Irish beating back the rest
of New York's populace. It was entitled 'The Slaves of the
Greeks.' Nast had good reason to feel strongly about the
riots. He had marched with his own regiment on the day
of the trouble. He indicated his anti-Irish sentiment by depicting all the Irishmen in his cartoons with the faces of

grinning baboons. In another panel, he showed an Irishman wearing a cleric's hat with a Roman cross on its side,
waving a sword. To the left of the cleric was another, uglier,
baboon-faced Irishman waving a shillelagh. Hall, Sweeny,
Tweed, and other public officials were groveling on their
knees before them in surrender.

One of the pieces of verse was entitled 'Pat's Complaint'
and was probably written by Nast. It read:

Oh, have ye heard the tidings? It's disgusted quite I am!
Our boasted rights and freedom is all a fraud and sham;
The Orangemen parade the day with banners, drums, and
    guns,
To overawe ould Ireland and her poor, down-trodden sons.

Sure those noble-minded gintlemen, O'Kelso and O'Hall,
Had forbid thim bloody Orangemen that they should march
    at all,
Lest in their pride and madness they might, belike, waylay,
And slaughter ivery Irishman they met upon their way.

It was, d'ye see, a splendid plan whereby to kape the peace,
Without the need of calling out the soldiers and the p'lice
For if thim coward Orangemen would just kape out of sight,
There'd be no provocation to massacre and fight.

But now they'll go parading down in all their rage and
    pride,
With soldiers and policemen to guard on ivery side;
And ivery son of Ireland must hide his peaceful head,
And skulk away in cellars in terror and in dread.

In the same issue with this Orange riot cartoon, Nast
published another cartoon indicating that he was continuing
his attack on the Tweed Ring. It was called 'The New

Horse Plague,' and showed Hall, with the body of a sick mare, standing in a luxurious stall while Tweed and Sweeny regard him mournfully from the next stall. (There had been an outbreak of a horse disease in various parts of the country.) The sub-caption read 'Tweed's Mayor (mare) has it so badly that recovery is doubtful. Alas! They know how it is themselves.'

IV

Hall must have turned with a frightened heart from the tragedy of the Orange Day riots to the unremitting editorial battle being waged on him by the *Times* and *Harper's Weekly*. He had found it easy to go along — too easy. Now the descending path, strewn with tag ends of Latin, held danger at the end. The reader of books must have remembered Johnson's variation of Virgil — 'Hell is paved with good intentions.' Of what avail were they now? In his own paper he employed various tactics to defend himself. The laughing-it-off technique, so often used by officials under attack, was not effective. 'Shocking levity,' Hall wrote in the *Leader* — 'the lightship at Savannah has gone astray. Counts at Newport are at a discount.' The *Times* promptly reprinted his puns. Perhaps in making fun of society, Hall knew that his standing with the 'respectabilities' was rapidly ebbing. In his diary for 29 July, the very respectable George Templeton Strong wrote: 'The New York *Times* continues its revelations, which are making an impression that I hope will last. Mayor Hall replies at last, feebly and irresponsibly, severely criticizing motives of the editor. These disclosures of Tammany's iniquity may now be considered as taken pro confesso. . . . The feeble defense of Oakey Hall is contemptible. He might have been compelled to sign these flagitious warrants by a mandamus; possibly. But why did he interpose no objection, make no resistance, or public protest, and at least warn the community of these enormous frauds to which he now pretends that "the law" compelled him to be an accessory?'

In a more serious vein, Hall wrote that he himself was gathering information about the city's financial condition and 'these statistical tables were . . . in progress when the Corinthian type of the *Times* fired its volley of secret account bullets. Corinthian type and startling headlines are tremendous influences of public opinion. If any paper should print in gigantic type, "The cholera has come," I believe its readers would collapse before tea time, when if the announcement was in brevier [a small type used in breviaries], no effect could be found.' A reporter for the *Herald* asked when, exactly, would his reports on the city's finances be published. 'Festina lente,' Hall said, smiling — make haste slowly. His Latin returned to plague him.

Two direct retaliatory measures were made against the *Times* by the city administration. In the *Leader,* city employees were asked not to use the restaurant in the basement of the *Times* building. 'Decidedly,' the *Times* replied in an editorial, 'the city authorities are carrying on a defensive warfare in a dignified manner. Quos Deus vult perdere, etc. as the accomplished and learned Mayor would say.' Also, a *Leader* editorial questioned the right of the *Times* to the property on which its building stood. The land had once been owned by the Brick Church and, for a time, title to it had been held by the city. It was a foolish maneuver and came to nothing. Whether Hall was responsible or not the record does not show, but he was blamed for the editorial.

There was a good deal of vituperation among New York papers over the Tweed Ring exposures. It had been reported that the *Times* was owed $13,764.36 by the city. The *Herald* called the *Times* and *Harper's* 'Humbug Reformers' and said that the whole campaign was being conducted 'with the intention of having their silence purchased by what they call the "Ring." ' The *Sun* directed its fire specifically at the editor of the *Times,* saying, 'The decline of the New York *Times* in everything that entitles a paper to respect and confidence has been rapid and complete. Its present editor, who was dismissed from the London *Times* for improper conduct and untruthful writing, has sunk into a tedious monotony of slander, disregard of truth and blackguard vituperation. . . . Let the *Times* change its course, send off Jennings and get some gentleman and scholar in his place, and become again an able and high-toned paper. Thus it may escape from ruin. Otherwise it is doomed.' The New York *Post,* edited by William Cullen Bryant, said, 'If we were dishonest or disingenious partisans we should probably do as the *Times* and *Harper's Weekly* do, and our praise and our blame would presently count for no more than theirs with honest and intelligent men.'

Some papers defended Hall. He had many friends among the newspapermen of the town. The New York *Globe* printed an editorial called, 'A Word For The Mayor,' and it was reprinted in the *Leader.* It must have been like balm to Hall's heart.

'A great many people think the Mayor is a dead cock in the pit,' the *Globe* writer said. 'This is a mistake. His term of office does not expire until the first of January, 1873; and he has too much power, and is too capable a man not to regain a good share, if not all, of the ground he may have lost. But it is not so certain that the Mayor has lost ground. Just now he is very unpopular in respectable circles, but respectable circles have very little to do at the ballot-box. If the men, who do business in Broad Street, Wall, and Broadway, and live on Fifth and Madison Avenues, controlled the ballot-box, Oakey, judging by the present storm in those quarters, might fare hard. But we all know that it is on the East and West sides of the town where the voting population live. And here the Mayor is stronger than ever. There has always been a faint taint of Know-Nothingism about his Honor, and those who have watched matters carefully for the last six months have noticed a growing dislike to the Mayor on the part of the Irish Democrats. But now the feeling is different. All through the East side, on the night of the riot, there was the greatest enthusiasm for the Mayor. Young men, who belonged to the Young Democracy, were drinking his health and shouting, "Who says Mayor Hall is a Know-Nothing?" If a vote for Mayor was taken today, Hall would poll more votes than he did last fall. And when the reaction sets in, and people begin to see that the Kelso order was issued in good faith and with the sole intent to preserve the peace, the "respectables" will also think that after all the Mayor was about right, and it is well enough to go for him. Mayor Hall is therefore by no means dead. He is stronger in the city than ever. In the country (nationally) he has lost ground, which it will take him a long time to recover, and it would now seem impossible for him to succeed Hoffman or reach any position dependent upon the suffrages of his party outside of New York. But time works wonders with the animosities of men, though this Orange feud is the longest lived of almost anything recorded of human hate, and the Mayor may yet be Governor, Senator, and President. Who knows?'

But the dislike of Hall, on the part of at least two men, seemed to increase rather than diminish. Thomas Nast began not only to include the Mayor in his full-page cartoons ridiculing Tweed, Connolly, and Sweeny, but drew separate cartoons especially directed at him. They began after the Orange riots. Louis John Jennings, editor of the *Times,* also singled out Hall for withering personal attacks. No city official ever had, or probably ever will have, two such skilled artists of derision and abuse working on him simultaneously.

V

Jennings had come to New York in his early forties as a correspondent for the London *Times* and, not long afterwards, had fallen in love with and married a popular American actress, Madeleine Henriques. In 1869 he became editor of the *New York Times*. Reading one of his most contempt-ridden editorials about Hall, 'We Keeps A Hartist,' one wonders if it is not as revealing of Jennings as it is of his victim. In any event, it is a classic of its kind. Jennings could also quote — with a vengeance.

'It was a London barber, we believe,' the *Times* editor wrote, 'who, inspired by a noble ambition to distinguish himself from the vulgar herd of his fellow-craftsmen, announced to the genteel world that — using the royal pronoun — "in our establishment for the prosecution of the tonsorial art we keeps a hartist." . . . Outside the honest but humble callings, too, the need has been acknowledged of someone who could throw over unpleasant details and ugly facts the charm of manners, who could keep clean hands while doing the dirty work, who could give fine names to foul things, and use the grand old name of gentleman as a mask, behind which to do most ungentlemanly deeds.

'Just as the fops had their Pelham, the murderers their Eugene Aram, the "gentlemen of the road" their Claude Duval, the seducers their Lovelace, so the Ring of New York has its Oakey Hall. He is the "artist" of the great organization of swindlers that has the honest hard-working citizens of New York under its heel. His companions in crime are a low set — mere jailbirds on a bender — who have no other thought than how to get the greatest possible amount of animal enjoyment out of their ill-gotten swag. They are men who make no pretension to respectability, who never knew what it is to be respectable and never had a desire to know; who only wish to be, and to be thought, rich, and who live for no other end than to get as much champagne, and oysters, and women, and horses, for their money as it will buy. . . .

'But Oakey Hall looks higher than the men he has so long made his bed with. As the Turveydrop of the Ring, he must turn his attention to other things. . . . To the other members of the firm — the right to keep racers and trotters, the strong food of the harem, the relaxation of champagne suppers and euchre after the arduous labor of pocketing and investing their stealings; but to Oakey, the duty of amusing the elegant society of Shoddyville with conversation on Shakespeare and the musical glasses, while his industrious friends were making way with the cash boxes of his refined victims. His part was to play at the gentleman and scholar. He has written books, so the trunkmakers say. And plays, too, "Humpty Dumpty," among others, or so 'tis whispered in "the fust colored suckles". . . .

'How admirably the Ring understands the distribution of labor! While the Boss keeps the "gentlemen" of the Democratic party in order — snubs Seymour's nose, tweaks Tilden's ear, treads on Hoffman's toes, and bullyrags the rank and file; while Sweeny does his best to keep the laborers in a riotous frame of mind, and having got the quiet citizens into a big scare, rouses his serfs into new enthusiasm by doling out, with a great show of magnanimity, a modicum of money he has himself robbed them of; while Hilton is maneuvering to get his lots cleared of stone at the city's expense, and Barnard, for his part, look you, is gone to pray; and Vanderbilt is sitting, a while after dinner, on one of his ferry-boat boilers, picking his teeth for recreation; and while the whole foul, noisy crowd of sinecure vultures are fattening at their ease on the fair body of our city, the elegant posture-maker of the Ring endeavors to divert the public attention from the doings of his mates, by dressing up — now in a suit of green, now in a suit of check; by going round to seven

theatres in a night, to show "his friends, the people," that
there is no truth in the newspaper story that he had run
away from the city. . . .

'Oakey Hall plays well his part. He is a shallow-pated
charlatan, 'tis true, but he has wit enough to serve his
masters, and impudence enough to keep the easy-going,
average New York at bay. . . . As the "Honorable" Oakey
Hall — they are all honorable men — as "our worthy
Mayor," he will long keep his place in the new Rogues
Calendar. He will soon take his leave of us — and there's
nothing that we would more willingly part withal — but will
he be forgotten? We trust not. The *World* will write his
eulogy in very choice Italian, and future Rings will learn
by his splendid example how useful it is for a gang of
thieves, no less than for a mere barber, to keep one member
of the fraternity to do the ornamental while they do the
useful, to cover their swindling with his suavity, and, like
another Claude Duval, to lead the fine people gracefully
from the coach to dance a corranton upon the heath while
the ruder villains search the baggage for plunder at their
ease.'

It is small wonder that Hall was finally driven, on 21
August 1871, to sue the *Times* for libel. It was the end of
what had been over the years a reasonably good relationship.
In later years Hall wrote that he had helped George Jones,
the *Times* publisher, set up the first issues of the paper when
Jones had founded it in 1851. In the *Leader,* Hall recalled
the long and pleasant association he had had with Jones and
noted that, following the Ring exposures, 'Immediately, he
[Hall], who had been a twenty-year-old friend of the living
proprietor of the *Times* [Jones], equally long an intimate associate with the deceased partner, and one of the latter's
pallbearers [Raymond]; he, who had been once regarded as
a valued correspondent of the paper; he, who had penned, at
the request of its editors, through a long series of years,

literary criticisms and editorial paragraphs; he, who had received pleasant and often undeserved praise in its columns for oratory or published volumes — he, this once-be-praised Mayor, began . . . to grow daily into a monster.

'He became . . . a man of low association; his humor was now puerile; his wit now feeble; his style was now inelegant and ungrammatical, and even the dramatic effervescences of his pen that had been time and again fulsomely praised in the *Times* were raked over, in order to furnish sparkle for the *Times* ridicule.'

In replying to *Harper's,* Hall did not attack Nast except to speak of the weekly's having caused 'Tweed to soar in some Nasty heaven of invention, an angel winged with gold.' Again, in the *Leader,* in an editorial entitled 'A Penny Or A Paper,' he said that 'these gray-bearded Harpers' reminded him of little boys climbing to the windows of the Philadelphia train, demanding a penny or a paper and then cursing the passengers when they didn't get what they wanted. 'So long,' he said of the Harper brothers, 'as the city authorities could be enticed into giving them "a penny or a paper," into sending them advertisements, or buying from them tons of school-books, irrespective of age or sex, their most sweet voices would incessantly salute "Mr. Government" . . . the Mayor would be hailed by them Augustus Optimus. . . .'

VI

Nast was a German immigrant who, with his mother and father, had come to the United States in 1846, when he was six years old. They settled on Greenwich Street in Greenwich Village. As a child, he suffered a feeling of inferiority among the Irish-American children by whom he was surrounded. Not only was he German; he was a sensitive child more interested in drawing than in joining a gang of neighborhood toughs.

In 1871 Nast was a competent on-the-spot artist who illustrated the news as much as news photographers do today. The Tweed Ring scandals gave him his big opportunity. In many ways, the smaller, special cartoons Nast drew of Hall were his cleverest, as they were the most barbed. Because he was far more colorful, far more complicated, than any of the Tweed Ring, Hall was an interesting subject for a journalistic artist like Nast. To begin with, Hall's appearance was unusual even for his day, when gentlemen didn't wear uniform clothes and keep their faces uniformly shaved and their hair uniformly cut. His beard, his long wavy hair, his pince-nez with its black ribbon, were made to order for a satirical cartoonist. The glasses 'drooped' slightly like a walrus mustache and Nast accentuated this, making the droopy pince-nez his trademark for the Mayor. He always put them on Hall regardless of the predicament in which he drew him — as a horse, as Touchstone, as a patient sick in bed.

During August, 1871, Nast devoted two of his four cartoons on the Tweed scandal to Hall, both depicting him as a sick horse. In the other two, cartoons attacking the entire Tweed group, Hall was likewise included. On 19 August, for example, Nast published one of his more celebrated panels, entitled 'Who Stole the People's Money? Do Tell. 'Twas Him.' In it, Hall was shown jerking his thumb at Connolly who was jerking his thumb at Sweeny who was jerking his thumb at Tweed and so on, so that in all, fifteen city officials and contractors, standing in a circle, were each indicating the man next to him as being the guilty one. On the last Saturday of August, Nast drew full length portraits of 'The President of the United States and His Cabinet For 1872.' Hall was pictured as Attorney General. He was standing with his right hand in his vest, Napoleonic style, and with a broom in his left hand. Back of him was a sign which said,

O K HALL
NOTICE
all kinds of dirty work done here
and things made as clear as mud

Jim Fisk was pictured as Secretary of the Navy, Connolly as Secretary of the Treasury, and Peter B. Sweeny as Secretary of State (and church). John T. Hoffman was indicated as President, but he was shown as a wraith-like figure behind 'Boss Tweed.' In the background was a portrait of Washington, weeping. The new seal of the United States was to contain, according to Nast's drawing, a baboon-faced Irishman and Irishwoman and an eagle calling out, 'What are you going to do about it?' (It was Tweed who, when asked by a reporter about the *Times* exposures, had snorted: 'Well, what are you going to do about it?') The inscription on the seal was 'Tammany Ring; As True As Steal.'

Nast even extended his ridicule of Hall to anyone who did not share his view of the Mayor of the city. Because James Gordon Bennett of the *Herald* and Horace Greeley of the *Tribune* did not immediately condemn Hall, he lampooned them. He showed Greeley and Bennett with a bucket, holding brushes, while they slapped whitewash over Hall. Bennett and Hall were friends and Bennett's *Herald* had once said of the Mayor, 'He calls a spade a spade and Horace Greeley a humbug.' But even after the *Times* exposures were well under way, Greeley wrote: 'We have scrupulously refrained from the intemperate style of attack in which the *Times* has of late profusely indulged because words thus used lose their force and because we did not have proofs to warrant charges which nevertheless we have often believed to be true.' Some New Yorkers said his restraint

Because Horace Greeley (left) and James Gordon Bennett, the younger (right), failed to join in the attack on Hall, Thomas Nast included them in this cartoon published in *Harper's Weekly*. He labeled them THE RIVALS and quoted them as saying, 'Let's see who can lay it [whitewash] on thickest.'

was motivated by pique that the *Times* had scooped him on the Ring disclosures. Nast drew a cartoon of Greeley standing in tears over the sick body of a horse which bore the face of Hall, still wearing his pince-nez glasses. Greeley was labeled as 'The great American farmer troubled with the milk of human kindness again.' Shown in Greeley's pocket was a copy of the *Tribune* with the headline: 'You lie. Everybody lies except H.G.' Nast was alluding to Greeley's habit of continually writing as if he alone in the country printed the truth. In Greeley's other pocket was a document marked, 'City Franchises; $10,000.' It had been charged that Greeley had accepted certain concessions from the city administration.

Eventually, Greeley attacked Hall, calling him 'a joking cheat' and, later, 'a gibbering mountebank.' By the end of the year, Greeley was to write of Hall: 'We don't say you are a thief but we do say you were one of a gang of robbers who had the hands of the victim tied while the rest picked his pockets.'

Hall did not reply to Greeley's statement regarding him. In fact, one of his strategies was to pretend that he was oblivious to all the attacks on him. He often told reporters who asked him about some new attack that he followed the practice of the late Abraham Lincoln by turning to another part of the paper when he saw that his name was mentioned. This was indeed an extraordinary statement in view of the fact that Hall's scrapbooks, now on deposit at the New York Public Library, contain virtually every clipping from almost every paper that ever carried a line about him.

VII

The *Times* staff had analyzed the figures brought by O'Brien with patience and extraordinary skill, and the newspaper pledged its good faith that its disclosures were susceptible of proof. It published the startling information that James H. Ingersol, chairmaker, had been paid $5,750,-000 for furniture supplied to the new courthouse; Andrew J. Garvey had received nearly $3,000,000 for plastering the courthouse; one Keyser had received $1,250,000 for plumbing; and J. A. Smith, an unknown, had been given $750,000 for work of an unknown nature. A humorous note was struck by some of the fictitious names — but not the items after them — which the Ring had used to siphon additional sums from the city treasury. 'T. C. Cash' had received $64,000; 'Phillipo Donoruma,' $66,000.

That portion of New York City's public which could read was first astonished and then stunned by the revelations. The magnitude of the frauds was breath-taking. An aroused citizenry demanded action. A call for a public meeting was made for Monday, 4 September 1871, at Cooper Union. The auditorium was packed. Presiding was former Mayor William F. Havemeyer. Joseph H. Choate, then only thirty-eight years old, advanced to the edge of the platform flourishing a scroll. He held the scroll up for all to see and declared: 'This is what *we* are going to do about it!' For several minutes he could not proceed because of the wild applause that broke out. Then, reading from the scroll, he declaimed:

'Resolved — that the taxpayers and citizens of New York have learned with astonishment and alarm that the funded and bonded debt of the City and County has been more than doubled within the last two-and-a-half years; that the acknowledged indebtedness of the City and County is now upward of $113,000,000, being over $83,000,000 more than what it was when the present Mayor took his office, and that there is reason to believe that there are floating, or contingent, or pretended debts and claims, against the City and County, which will amount to many millions of dollars in addition, which will be paid out of the City and County treasury, unless the present financial officials are removed or their proceedings arrested.'

Choate read off eleven resolutions, and concluded with the twelfth: 'Resolved — that an executive committee of seventy members be appointed by the president of this meeting, whose duty it shall be to take such measures as shall be necessary or expedient to carry out the objects for which we are assembled.'

Thus was brought into being the famous 'Committee of Seventy,' which was to undo Tweed, the Ring, and Hall. It was headed by Choate, Charles O'Conor, and Samuel J. Tilden. Tilden had been a prominent Democrat and was a fellow member of Hall's at the Union and Manhattan clubs. Later, as a result of his activities in helping expose the Ring, he became Governor of New York and the Democratic nominee for President.

Hall was unfortunate enough to remark to a reporter: 'It will all blow over. These gusts of reform are wind and clatter. Next year we shall all be in Washington.'

Washington — if not the entire nation — must have felt alarm.

One of his friends, apparently seeking to create some favorable news about Hall, gave a story to the newspapers about his having saved a child from drowning. Hall quickly put the record straight.

'The newspapers have put me in a good deal of hot water lately,' he wrote, 'but I must disclaim the cold water heroism they have so generously given me credit for. I think the story of my romantic bravery is simply a clever hoax of that king of practical jokers, Alderman Jerome. I am an expert swimmer and have often jumped off docks and other places, and picked out drowning people, but I do not desire credit for an act not performed. The whole story is founded upon the simple incident of two little children floundering in a brook. They were in no danger, and were brought ashore without any display of heroism. If a bad pun will pun-ish the not pun-y act of the Alderman in relating his yarn, I will characterize it a (Je)rome-antic story.' Nevertheless, he must have been grateful for an opportunity to appear in the public prints as something other than an ogre.

During September, the attack on the Tweed Ring — and on Hall — grew more and more intense. On the second day

When *The Leader,* a Tammany-controlled paper, said editorially, 'The Democratic party is behind him [Hall],' Nast promptly drew this cartoon.

of that month, Nast published a cartoon of Hall being kicked in the pants by a boot labeled HONEST DEMOCRATS. The cartoon was entitled 'Which Nobody Can Deny,' and quoted a statement in *The Leader* that 'The Democratic party is behind him [Hall].'

111

VIII

The day after the Cooper Union meeting, John Foley, one of the Committee of Seventy, applied to Judge George Gray Barnard, a Tweed appointee, for an injunction restraining any further payment of money from the city treasury. Barnard signed the order at home where he was laid up with an attack of gout. A newspaper commented: 'It was generally thought that the Ring was sicker than the judge.'

Said Hall: 'Foley is a crazy fellow who, I have been told, claims to be a lineal descendant of the daring youth who fired the Ephesian dome. In its practical effect, the granting of the injunction is one of Judge Barnard's stereotyped jokes. . . . Foley thought that he had planted the nettle danger in the Court House; but from what I know of farming I think we shall pluck the flower safely from it.' He said all the fuss was merely a plot on the part of General Grant and the Republicans to gain control of the city administration for purposes of corruption. The latter was a well-aimed dart. Grant's administration in Washington was piling up an all-time record for Federal corruption.

George Templeton Strong was regarding Hall, at this time, with unusual interest. 'The New York *Herald*,' Strong wrote in his diary, 'reluctantly abandons the Ring to its fate, all but Oakey Hall for whom it still retains some tenderness. But it thinks that even Oakey Hall had better resign. The New York *World* itself is demoralized by this suicidal burglary and by the discord among its clients. Its brazen trumpet gives forth an uncertain sound. It is understood that Hall and Sweeny are in alliance, offensive and defensive, against Tweed and Connolly — skunk vs. rattlesnake.'

Connolly had learned that Hall and Sweeny were to use him as a scapegoat and immediately went over to the reform

Democrats. He conferred with Tilden and was told to hold on to his job. On Sunday night, 11 September, according to an official report the next day, Connolly's office was forcibly entered and the vouchers showing to whom city's funds had been paid were stolen. It was explained that the culprits had gained entry by cutting, with a diamond, a hole in a glass door while the watchman was out getting his supper. Actually, the thirteen bundles of vouchers had been quietly removed from an unharmed steel safe; their charred remains were later found in an attic in City Hall. Someone had made a bad blunder, for copies of the vouchers were safely in the vaults of a New York bank.

Hall immediately wrote a letter to Connolly in which he said: 'With great personal reluctance I officially reach the conclusion that the exigency requires your retirement from the head of the Finance Department, in order that I may place there another gentleman who will be enabled thoroughly to investigate its affairs and restore public confidence. . . . I am compelled to throw myself, therefore, as Mayor, in this unexpected and sudden emergency, upon your magnanimity, and ask, under the circumstances, for your resignation.'

Hall delivered the letter in person at eleven o'clock at night at Connolly's house. The next day Connolly wrote Hall: 'Similar verbal requests, from yourself and others, have been, within the last few weeks, received and delivered. . . . My official acts have been supervised and approved by your superior vigilance. So far as my administration is questioned, equal responsibility attaches to yourself. . . . I am unwilling to submit myself a vicarious sacrifice to satisfy the hungry appetite of adversaries for a victim, or at this juncture and under these circumstances betray weakness of position or fear of rigid investigation by tendering my resignation. . . . When my past administration shall be vindicated. . . . I shall not fail to act as may seem to be demanded by the changed circumstances which may then exist.

'Very respectfully, your ob'dt servant
'Richard B. Connolly, Comptroller.'

Writing in his diary on this exchange of letters, Strong said: 'Even Mr. Oakey Hall sees that someone must be thrown overboard; so he writes to Connolly (in very bad English), inviting that functionary to make a martyr of himself for the sake of his endangered confederates and resign. This invitation is enforced by this morning's *World* with the statement that "if the Comptroller's resignation be not received before night, New York will be too hot to hold him." Mr. Hall makes a strong appeal to Connolly's "magnanimity" and we have that "magnanimous" official's response in tonight's *Post*.'

Both Hall and Connolly now acted quickly. Hall appointed General George Brinton McClellan, the Civil War hero, as comptroller. Connolly appointed as deputy comptroller the very respectable Andrew H. Green, who was acceptable to Tilden. 'Thereupon,' Strong noted in his diary, 'Mr. Oakey Hall (who must have lost his head altogether), forgetting that he wrote to Connolly a week ago that he had no power whatever to remove him, writes him again that he considers this appointment (Green) possibly equivalent to a resignation and that anyhow he holds the comptrollership vacant. So he invites General George B. McClellan to take that position. McClellan will hardly be such a fool as to take it.'

Connolly moved out of the office, and so did the guards he had stationed around the office to protect him. The reformers sent a new set of guards to the comptroller's office to protect Green, who had moved in. As Strong predicted, McClellan, 'that cautious campaigner . . . declines the comptrollership, of course. Hall should have foreseen he would do so. Who can be Hall's adviser? Every move of his is a gross blunder.'

IX

At this juncture, when the whole town was abuzz with excitement, the rumor was heard, according to Matthew P. Breen's memoirs, that Hall had gone mad and had to be held down by four men who took him to his Forty-second Street home every day in his carriage. Strong heard a similar report and wrote in his diary: 'Rumor that Mayor Hall had collapsed and recalled his circular letter refusing to recognize the comptroller and deputy comptroller; also, that he has not. He has made himself supremely ridiculous and contemptible during the last ten days.'

The rumors were not true, and when reporters found Hall and asked him how he felt about his failure to get General McClellan into the comptrollership, he said: 'Gentlemen, some of you yesterday said that I had received a severe check, and, in testimonium vertatis, I have, as you see, put on a check suit.' He had.

Nast was quick to answer Hall's attempt to laugh off the Green incident and drew a cartoon entitled 'An Awful Dose.' It showed Hall sick in bed with a doctor sitting at his bedside taking his pulse. On a table was a bottle marked 'Green Bitters.' Below was the two-line caption:

Tammany Haul — Now that I have swallowed that horrid 'Green' stuff, will I recover?

Dr. N.Y. — Oh, dear, no. That was only a Tonic. Nothing will save you, you're so far gone.

Nast continued to include Hall in his full-page pictures of the Ring. He showed the Mayor as one of a group of vultures perched on the side of a craggy mountain 'waiting for the storm to blow over,' an illusion to Hall's statement about the reform movement. He also showed Hall as one of the four Ring members looking as if they were being seen in one of those freak mirrors which make one's body look as thin as a toothpick. The title was, of course, 'Too Thin, We Know Nothing About the Stolen Vouchers, We Are Innocent.' And he showed Hall and Sweeny, Connolly and Tweed, standing under the shadows of four hangman's nooses. Another cartoon showed them as striped tigers behind bars.

It was at this time that Tweed was reported to have said: 'Let's stop them damn pictures. I don't care so much what the papers write about me — my constituents can't read; but damn it, they can see pictures.'

Nast told his biographer, Albert Bigelow Paine, that a representative of Tweed and his group tried to buy him off. A lawyer friend of Nast's casually mentioned to him one day that a group of wealthy businessmen wished to send him abroad to study art under the world's masters. The following Sunday an executive of the Broadway Bank called at Nast's home and after talking about various matters said, 'I hear you have been made an offer to go abroad for art study.'

'Yes,' Nast said, 'but I can't go. I haven't time.'

'But they will pay you for your time,' the banker said, 'I have reason to believe you could get a hundred thousand dollars for the trip.'

Nast asked if he thought he could get two hundred thousand. The banker said, 'Well, possibly. I believe from what I have heard in the bank that you might get it. You have a great talent; but you need study and you need rest. Besides, this Ring business will get you into trouble. They own all the judges and jurors and can get you locked up for libel. My advice is to take the money and get away.'

'Don't you think I could get five hundred thousand to make that trip?'

'You can,' the bank official went on, assuming that Nast was an excellent negotiator. 'You can get five hundred thousand dollars in gold to drop this Ring business and get out of the country.'

'Well, I don't think I'll do it,' Nast said, laughing. 'I made up my mind not long ago to put them behind bars, and I'm going to put them there.'

'Only be careful,' the banker said, 'that you do not first put yourself in a coffin.'

Hall never referred to Nast in his voluminous retrospective writings.

6

FIRST GRAND JURY TESTIMONY

I

BOMBARDED BY THE PRESS, besieged by reporters, embarrassed in the presence of his family and friends, Hall must have found in the next development of the scandal a measure of relief. The District Attorney, forced by public opinion and the private pressure of public men to empanel a Grand Jury, summoned fifty citizens to the County Court House, back of City Hall, from which so much of the plunder of the Tweed Ring had flowed. From this group, twenty-two were to be selected to hear testimony as to the guilt or innocence of the Mayor of New York.

Selection of the jurors began on Monday, 2 October 1871. Although it was widely reported at the time that Hall's uncle and cousin were on the jury, the official list shows no Halls. The jurors finally chosen were all men of some standing. Most of them lived in downtown Manhattan. They were merchants, a printer, a mechanic, a builder, a photographer, and an artist. A rejected juror was George Jones, 30 West 37th Street, publisher of the *New York Times*.

On Thursday morning, the 19th, hearing of testimony commenced. The first witness was Andrew H. Green, who had been appointed by Connolly on Tilden's advice and whose appointment Hall had tried unsuccessfully to block. Green testified that he did 'not know of any act of Mr. Hall's in support of the accusation.' He was followed on the stand by A. S. Cady, who served as a clerk in the comptroller's office. After testifying as to the procedure used in paying out the city's money, he was asked if he knew of any bills against the city which were exorbitant in sum.

'I have heard that spoken very frequently inside and outside,' he replied.

'Do you know,' Cady was asked, 'of your own knowledge of any bill that has been fraudulent?'

'Not of my personal knowledge,' he replied.

The next witness to testify was the chairman of the Committee of Remedies for the Committee of Seventy, Henry F. Spaulding. Like most of the witnesses who testified before the Grand Jury, Spaulding was of little use in providing any specific facts.

'You made a complaint,' the District Attorney said, 'against Mr. Hall, charging him with some sort of offense; will you state any facts in regard to the matter?'

Spaulding: 'I have no facts of my own knowledge; my complaint was made on information and belief.'

District Attorney: 'Can you state anything else in regard to this case which throws any light upon it for the benefit of this Grand Jury?'

Spaulding: 'I have not any evidence in my possession.'

District Attorney: 'Then you do not know that the Mayor did connive at any fraud, or that he has been guilty of any misdemeanor?'

Spaulding: 'I stated before I did not know of my own knowledge; it is all on information and belief.'

Probably the most interesting witness to come before the Grand Jury was William S. Copeland, a bookkeeper, who had gone to work in the county auditor's office early in January,

1870. He was, in effect, a spy for former Sheriff James O'Brien, who was out to expose the Tweed Ring because he had asked for $350,000 as his rightful share of the graft but had been turned down with nothing.

Copeland was questioned about the signing of the warrants for payment of various items in connection with the new County Court House, for which the city appropriated $250,000 but which cost the taxpayers a sum several authorities placed as high as $12,200,000. Asked about a bill for windows in the Court House, Copeland said he had noticed that 'it was enormous, in my eyes; there was only a hundred windows.'

District Attorney: 'Do you think Mr. Hall knew anything about that?'

Copeland: 'I should think he would; he has to put his name to it; he would have to be blind not to see it; it was before his eyes; he could not avoid seeing what he was signing.'

Copeland said he had been discharged from the comptroller's office for 'political reasons.' Asked what they were, he said: 'I am a friend of Mr. O'Brien and of course when the troubles arose between Mr. O'Brien and Mr. Connolly I was amongst those that were discharged.' He then went on to tell how he came to discover the frauds.

'What called my attention to it, in the first place,' he said, 'I was given a book in January, 1870; the bookkeeper gave me a book, called the Record of Vouchers, to write up, which contains all the accounts under the different heads; when I was copying it from the audit book, where the amounts are entered first, when I came to this account of County Liabilities, he [Lynes, the bookkeeper] came to me and said that Mr. Watson, or the Comptroller, would be very angry if he knew anybody but him wrote that account; I thought it very strange I could write all accounts in the book and not that; I thought I would inspect that;

this was in January, 1870, when I first went there; so I looked over those accounts afterwards to see what was so wonderful in this account that he did not want me to write it; I saw Keyser forty and fifty thousand dollars, and Mr. Ingersoll for this, and no other thing hardly in that account but these claims; I guess there must be something in that; I had the curiosity to look further into the matter, and I discovered that there must be something wrong.'

District Attorney: 'What did you discover that was wrong?'

Copeland: 'These things were not sworn to; they were for enormous amounts for furniture and plastering, which, in my idea, never was in place.'

District Attorney: 'Have you a knowledge that Mr. Hall knew anything about this?'

Copeland: 'Nothing more than that his signature was attached to the warrants. I know that I never sign anything without reading it, and I suppose Mr. Hall knows more than me. I do not think that Mr. Hall, nor Mr. Connolly, or anybody else would sign away one hundred thousand dollars in warrants, without looking to see what it was about. I know, simple a man as I am, I would not sign such things without looking at them.'

The District Attorney did not fully accept Copeland's description of himself as a simple man. 'In the performance of your duties,' he said, 'over some memorandums or vouchers, you were copying them off; what did you copy them off for?'

Copeland: 'Because I thought I might want to use them at some future date to give them away.'

District Attorney: 'What motive had you for doing it?'

Copeland: 'It was more for curiosity than anything else, for the time being.'

District Attorney: 'Still knowing these things were going on, why did you not report them?'

Copeland: 'I would think when I was in a place it would

not be right to do a thing of that kind; it would be going against my employer.'

District Attorney: 'You made this statement for political reasons and were not impelled by patriotic motives in the matter?'

Copeland: 'No, I did not make that for political reasons. You asked me why I was discharged. It was nothing about these things.'

District Attorney: 'What was your motive in volunteering to bring this matter before the public?'

Copeland: 'I felt a little "sore," as they say, considering that I worked diligently in the office and that I was discharged. I done my duty right enough, and I thought it was rather wrong to have me discharged.'

District Attorney: 'How long whilst you were in the employ of the city government did you know of these so-called frauds — how long have you hidden that in your political breast?'

Copeland: 'I cannot say as to the whole of them, but I knew it when I had been in there two months.'

District Attorney: 'When did you first tell anybody?'

Copeland: 'I think it was along in November or December; it was in the fall of 1870.'

District Attorney: 'Who did you tell?'

Copeland: 'I told Mr. O'Brien.'

When William F. Havemeyer, the sugar merchant, took the stand, he was obviously annoyed. Twice before he had been called by the people to serve as Mayor after a wave of reform. He had been subpoenaed to appear before the Grand Jury and probably didn't like it. He had the air of a man who could well say, 'I've been through all this before.' He was asked if he could 'throw some light upon this complaint against Mayor Hall?'

'I do not know anything,' Havemeyer said. 'I do not think I would know Mr. Hall if I should see him; all I know is what I read in the papers in reference to his connection with the transactions which are exciting the attention of the public just now.'

He testified to the signing of vouchers when he served as Mayor. 'Well,' he said gruffly, 'I never signed anything but what it was all right, that I will assure you.' He then went into a rather lengthy discussion of how he spotted that some coffee for the Almshouses was charged to the city as 1,600 pounds of St. Domingo coffee. Havemeyer said he thought it was Rio coffee, which was cheaper. It turned out to be damaged coffee bought at auction by 'a very respectable grocer, he made a great noise about it. Well, said I, if this is all right, let me see your books. That he declined to do.' Havemeyer remarked, as he continued his testimony, that 'we raised by tax two millions of dollars to pay the whole expense of the city government.'

Richard A. Storrs, clerk in the County Bureau, testified that Hall had returned some of the vouchers sent him by the County Auditor to be signed, but he didn't remember why.

Henry G. Stebbins, a broker who was chairman of the Committee of Seventy, testified that he knew of no fact that 'threw any light on this complaint . . . against Mr. Hall.' A juror interrupted to ask, 'Do you know that this Committee of Seventy have any positive evidence before them tending to criminate or convict Mayor Hall under these charges?' Stebbins said he did not.

District Attorney: 'And you, Colonel Stebbins, do not know that Mayor Hall had been guilty of a misdemeanor from any fact that you know?'

Stebbins: 'Not on the case as it stands today before my mind.'

Samuel J. Tilden, the Democratic party leader who had aligned himself with the anti-Tammany reform movement, took the stand. Of all the witnesses before the Grand Jury, it was felt that Tilden would be most likely to contribute something of value.

District Attorney: 'Do you know any fact of your personal knowledge that you can state to this Grand Jury which will throw any light on the complaint against Mayor Hall?'

Tilden: 'I do not. I know Mr. Hall's alleged participation in the auditing of $6,312,000 county liabilities.'

Tilden was then asked if Hall received any of the six million. 'Not so far as I know,' he replied. 'I cannot say negatively that it was not Mr. Hall, but I can say I have no evidence that it was Mr. Hall.'

Asked how much of the six million the city lost, Tilden said he thought it was all. He said that $5,700,000 had been deposited in the names of three people.

District Attorney: 'Was the money deposited in an individual or official capacity?'

Tilden: 'Individual.'

District Attorney: 'And Mr. Hall is none of the parties?'

Tilden: 'No, sir.'

District Attorney: 'Do you think Mayor Hall exceeded his authority, or neglected his duty, or that he knew that those checks were fraudulent?'

Tilden: 'Of course, I have not any knowledge about that . . . but my opinion is, of course, that the auditing was not a ministerial but a judicial duty.'

District Attorney: 'What was your answer?'

Tilden: 'I say that the auditing of these claims, by the three gentlemen appointed to audit them, was not a ministerial duty, but a judicial duty, in which they were bound to look into the validity of the claims, and the amount of those claims, and were answerable in good faith for the performance of that duty.'

No more witnesses were heard by the Grand Jury until Tuesday of the following week. Meanwhile, on the Saturday before the Grand Jury reconvened, another Nast cartoon directed at Hall appeared in *Harper's Weekly*. It was a drawing of twelve identical heads of Hall and looked like a sheet of postage stamps. It was entitled 'The Grand Jury?'. Apparently Nast had assumed that the Grand Jury was not going to indict Hall.

II

On Tuesday, 24 October, the Grand Jury again listened to testimony. John H. Masterson, who described himself as 'a mason, builder and contractor,' testified that plastering for which the city had been charged about a million dollars he would have done for $50,000. He testified that he had 'plastered Tammany Hall, the Union Dime Savings Bank and several other large buildings.'

Apparently Hall had signed the vouchers without affidavits being attached to them. District Attorney Garvin came into the hearing room and explained that in signing the vouchers without affidavits attached to them Hall was committing 'a statutory misdemeanor.'

'He has got,' Garvin said, 'to do it wilfully and knowingly with intent to convert the public property. If he does that he is guilty of a misdemeanor.'

Ex-Sheriff James O'Brien, who had turned over the secret accounts to Jennings of the *New York Times,* now took the stand. He was asked if he 'knew of any peculation or any appropriation of the public funds by Mr. Hall, so far as he is concerned.'

O'Brien replied, 'No; as far as Mr. Hall is concerned, he signed those warrants. It looks to me that a man of Mr. Hall's position would not do it without he would be patted on the back, that he would be made Governor, or that he would have some emoluments.' A juror interposed to ask, 'That is simply a matter of opinion?'

'No,' O'Brien said, 'I should think a smart man like Mr. Hall would detect those warrants; he was in a position to do it.'

'I understand,' a juror interposed again, 'of your own personal knowledge you know nothing of the misdemeanor on the part of the Mayor.' O'Brien replied, probably rather sheepishly: 'No, only what I see in the newspapers every day.' After a few more questions O'Brien was dismissed.

George Jones, publisher of the *New York Times,* the paper which had published the Tweed Ring frauds, followed O'Brien on the stand. He said he'd been a newspaper publisher for twenty-one years.

'I have the information,' Jones said, in reply to a question as to what he knew about 'this complaint against Mr. Hall,' 'that all people have, who have read the statements, and have opinions as to the credibility of those statements; I have no personal knowledge.'

The spectacle of the publisher of a newspaper that was the fountainhead of the Tweed Ring exposures claiming to know nothing personally about the facts of the scandal seemed to irritate the jurors.

'I have read editorials,' one juror said, 'probably two or three months in your paper, on this question; the paper has not ceased almost daily to brand Mr. Hall as a thief. Can you give us of your own knowledge any information that will help us to come to a conclusion that he has proved himself to be a thief?'

Jones's replies to the questions he was now asked by the Grand Jury have been useful to students of journalism in the United States, however unsatisfactory they appeared to the jurors.

'There is a difference,' Jones said, 'between me as an individual and the newspaper; the newspaper is an impersonality; I am an individual. I do not propose to answer any

126

questions in relation to the paper. I am here as an individual.'

The juror who seemed most anxious to prevent Jones from hiding behind the impersonality of the *Times* was Isaac J. Oliver, a prominent New Yorker.

'You will understand,' Oliver said, 'that we are expected to perform a certain duty, and there is no man here that proposes to swerve one hair from what he believes to be a strict, conscientious discharge of that duty.'

Jones: 'I stated to you that the *Times* and George Jones were not identical things.'

Oliver: 'Have you in your possession any such evidence?'

Jones: 'I have the same evidence the public has had and has been published.'

Oliver: 'Have you any control over the columns of the newspaper called the *Times?*'

Jones: 'I do not propose to go into the interior working of the New York *Times*. . . . I tell you very plainly that the *Times* and myself are two parties. The New York *Times* is responsible for what it says at law.'

Oliver: 'Can you tell us the man who wrote those articles?'

Jones: 'No, sir.'

Oliver: 'Can you tell us the party who wrote the articles which you published?'

Jones: 'There were a great many who wrote them.'

Oliver: 'Referring to the charge against Mayor Hall?'

Jones: 'There is a great many.'

Oliver: 'Mr. Jones, does not everybody who sends you an article for publication accompany it with his name, and don't you hold him responsible?'

Jones: 'I told you I don't propose to give you anything of the interior working of the *Times*, neither shall I.'

Oliver: 'What I want is simply this: we are examining witnesses here. Among the witnesses are the most distinguished and prominent men of our city, men whose word alone without their oath would be sufficient for us — we want to get at the truth. We want you to answer this — not in regard to your newspaper, but without regard to it — can you give us the name or names of any person who knows that Mayor Hall has corruptly discharged the duties of his office — that he has been guilty of a misdemeanor, that he has wrongfully and corruptly allowed the public moneys to be appropriated and paid to parties without a proper equivalent being given therefor?'

Jones: 'Yes, sir; I suppose, in answer to that question, it would be proper to say that it is known to the whole city that public moneys have been drawn from the city treasury by the signature of Mayor Hall, for which no equivalent has been returned. There is a flood of evidence which is open to you and to every gentleman here as well as to me.'

'I would like to ask Mr. Jones,' Oliver said, still hopeful of getting Jones to admit he knew something about the guilt or innocence of Hall, 'if he has in his possession any evidence on which he bases the charge made through the *Times?* Now, we are seeking after information. If Mayor Hall has been guilty we want that made clear to us by testimony, and we cannot act from any other standpoint except truth. Now, according to your own knowledge, can you give us any information yourself that you know will help us to come to a conclusion in this case of Mayor Hall?'

Jones was insistent that he was not responsible as an individual for what the *Times* had said despite the fact that he was the paper's publisher. 'I have answered that already'; he said, 'I have said that I could not, as an individual.'

Oliver: 'Can you give us the name or names of any persons who are cognizant of this misdemeanor, or who can give us any information on that point?'

Jones: 'I cannot give you the names of any one that furnishes information to a newspaper.'

Oliver: 'What we want . . .'

Jones: 'I see what you are at; you want me to give you the names of persons who give us information.'

He did not give them.

Hall's law partner, Augustus L. Brown, took the stand and testified that the signatures on the warrants shown him did not seem to be those of Mayor Hall. 'There is a peculiarity about the "K" which is different,' he said. He was questioned by George J. Forrest, foreman of the Grand Jury. Forrest began by asking Brown if he knew Mayor Hall's circumstances. 'Very well'; Brown replied, 'I think no one knows them so well.'

'Will you say to the jury,' Forrest asked, 'to what extent he is a man of fortune?'

Brown said he had been Hall's business partner and intimate friend for eighteen years; that Hall 'hardly kept any bank account; I kept it entirely for him. I should think today he is a man worth from sixty to seventy thousand dollars in all; I think I know all his property.' He said Hall had paid 'twenty thousand for a twenty-year lease on a house on Forty-Second Street with a forty-foot frontage.' Five years of the lease were up. In the basement, he said, was a 'miscellaneous library of uncertain value' which might bring at auction eight or ten thousand dollars. His law library at his office was insured for fifteen hundred dollars. In New Jersey, he owned a house he had purchased five years before for '12,000 before he was Mayor.' Because Hall had a large family, about a dozen people, Brown said, he had made about $4,000 worth of additions to his summer house. He said that Hall was still a member of the law firm of Brown, Hall & Vanderpoel and that he 'receives a pretty considerable remuneration from that firm.'

Forrest said that it had been represented in the papers that Hall had made deposits of 'as high as two hundred thousand dollars' within the last thirty days. 'I now under my oath,'

Brown replied, 'state that if Mr. Hall were to die today, and everything he had in the world sold, and his little debts around paid which he owes, I do not believe, so help me God, that he would have sixty thousand dollars in the world.'

While Brown was still on the stand it was noted that Hall had, in his answer to the complaint, made a sworn statement to the effect that he had signed the warrants without making any further inquiry than that afforded by the previous approvals of the Comptroller and the Auditor, and that during the two and half years he was Mayor, 39,257 warrants had passed through his office.

The next witness was Edward Bull, who said he had been a carpet dealer for twenty-five years. He said that he had examined the carpets in the new courthouse and that their value was $12,000. The cost to the city of the carpets had been $221,799.48.

Robert B. Palmer, cashier for the Tenth National Bank, took the stand and testified that Mayor Hall had had a personal account in his bank since early in 1870 and that his balance had averaged less than $5,000. The largest deposit, he said, was between $27,000 and $28,000, and remained in the account only a day or two.

'I have read in the paper,' Palmer said, 'that he had $250,-000 or $300,000 in the bank, which is absurd; it is not the case; it is untrue, and never has been; the largest transaction we ever had was this one case; there may have been one or two cases approximating to it.'

The last important witness to testify was William A. Booth, one of the Committee of Seventy. As Chairman of the Booth Committee, made up of prominent citizens and aldermen, he had reported that the city debt had increased by almost $60,000,000 during the nineteen months that Hall had been Mayor. He said that he knew of no evidence 'as to any misconduct of Mr. Hall in regard to peculations or appropriation of the public funds to his own personal account.'

'Nothing in all my investigations,' he said, 'have shown or given me a knowledge that he either has been corrupt or that he has connived. . . . I think Mayor Hall has been very derelict in duty; I do not know that he has misappropriated a dollar of the funds or that he has done it with an evil intent or a guilty knowledge.'

Booth said that on many of the very large number of warrants Hall signed there were no affidavits attesting to their validity, which was required by law. He said the evidence his committee had gathered showed that the city had paid out $7,000,000 for $700,000 worth of value. Inasmuch as many of the amounts for large sums were made out to the same person, Booth felt, they 'ought to [have] put [Hall] on his guard.'

A final witness was Edward W. Baxter, furniture manufacturer, who testified that the furniture in the new courthouse was 'not exceeding in value $97,000.'

On Wednesday, 25 October 1871, the Grand Jury 'by a vote nearly unanimous . . . dismissed the charge against A. Oakey Hall, Mayor of this city; but . . . find that A. Oakey Hall has been careless and negligent in the discharge of his duties, in affixing his signature to the warrants without giving the vouchers that consideration which the public interests demanded.'

A few days after the verdict, Nast published a cartoon of a small horse suspended in the air by a hammock slung around its belly, and obviously very sick. The head of course was Hall's, complete with pince-nez and beard. The caption said: 'Our Mare Still Lives.'

III

Tweed ran for State Senator that November and, despite the Ring disclosures, was re-elected. Connolly and Sweeny fled — Sweeny to Canada, Connolly to Paris. Hall stayed on as Mayor. The reformers still entertained hopes of prosecuting him on the basis of the 'careless and negligent' phrase in the Grand Jury minutes. A reporter for the *Sun* called at City Hall to check a rumor that Hall had been arrested. 'After making the requisite number of raps,' the reporter wrote, 'at the side entrance to the Mayor's office, I was admitted and said, "I called in reference to a rumor about your arrest floating around town."

' "A friend," Hall replied, "asked if I had given bail. I replied that I did not wish to exert a baleful influence." ' The reporter said it was also rumored that bail was to be a million dollars. 'Here,' the reporter wrote, 'the Mayor pulled the lapels of his frieze coat (he said he wore a freeze coat yesterday) and said, "The proper person to see is Judge Brady." ' When the story was printed in the *Sun,* the headline read: 'WILL MAYOR HALL CRACK A HIDEOUS JOKE AT HIS OWN FUNERAL?'

Nast's attack on the Tweed Ring reached its height on 11 November when he published what has become one of the most widely known cartoons in American history. It was a double-spread picture in *Harper's Weekly* of a crowd-filled Roman amphitheatre. In the Emperor's box was Tweed and the other members of the Ring dressed in Roman togas. Tweed's fat face and bald head adorned with palm leaves suggested Nero. Oakey Hall was in the background with his pince-nez giving an anachronistic touch to the scene. In the arena a huge fierce tiger baring its teeth was about to attack a maiden labeled THE REPUBLIC. In the background were the bodies of Mercury and Justice already slain by the tiger. The title of the cartoon was 'The Tammany Tiger Loose.' This cartoon fixed in the public mind, perhaps for all time, the tiger as a symbol of not only Tammany Hall but other big-city political machines as well.

That same Saturday, Nast had a special cartoon about Hall, but the subject was remote from the Ring scandal — the visit of the Grand Duke Alexis to the United States. As a result of czarist oppressions then going on in Russia, influence had been brought to bear on Hall not to honor the Grand Duke. The cartoon showed Hall in a silk top hat pushed down over his eyes, a cigar clamped between his teeth, and his arms folded high on his chest facing the Grand Duke in an obviously defiant manner. The Grand Duke was shown in his long Russian greatcoat lifting his cap graciously to the Mayor. The caption was:

'For this relief much thanks!' Shakespeare.
Mayor Haul — 'I will not receive you in
an Official Capacity.'
Grand Duke Alexis — 'You do me honor.'

A few days later Tweed was arrested. One of his friends, Sheriff Matthew T. Brennan, handed him the arrest warrant in the Boss's luxurious office in the Court House. Brennan raised his hat and, according to the *Tribune,* 'merely nodded to Mr. Tweed, bade him "Good-day," and laying his hand tenderly on his shoulder, said, laughingly, "you're my man." It seemed like a deliciously cool joke and, judging from the faces, it was.'

Nast's cartoon on 18 November depicting Tweed's arrest showed Hall standing directly in back of Tweed. Sweeny was sitting beside the Boss at his desk. In the background was the buxom figure of Justice who was saying, 'I'll make some of you cry yet.' Tweed was smiling, Sweeny looked as if he were about to whisper something to Tweed. Hall looked both puzzled and worried.

The *Times* and *Harper's* continued to rail at Greeley of the *Tribune* and James Gordon Bennett, the younger, of the *Herald* for not having denounced Hall in the editorial columns of their papers. In 9 December Nast printed, in *Harper's Weekly,* a full-page cartoon showing Hall standing on the steps of City Hall (labeled 'The Hall of Honesty') with his two vest pockets pulled inside out and in the act of showing the insides of his pants pockets. Greeley, dressed in a long baggy overcoat, was shown flashing a lamp on Hall's face. The title was 'H. G. Diogenes Has Found the Honest Man,' and under it was this caption:

> H.G.D. — Whoever says you ain't is a vulgar
> braggart and liar, chattering slander with as
> little sense as a magpie.

Hall was a sorely pressed Mayor and must have felt his vindication by the Grand Jury an empty verdict indeed. He told a reporter for the *Times* he was 'casting my political skin.' The *Times* listed a total of $205,500 in fees paid by the city to Hall's law firm — Brown, Hall, and Vanderpoel. The timing of this information carried overtones of fraudulent dealings, probably unjustly.

Greeley was finally forced to take a position. 'We do not endorse it (the crusade),' he wrote, 'neither do we discredit it. We are not in possession of facts that would warrant us in making charges. If it be justified by facts, Messrs. Hall and Connolly ought now to be cutting stone in a state prison. The *Times* deserves the thanks of the community.'

Meanwhile, Mrs. Andrew J. Garvey, the wife of the plastering contractor, who had sailed with her husband to Europe, returned to New York. She told reporters that her husband who had reportedly received millions from the city for contracts for plastering, kicking back half the money to the Ring, would return to the United States shortly. She said he had instructed her to say that he would disclose all he knew if he received immunity from prosecution. She said that her husband's revelations would not only implicate Tweed but also Sweeny and Hall. A reporter for the *Herald* showed Hall a clipping about Mrs. Garvey's return. All the interviews with Hall, at this time, indicate there was a good deal of curiosity as to whether he would be able to main-

By December, 1871, Nast was still lampooning Horace Greeley for his failure to join the *Harper's Weekly* attacks on Hall. Here he labeled Greeley, 'H. G. Diogenes [who] has found the honest man.'

tain his manner of amused unconcern. This interview was no exception. Hall read the slip, the reporter wrote, and 'seemed somewhat annoyed — much more so than usual. He knit his brow, bit his upper lip, and gave his head a slight oscillation while gazing at the slip. Then he said:

'My fair-haired young friend, I can tell you and I can tell anybody — tell the entire world — that there does not live a man, nor has any man died, who can or ever could make any revelation which would implicate me in any dishonorable professional or official act, nor impugn my professional or official integrity. . . . I can't say whether Mrs. Garvey has made any such statement or not; and as to those statements of my being implicated I am certain no man can make any, much less substantiate them.'

IV

How Hall appeared to the 'respectabilities' is suggested by George Templeton Strong's diary for 2 December 1871: 'Oakey Hall, once so jaunty and cocky, is said to be sadly wilted down, like a broken lily, in fact. His wife and daughter in Europe are driven from one hotel to another by people who point at them as the family of one of the Great American Swindlers. One can't help pity the poor things. Hall himself, who had a kind of social position once, is now very generally cut, as he deserves to be.'

Not only was Hall being cut by the 'respectabilities,' but some of them wanted to express their disapproval in more tangible form. So far, in the public prints, Hall had been able to appear to be laughing off the extravagant charges made against him. His 'social position' — which was extremely important to him — was infinitely more vulnerable. It had taken him years to achieve the place he occupied in New York society. In a moment it could all be swept away. Naturally, it distressed him to realize how unpleasant all this was making things for his wife, and for his children, who were just reaching adulthood. Up until now his political life had been a thing apart. His wife, the former Katherine Louise Barnes, had maintained an impregnable social position. She and all her children were parishioners of the fashionable Trinity Chapel and were intimate friends of its Rector, the Rev. Stephen Tyng. They were all included in The List, the Social Register of the day. Mrs. Hall never received her husband's political friends — or their wives. Descendants of Hall remember that it was said that 'Mother Barnes-Hall would not have Tweed or any of those politicians in the house.' It is probable that Tweed knew this, which may help to explain his later implicating Hall in the Ring stealings.

The attack on Hall among the socially entrenched of New York was expressed in a move among members of the Union Club to have him expelled. It was the most socially powerful club in New York. 'But for the fact,' Reginald Townsend later wrote in *Mother of Clubs,* a history of the first hundred years of the Union, 'that original members of the Club were men of unimpeachable character and standing and represented the best families in the city, the Club might not have survived.'

Under the club's constitution, its government was in the hands of twenty-four members who were authorized, under paragraph 6, 'To admit and to expel members by ballot; one adverse ballot in ten excluding, and a two-thirds vote of a meeting in favor of expulsion, expelling.' This committee was also authorized, under paragraph 13, 'To put an end to membership for any conduct of a member not in violation of the constitution or the rules, but improper and prejudicial to the Club.'

This wording was obviously open to wide interpretation. What constituted, for example, improper conduct, or conduct prejudicial to the club? Did paragraph 13 also require a two-

thirds vote or a unanimous vote? In later years, the Union
was to learn the hard way, through the courts. A member,
charged with making a slurring remark about a lady, was
expelled, took the case to the law courts, and won.

On Wednesday night, 5 December, by a vote of twelve to
ten, the governing committee of the Union Club voted to
expel Oakey Hall from membership. Absent from the meeting were Isaac Bell and Moses H. Grinnell. (Hall was apparently able to find out how the members present voted, for he
put it down in his Union Club yearbook for 1871.) Among
those who voted for the resolution to expel him were William
Cutting, Henry S. Fearing, George Griswold Gray, James W.
Clendenin, and Philip Schuyler. Among those who voted
against the resolution were William H. Appleton, Edwin A.
Post, August Belmont, Denning Duer, J. Grenville Kane,
and John Romeyn Brodhead.

The day after the meeting Hall wrote a letter to the president and governing committee of the Union Club:
'Gentlemen:

'The Governing Committee, last night, by its constitutional
vote, denied the efforts of (what you must pardon me for
characterizing) a Cabal to expel me. I learn, this morning,
that every acquaintance whom I had upon the Committee
voted for the denial. Thereby the minority, which can protect a Member against Club menace (in the same method
whereby a minority can protect a Club against menace of
unacceptable candidacy) have maintained my club position.

'But, the discussions over my connection with the recent
public events, which were had as well within the Committee
room as outside of it, and even in the partisan press; also the
chivalric zeal of my friends that was pitted against the harsh
criticism of those who were not my friends; all evidence to me,
that, however much I may personally value the pleasure of club
association or Union Club privileges (in company with the
thousand members — "of many minds who can't agree") I

ought not to continue (& in Club history there is abundant, and approved & honorable precedent for such a course) as a subject of discord in a club that is exclusively social & not political. Its social amenities have been, & are likely to be for a long time, disturbed quite as much by the partisanship of my numerous friends among those thousand Members as by the undeserved criticisms of those with whom I have not the honor of acquaintanceship. Moreover, message has been sent me that my adherents may be aggressively (& as I fear offensively) attacked in certain press quarters so long as I remain. I owe it to them to make a sacrifice, & become contented to submit for a time to possible distorting of motives that my enemies will probably make. Therefore, being now relieved by the action of the Committee from pressure of menace I am free to act upon the foregoing reasons. I now therefore after ten years of membership resign from the Union Club.

'Without any rancorous feelings towards the strangers to me who have had I admit, (but only) *prima facie* pretexts for harsh attacks,

'Believe me very truly your
'Obedient Servant
'A. Oakey Hall.'

Hall did not immediately mail his resignation because his friend Recorder Hackett told him a meeting of the entire membership of the club was to be called. Notice of the meeting was sent out by Oliver K. King, secretary, on 13 December. 'A Special Meeting will be held,' the notice read, 'at the Club House on Friday, December 29th inst., at 8 o'clock P.M. for the purpose of taking into consideration the question of the continuance of Mr. A. Oakey Hall's membership. By order of the Committee.'

In many a brownstone-front house, in drawing rooms warmed by iron grilled fireplaces, ladies and gentlemen of New York's upper families discussed the question of whether

Oakey Hall should be expelled from the Union Club. It was the day of Victorian morality. Family-proud New Yorkers of entrenched wealth took a sharp view of the slightest suggestion of any lack of personal integrity or honesty among them. Their business ethics might be rough and tumble, the wages paid those who worked for them might be at less than subsistence levels. But a man's honesty must be beyond reproach, his word his bond. Apparently, most of those who knew Hall or who knew the circumstances of his connection with the Tweed Ring stood by him. In his Union Club yearbook he noted those among the members whom he believed he could count on to back him up. He marked the names of five Cuttings. The sixth, William Cutting, a member of the governing committee, had already voted for his expulsion. He also marked the names of J. Schuyler Crosby, Henry Clews, John L. Cadwalader, Henry L. Brevoort, Albert L. Beeckman, John J., William, and William Waldorf Astor, Perry and August Belmont, James Gordon Bennett, Jr., Benjamin L. De Forest, Joseph W. Drexel, John H. and William E. Iselin, Samuel W. Johnson, Henry Redmond, and Andrew H. Sands. Hall could count on a brilliant array of the sons of New York's first families to stand by him but, in numbers, they were not enough.

On Friday evening, 29 December, shiny carriages pulled by high-stepping horses, driven by high-hatted coachmen, pulled up at the entrance to the Union Club then located on Fifth Avenue at Twenty-first Street. Their passengers hurried into the Corinthian-columned 'brownstone mansion' — only to emerge almost immediately. The meeting had been called off. Oakey Hall had agreed to resign. It was later reported in the *Times* that August Belmont and other friends of Hall had taken a pre-election poll and learned that his expulsion would be sustained. They had persuaded him to resign and the governing committee to call off the election.

A more detailed and probably more exact report on what transpired among the club members was reported in George Templeton Strong's diary for 2 December. Strong was not a member of the Union, but had five relatives who were. One of them was on the board of governors.

'A general meeting of the Union Club,' Strong wrote, 'is called for Friday night to consider a resolution that Oakey Hall's membership is prejudicial to the character of the club. There are sixty-five signatures. Oakey Hall feels this very keenly and has been begging and praying O'Conor (Charles O'Conor, a member since 1853) to help him — talking about his young daughter whose prospects would be blighted by the infliction of a social stigma on her papa, and so on. O'Conor has been rather melted, I regret to say. Belmont's enthusiasm for Oakey Hall seems to have cooled down a little. Hall wrote yesterday to Denning Duer, acting president of the club, that he feels he is "unwilling the serenity of the club should be imperiled" by differences of opinion on a merely personal question; and that in case the proposed meeting should happen not to take place, he would like this to be considered as his resignation.'

Hall sent the letter of resignation he had previously written, but added a 'Memorandum' dated 31 December.

'The above,' he wrote, 'was about to be sent when I learned on its day of date from Recorder Hackett that a call had been started for a Club meeting about this matter. Of course my self respect withheld the note upon the new pressure. The Governing Committee, however, after granting a call, revoked it, and the above now leaves my custody. I beg to add that it would have been forwarded although I had been there constitutionally sustained as I had been by the Committee — in such a case the first submitted reasons were equally weighty.'

On 4 January, Oliver K. King, secretary of the Union Club,

Hall's protestations of his honesty in the fall of 1871 resulted in Nast's drawing him in the role of HONEST HAUL AS RICHARD III, quoting the 'secret mischiefs that I set abroach' speech.

returned Hall's resignation to him with the accompanying note:

'Sir. I am instructed by the Governing Committee to return to you the enclosed letter of date Dec. 6th which you addressed to the President and Governing Committee, the document being in the opinion of the Committee disrespectful to them. I am Your obe't Sv't Oliver K. King, Secretary."

The Union Club had had the last word. In its official records showing the date of admission of its members, there was added to Oakey Hall's card the words: 'Expulsion laid on table. December 5, 1871.'

Christmas week, 1871, was a sad one for Hall. On 29 December, Hall's paper, *The Leader,* appeared for the last time. On Saturday, the day before New Year's Eve, Nast published a cartoon showing Hall in Shakespearean dress. It was entitled 'Honest Haul as Richard III.' The caption was Shakespeare's:

> I do the wrong, and first begin to brawl.
> The secret mischiefs that I set abroach
> I lay unto the grievous charge of others. . . .
> But then I sigh, and, with a piece of scripture,
> Tell them that God bids us do good for evil:
> And thus I clothe my naked villany
> With odd old ends, stol'n forth of holy writ,
> And seem a saint when most I play the devil.

7

THE RIOT OF THE ALDERMEN

I

HALL'S FOURTH and last year as Mayor of New York City began with a virtual riot in that traditionally riotous and occasionally ridiculous branch of the city government — the Aldermanic chamber. The Tammany or Tweed Board of Aldermen and assistant aldermen had been defeated in the October, 1871, elections by a slate of candidates put up by a fusion ticket of the Republican party and the Apollo Hall Reform Democracy, controlled by Samuel J. Tilden. The Committee of Seventy had also endorsed this slate.

The problem of the reformers was to make sure the new members of the Board of Aldermen would be allowed to take their seats. They knew that Tweed had obtained passage in the state legislature of a new city charter which clinched Tammany's hold over the city government. Tweed had also had an act passed by the legislature in 1871 which extended the term of office of the old Board of Aldermen for one year. Although this act was patently unconstitutional, the reformers quite rightly suspected that the Tweed machine would, by some legal device or maneuvering, attempt to continue the old board in office. Henry Lauren Clinton, counsel to the Committee of Seventy and active in the reform wing of the Democratic party, mapped the strategy whereby the new board would take office without incident.

Clinton's first move was to obtain from Judge Brady in the New York Supreme Court a writ of prohibition forbidding Mayor Hall to appoint any of the 'holdover' aldermen or assistant aldermen to serve during the new term beginning at noon 1 January 1872. He was forbidden 'to recognize them or to recognize any but those who were elected in the October elections.' Clinton also obtained writs for each and every alderman and assistant alderman forbidding them to receive any appointment for the new term. On Saturday afternoon, 30 December, the writ of prohibition was served on Mayor Hall. The president of the Board of Aldermen, Thomas Coman, learned that the writ had been served on the Mayor but he did not know that writs had also been obtained against all the old aldermen and assistant aldermen. Coman had planned that when the board members met on the last day of their terms they would vote to impeach Mayor Hall, whereupon he, Coman, would become acting Mayor; then, just at noon, the old board would resign and the acting Mayor would appoint all those who resigned to replace themselves. Thus, the old board would be in and the new board out. The new board would go to court to get an order permitting it to take its rightful place in the city government, but this might take a long time. However, the reformers had anticipated that this would be the Tammany strategy and prepared accordingly.

On Monday morning, 1 January, the old board met in the aldermanic chamber. Mayor Hall remained in his office at the other end of City Hall. The spectators' gallery in the aldermanic chamber was filled to overflowing. The special complement of City Hall guards and policemen, assigned to keep order in the chamber, had to caution the crowd continually to stay behind the iron guard rail which separated the public from the aldermen's desks.

Clinton stationed himself along with his cohorts, each of them armed with Supreme Court writs, at the entrance to the chamber which was guarded by 'a stout, muscular sergeant-at-arms.' A few minutes before noon, Coman, as was expected, moved to impeach Mayor Hall and the motion was unanimously passed on an aye and nay vote. The board members then resigned in a body and the acting Mayor, Coman, appointed them to fill the vacancies they had just created. A motion was then made to 'adjourn the board sine die,' and it was seconded by George Washington Plunkitt who was later to achieve fame as the author of the phrase 'dishonest and honest graft.'

As this motion was voted on, A. R. Lawrence, one of the counsel to the new board, stood up and warned the members of the old board that they would be in contempt of court if they tried to form themselves into a new board. The members tried to howl him down. The clerk rapped his gavel for order but Lawrence continued to speak out. 'It sounded like a magistrate reading the riot act to a seditious mob,' according to the *World* reporter. 'Mr. Lawrence grew a little pale in the face for he did not know how soon an inkstand might be hurled at his head. People sitting near him began to vacate their places, lest the missile, should it come, might damage them also.'

Meanwhile, at the entrance of the chamber, at exactly three minutes before twelve, 'a small-sized young man emerged from the door, which was opened but a little way to let him out.' This was the opportunity Clinton was waiting for and he put his shoulder against the door and held it open. He called out the warning Lawrence had already given — that the board would be in contempt if it attempted to organize for the year 1872.

'Why the hell don't you shut the door?' one of the old aldermen called from the chamber. The sergeant-at-arms tried to comply, but Clinton had placed himself between the door and the frame and, according to the *World* reporter, now shouted: 'Resist me if you dare. We are here to demand admission as the duly elected Board of Aldermen for the year 1872. Your time is up. You must adjourn and vacate this room.'

The sergeant-at-arms said he didn't care for the writ. Clinton told one of his assistants to put down everything the sergeant-at-arms said. 'What is your name? What is your name, I say? I demand your name.' Someone called out his name was Munn.

'Ah,' said Clinton, 'your name is Munn, is it? I'll make you regret your action today, sir, of resisting the Supreme Court.'

'Well, I can't help it,' the sergeant-at-arms, now somewhat intimidated, said. 'You can't blame me in working for my friends.'

After a struggle of five minutes Clinton broke into the chamber, calling out, 'Follow me' to his clerks and those members of the new board who had not already gained admission through another entrance. According to the *World* reporter, 'Mr. Clinton's clerks sprang for the aldermen, in order to serve them with copies of the writ and accompanying papers; they, in order to avoid service, leaped from their seats, rushed around the room, knocking over chairs, desks, and tables, the clerks in hot pursuit and managing to serve the papers by throwing copies in their faces or inside the collars of their coats and vests. While these proceedings were in progress, the newly elected aldermen, following Mr. Clinton, rushed inside the railing and occupied the seats which had just been vacated. Some of the old aldermen, in order to avoid Clinton and his cohorts, made a rush for the door. But Mr. Clinton called out to his clerks to follow them, crying: "Serve them! Serve them!" A few of the bravest of the old aldermen resolved to fight it out to the last, and had entrenched themselves behind the president's desk. As the head of the attacking party came in those men shouted, "Put them out! Put them out, I tell you!" But they soon came in such strong numbers that all hope of resisting by force was abandoned.'

According to the *Herald* reporter, one of Clinton's clerks, a boy named Shields, 'small, energetic and wiry,' attempted to serve Alderman James Irving with a writ. 'The alderman, true to his nature, struck the boy. Two reporters stepped between them, and restrained the alderman.' Shields, according to the *World* reporter, accused Irving of striking him. 'Mr. Clinton, hearing the discussion walked up and said, "What's that? Did he strike you? Can you swear to that? Are you not mistaken?" And then, turning to Irving, who stood like a huge coarse giant, his eyes flashing as sharp as the rays from the big diamond on his shirt-front, his hands in his overcoat pockets, and a cigar in his mouth, he said: "I know you too well to believe that you would strike a boy!"

' "Why, good God! I ain't had my hands out of my pockets! What is the fellow talking about?" Irving replied.

'Shields repeated his charge to the alderman. "What did you say?" said the alderman, bending over the young twig who was a mere baby beside his antagonist. "Did you say I struck you?"

' "Yes, sir; I do say so. You struck me, big as you are."

' "You're a G — d —— s —— liar!" quoth the city father.

'Alderman George Washington Plunkitt walked over and told his friend, Irving, "Hold on, Jim. Don't get yourself into trouble." '

The *World* reporter noted that Irving then said, 'I swear I didn't by (fearful oath) I didn't.'

'You are a (obscene oath) liar,' Shields replied.

'By (oath) I didn't take my hands out of my pockets,' Irving insisted. 'Whoever says so is a (shocking oath), and I'll put a head on him.'

According to the *Herald* reporter, Irving then 'ran off to the president's chair, as though he thought that sacred place would save him from arrest. The limb of the law pursued him there and gave him the writ, which he indignantly took. Some of the "bullies" of the board shouted, "Turn him out!" and a tall, black-mustached messenger of the court (friendly to the old aldermen) caught the young man as he was crossing the chamber to serve some fleeing aldermen. The messenger struck him, and lifted him up, evidently with the intention of throwing him over the railing. A reporter went up to this pugilistic individual and advised him not to do that, for he was assaulting a messenger of the Supreme Court. The man had sense enough to disobey the orders of his superiors, and he let go his hold of the process-server.'

Shields went about his duties of serving the other aldermen. More police arrived. Order was restored and the new board proceeded to organize.

A committee of three was appointed 'to wait upon the Mayor and inform him of our organization and that we are ready to entertain his personal presence.' According to the *Sun,* the committee returned 'with a little man in elegant gray clothes, who was accompanied by Colonel Joline. "The Mayor!" cried one of the officers, and there was a profound silence. Mr. Vance (one of the committee) coughed, and bowed to the Mayor. The Mayor made him a profound bow.

'The Mayor (coughing violently, and looking quite pale, as if something had very much annoyed him) — "Mr. President, if you will allow me but a few words. I came to the office of the Mayor of the City of New York at the hour of noon, prepared to disobey the writ of prohibition which was served upon me last Saturday, because I was instructed by counsel learned in the law that it was, upon its face, null and void, because a writ of prohibition could only issue to a court on a motion in a higher court. I came for the purpose of solving all legal doubt, and for the purpose of performing a pledge which I have long ago entered into, of appointing the old Board of Aldermen and assistant aldermen (here his Honor drew some breath and adjusted the splendid velvet collar of his coat). I found that they had seen fit, on their part, without seeking a conference with me, without appearing to seek a conference with me, to take hostile action against me, both personally and officially. You are, therefore, in accord with me, and I have an opportunity to do as I please.

' "You have two titles for the office of aldermen. If you are elected, that's one title; if you are not elected, why then you are appointed. (Laughter, and Mr. Hall looked as he does when he has committed an atrocious joke.) Gentlemen, I appoint you as aldermen, and I'm prepared to administer the oath of office to you."

'Colonel Joline took out of his hat a half-dozen blanks of oaths of office and, with the tone of a pastor, Mayor Hall swore them in. Then he made a profound bow to Mr. Vance and went from the room, holding his silk hat high in his hand.'

Later, the new Board of Aldermen voted to rescind the resolution to impeach the Mayor which had been voted by the old board.

The reformers had taken over.

In the two weeks following the events recorded above, Nast drew two cartoons featuring the city's chief executive. In one, a denuded thorn bush was growing out of the dome of City Hall. At the top was Hall's head. Pieces of thorn were falling off. On them were small heads of Tweed and Sweeny. In the background Connolly was shown behind prison bars. The caption was 'Last of the Four' with the following inscription:

'Tis the last 'Thorn of Tammany' left blooming alone,
All 'His' lovely companions are faded and gone.
I'll not leave thee, thou lone one, to pine on the stem
Since the lovely are sleeping, go sleep thou with them.

In the other cartoon, Hall was dressed in the costume of Touchstone, sitting on the floor, reading a large volume of Shakespeare. The caption was:

Tammany (OK) Hall Jester (Reads). ' "Where ignorance is bliss, 'tis Folly to be Wise." I am in Blissful Ignorance of Every Thing that has happened since I have been Mayor of New York.'

II

A week after the reformers had taken over the Board of Aldermen, Big Jim Fisk, one of the great roisterers of the day and an official of the Erie Railroad, was walking down the inside stairs of the Grand Central Hotel on Broadway just below Astor Place. At the foot of the stairs, with a pistol in his hand, stood Edward S. Stokes, a rival for the affections of an actress named Josie Mansfield and known as the 'Cleopatra of Twenty-third Street.' Fisk had set her up in a house on Twenty-third Street, a few doors from the Grand Opera House at Eighth Avenue which housed the offices of the Erie Railroad and also served as a place of entertainment for friends and a large acquaintance of chorus girls. Stokes fired twice at Fisk and wounded him. He died a few hours later. At Fisk's bedside was Boss Tweed, a friend and fellow stockholder in the Erie Railroad.

The indignation of the city, particularly from the quarters inhabited by the reformers, turned on Mayor Hall. It was unfair, perhaps; but horror and anger made a hash of logic. The Ring had been involved in corruption and fraud; now violence had been added to its sins. Tweed was a friend of Fisk's, and Hall was an associate of Tweed. The Mayor must go — so said the reformers. Members of the Committee of Seventy conferred with Hall and suggested he resign. He spurned their suggestions. It was proposed that he meet Tilden at the house of a common friend. (The friend was generally believed to be Manton Marble of the *World,* a member of the Union Club.)

'We met,' Hall wrote later. 'Mr. Tilden offered to use his influence to prevent any legal prosecution against me for "neglect of duty" if I would resign. Fortunately, as a matter of precaution, I took with me a confidential friend, as a possible witness, who is yet alive. I at once refused, as I had refused other overtures.'

Tilden had investigated Hall's affairs rather thoroughly. Back in October, 1871, Tilden had in his possession a letter from someone who signed himself 'G.' 'If the Committee of 70,' the letter, addressed to Henry G. Stebbins, said, 'of which you are the Ch. desire the Ev. of A.O.H.'s complicity with the division of "Ring Spoils" let them Scrutinize the Bank Acct. of Mr. Wm. Edelstein the Law Partner of Tweed W. & a former clk, with B.H. & V. in the 10th National Bank.'

Edelstein turned out to be one of the lawyers for Tweed. He had a large bank account, but then so did many of the lawyers who defended Tweed. Tweed's lawyers, incidentally, included some very distinguished names — Elihu Root, David Dudley Field, and John Graham. Apparently it was possible for a lawyer to accept a portion of a client's ill-gotten funds and still maintain his respectability. Tweed later testified that he paid out $400,000 in legal fees and expenses. Some of this went to Hall's two law partners, Aaron J. Vanderpoel and Augustus L. Brown.

Tilden had also obtained a transcript of Hall's account in the Tenth National Bank of New York. It showed that, while Hall had no large balance, from 1 March 1870 through July, he had deposited $102,693.48 and drawn out $93,345.30. His withdrawals were marked 'Ex' and 'Office.' On Tilden's copy of the transcript was a notation opposite Hall's 5 August withdrawal of $6,528.50 which read: 'W. M. Tweed pays of. same acc't same day.' Hall had deposited $6,750.00 on 2 August. In a breakdown of the 'Deposits as they appear in

Ledger' sheet, it was noted that the $6,750.00 deposit was $5,000 in 'Bills' (probably cash) and two checks — one for $1,125 and one for $625. What the exact nature of the transaction was, the records do not reveal.

There were other circles in which Hall's popularity was as great as ever, particularly those in need of an amusing speaker. He was invited to the annual Franklin Banquet, held on 17 January at Delmonico's, Fifth Avenue and Fourteenth Street. One of the members of the committee of arrangements for this affair was Fletcher Harper, Jr., a part owner of *Harper's Weekly,* in whose pages Nast was continuing to attack Hall. Henry Ward Beecher and Horace Greeley were among the honored guests, and Hall sat between them. He was 'cheered' when he got up to speak, according to the *World.* He paid the usual tributes to the Philadelphia printer and the printing profession, to which his audience chiefly belonged. Then he spoke indirectly, but feelingly, of himself, saying he 'was not willing to discharge an old compositor because he has mixed his type a little in his form.' It was a figure of speech his hearers could understand, and was perhaps as close to the truth about Hall's role in the Tweed Ring scandals as we can get. He had been compliant, and had become muddled.

He had good reason to be feeling sorry for himself. Another Grand Jury had been convened in November, headed by Lucius S. Comstock, a brother of that great Nestor of morality, Anthony Comstock, and there were persistent rumors that it was going to hand up an indictment against Hall. The strategy of the reformers, who were aware that it would be impossible to convict the Mayor of stealing money from the city treasury, had been to charge him with neglect of duty in failing to audit a specific account, a misdemeanor under the fourth section of an 1870 act of the state legislature. To top the rumors, there appeared on 3 February a Nast cartoon entitled 'Haul Turned Up. Here We Are Again.' It showed

In his New Year's address, 1872, on the state of the city's affairs, Hall asked for understanding of his many problems. Nast promptly drew him as a sandwich man, suggesting the text for his message.

a Jack-in-the-box with the bewildered face of the Mayor. Nast, apparently, had learned the Grand Jury's findings, and seeing his cartoon Hall must have known the truth at last. Unfortunately the minutes of the second Grand Jury are not available.

8

INDICTMENT AND FIRST TRIAL

I

THE EXCITEMENT IN NEW YORK was intense on Saturday, 10 February, the day the Grand Jury was to hand up its final report to Judge Gunning Bedford in the Court of General Sessions. Shortly before eleven o'clock a large crowd gathered; according to the Sunday *Herald*, never before had so much public interest been manifested. 'There was such an unusual pressure of respectable citizens and such a very infinitesimal element of the habitués of the place, that refusal for entrance was out of the question. As might be expected, the utmost decorum was observed. . . . While expectation was on tiptoe, awaiting the arrival of the Grand Jury, an important personage entered the room quietly and took his seat outside the bars, having all eyes directed to his. This was Mayor Hall, the chief magistrate of the city, whom rumor had also indicted, and truly so, as after events proved.'

According to the *Star*, Hall 'looked as cheery as might be expected.' Tweed was present with one of his attorneys, John Graham, who was 'looking as determined as ever.' The Grand Jury members filed into the courtroom. Lucius Comstock, the foreman, stood up and said they had found the last indictments and completed their duties. The secretary, J. H. Draper, then read a statement in which he said 'New York has suffered a loss of at least $20,000,000 through the venality and corruption of those they have indicted . . . Perjury, forgery, and similar crimes, are the means by which the treasury was robbed and the city disgraced.' Judge Bedford praised the jury, thanked them, and discharged them.

'Hall,' according to the Sunday *Herald,* 'amid breathless silence, rose and said: "If the court please, I have read in the newspapers for several days past that the Grand Jury had found indictments against me. I desire to know if that is the fact, and I am here, both as a counsellor of the court and as an individual, to answer it." ' The District Attorney said five indictments had been found against Hall and at Hall's request he read the Grand Jury's conclusion: 'Abraham Oakey Hall . . . did . . . unlawfully and corruptly neglect to audit the said claim or to examine into the validity and correctness of the said claim.'

Hall spoke immediately. 'It, then,' he said, 'is neglect of official duty. If the court please, I am here to answer that accusation and to make a motion. I have appeared twice before in this court as counsel for officials of this county charged with official misdemeanor. One of them was a judge of this very tribunal and the other was a former Mayor of this city. They were each absolved, as I expect to be. I desire, sir, to offer bail, and my bail is in court. And I wish to say that I shall make no plea to the irregularities of the Grand Jury which, as a lawyer and as a man, I conscientiously believe to have been many.'

Judge Bedford, after speaking of 'the distinguished position Mr. Hall holds in this community,' fixed bail at $10,000. Hall called out, 'Is Mr. Barnes in court?' Barnes, his brother-in-law, came forward and the 'bonds were made out without the least delay, and as soon as Mr. Hall and Mr. Barnes were sworn and the bail bonds were signed by the judge, they left court.'

The case against Hall was placed on the General Sessions Court calendar for Monday, 19 February. 'Future historians,' the reporter for the Boston *Post* wrote that day, 'will have to relate how . . . the Mayor of this city appeared at the bar of the General Sessions Court in answer to a criminal charge, and it will also be the duty of the coming chronicler to inform his readers how much popular sympathy and enthusiasm was manifested in Mayor Hall's favor, on that occasion. From the moment of His Honor's entry the inevitable handshaking commenced, and until the moment of his departure it was as much as the ushers of the court could do to maintain silence and order. There seemed a disposition among the persons present to break out into a good, hearty cheer for Mayor Hall.'

Attorney General Francis C. Barlow, who had superseded the District Attorney, was present for the prosecution. He asked, not without a great deal of oratory, that the case be postponed, but Hall immediately objected.

'The Mayor, in a calm dignified manner,' the Boston *Post* reporter wrote, 'waited until his turn came, and then never for one moment forgetting his good breeding, returned to Mr. Barlow quite as good as he gave, and placed that estimable gentleman in a perfectly white heat of passion. Barlow said Hall's insistence on the trial taking place immediately was "a trick to cover up his actions."

'This sally placed the Mayor on his mettle, for, drawing himself to his full height, he said, "I shall at least remember the dignity of the position which I hold in the community and confine myself to the case and to the facts. The Attorney General is here to represent the people and in due time, no doubt, will file with the court the only evidence of his authority, the fiat of the Governor. Whether he is here to represent the high office formerly filled by Van Buren, Ogden Hoffman, Levi Chatfield, Talcott and other distinguished men who have filled the position, or whether he is here as a volunteer, I do not care to question. But I insist on my trial being commenced today." Barlow here allowed his anger to get the better of his eloquence.

' "It is a scandal," Hall continued, "that an official should be suffered to rest under accusations, charging him with corrupt neglect of duty and have similar official duties to perform, when he claims and is ready for an immediate investigation. Therefore, in the name of the people whose servant they say I am neglectful, whose servant I say I am faithful, I shall insist upon my rights." '

His rhetoric was better than his grammar.

Barlow having said he would have counsel ready to try the case the following Monday, Judge Bedford stated that he would adjourn the case until then. On this, Hall remarked that 'if it were possible for my deadliest enemy to sit upon the bench I would still wish the case to proceed next Monday.'

According to M. T. Jugg, a writer for the *Star*, Barlow looked like 'a baby elephant, a regular calf. . . . His face is the fascimile of the labels on "Mother Winslow's Soothing Syrup," and as one of the jurors remarked, he acts like a sick monkey and smiles like a mild baboon. . . . His chief trouble is brains. . . . Or he might succeed as an undertaker.'

The trial commenced in the Court of General Sessions 26 February, the Hon. Charles P. Daly, Chief Judge of the New York Court of Common Pleas, presiding. Hall came to the sessions on horseback. He was, of course, impeccably dressed. The majority of those who attended were obviously friendly to the Mayor. There were seven lawyers defending Hall — E. W. Stoughton, John E. Burrill, James M. Smith, Ira S. Shafer, Thomas C. Buckley, ex-Judge Joel A. Fithian, and Aaron J. Vanderpoel, Hall's law partner. Three of them, Stoughton, Burrill, and Buckley, were members of the Union Club. The prosecutors were Lyman Tremain, Wheeler H. Peckham, and Henry Lauren Clinton. It was said they were each receiving fees of $10,000 apiece for their services.

Hall arrived on horseback for his first trial and a newspaper artist caught the event with pen and ink.

A mild sensation occurred during the examination of the third prospective juror. It was the opinion of this man that if Mayor Hall did anything wrong it was an 'error of the head, not the heart.' Hall took this occasion to make a little speech in which he said:

'The gentleman stands there simply as the embodiment, in what he has said, of the law. The law, looking down on the defendant, says, "You are innocent; first, of having neglected, and second of ever having wilfully or intentionally neglected to do your duty." That which the law, the Constitution, says in so many words, in England and in this country, is borrowed from the old Roman law, and that is what this juror says. He says he believes the defendant is innocent of any neglect of duty. The law has said that, and these gentlemen, upon the other side, are here to overthrow the presumption of the law. It may be in the forum of the newspaper a man is presumed guilty until he proves his innocence, but in a forum like this, it is exactly the opposite. It has been said that a juror should go into the witness-box with his mind as free from traces of suspicion, of doubt, of opinion, of impressions, as the old wax table of the Romans was before the iron of the penman traced one dot upon it. Is not that the condition of the gentleman's mind? He waits at the door of the jury-box for the presumption of law to be overthrown by the evidence which my friends on the other side will present.'

The juror, whose name was Romaine A. Lukomski, was accepted after thirty-five minutes of intensive questioning.

After six of the jurors were installed, the reporter for the *Herald* called them 'the six remarkable jurymen who never read newspapers, or, if they do, were incapable of forming an opinion on, or receiving an impression from, what they had perused.' The seventh juror was one Horatio Reed, a slaugh-

In March, 1872, at his first trial, Hall (center) rose during the selection of the jury and complimented one prospective juror on his having said he believed the Mayor had committed 'an error of the head, not the heart.'

terer. He was, according to the *Herald,* 'apparently an English-man, resident in this city thirty years and good old English beef stuck out in lumps all over his jolly old countenance.' He was asked if he had any bias against the Mayor. ' "I'm pretty sure I have," he said, pursing his lips and looking determin-edly at counsel.' Asked if he could render an impartial verdict, he said, ' "I think I could — in fact, I've no doubt on that point; but I could render a verdict in accordance with the testimony — yes, sir." ' He was accepted.

II

The opening address to the jury was made by Henry Lauren Clinton, a reform Democrat and one of the prosecutors of the Tweed Ring. Clinton had encountered Hall in court before, having defended Mrs. Cunningham whom Hall, as District Attorney, had prosecuted for murder. It was said that Clinton bore Hall considerable personal animosity because Hall had opposed him in inter-party political fights. They had known each other for twenty years and Clinton told the jury, 'Often have we crossed forensic swords. Many have been the trials of deep and absorbing interest in which we have been opposed, not a few of them equalling, if not surpassing, the present. Only a deep and stern sense of duty could induce me to appear here as the prosecutor of one who, at this bar, has so often and so successfully prosecuted others. . . . If I know my own heart, I have no personal ill feeling whatever in respect to this defendant. . . . I will disguise nothing from you, gentlemen. I will not deny that although we both belong to the same political party — he to one branch and I to another — for the last two years I have opposed him and those connected with him — the Tammany Ring. I have denounced that organiza-tion.'

Clinton's opening speech was, according to the reporter for

the *Star,* 'ponderous and in spite of that ingenious . . . he rather attacked a system than a man.'

Although it was apparent he was making political capital out of Hall's trial, Clinton protested that he 'would desire to keep politics as far as possible out of this case, yet we cannot ignore that which we all know, that a great reform movement recently swept over this city like a tornado, uprooting infamous abuses of long standing and scattering to the four winds the conspirators against the public welfare and the public treasury.'

Clinton told how the city's debt had risen from $36,000,000 to $97,000,000 in a little over two years and a half. He spoke long and eloquently about the courthouse 'worth but little over two million [which] has cost the city upward of fourteen millions of dollars.' At the end of his opening address, he reached his greatest flight of oratory — with a quotation from Shakespeare's *Hamlet* thrown in for good measure:

'In times like these, when corruption, like the pall of death overhangs our city; when fraud, brazen with success, defies a long-suffering, patient, plundered community; when larcenies are conducted on a scale of imperial splendor; when forgeries nestle in the bosom of justice; when amateur burglars convert the very temple of law into a theatre for the exercise of their skill and daring; when the signs of the times are read by the light of burning records; when names of high officials are encircled with a halo of infamy; our only hope is in an upright, independent judiciary, and an honest fearless jury. The eyes of the people of this great metropolis — the first city in America — are upon you. This whole nation is anxiously awaiting your verdict. The deep interest of not alone this nation, but of every civilized nation on the globe, in the result of this trial must admonish you of the importance of the rendition of a true verdict; a verdict which will show to the world that you have, indeed, been true to the great public interests involved in this case — true to the law, whose ministers you are — true to the cause of public justice committed to your keeping — true to yourselves. To each of you I say,

> To thine own self be true,
> And it must follow, as the night the day,
> Thou canst not then be false to any man

or to the community in which you live.'

Hall received some consolation at the beginning of the trial. Andrew C. Wheeler of the *World* and George W. Hows of the *Express* and other members of the Lotos Club wrote him: 'Recognizing your past ability as President of The Lotos Club and believing that your reelection would tend to its future prosperity, [we] beg, hereby to tender you a renomination, with the hope that you will honor us by accepting it.'

The prosecution centered its evidence of Hall's neglect of duty on a $41,563.42 warrant payable to Andrew J. Garvey for labor and materials for the county courthouse. This warrant was signed by Hall as Mayor, Connolly as Comptroller, and J. B. Young as Clerk of the board of supervisors, of which Tweed was president. Garvey had returned secretly from Europe, where he had fled, and Clinton had already conferred with him regarding his testimony. Garvey was to appear, without any previous announcement, at Hall's trial on Thursday afternoon, 7 March.

'It was arranged,' Clinton wrote later, 'that Garvey should quietly attend in the clerk's office without removing the disguise which he wore; and . . . on being called as a witness, he should remove his disguise, walk into the courtroom and take his place on the witness stand. This program was carried out. Had Garvey risen from the dead, and appeared in grave clothes, he could not have carried greater consternation into the ranks of the defense. The effect upon defendant's different counsel was peculiar and extraordinary. Poor Garvey . . . sat perched up in the witness-chair, facing his old comrades, tremulous with excitement, evidently making desperate efforts to maintain his self possession.'

According to the *Tribune,* 'No more dramatic incident ever occurred in a New York courtroom. . . . Andy Garvey walked rapidly through the door, up the steps leading to the bench, disappearing for a moment behind the broad sounding board in the rear of the Judge's seat, reappeared beside the witness-stand and grasped the Bible as he waited with head uncovered to receive the oath. . . . A buzz of astonishment filled the room. Many persons involuntarily rose in their seats and stared at the newcomer as if he were a ghost come from the grave to fright them . . . the room was a Babel of whispers. . . .

'As to Mayor Hall, his countenance, while tolerably composed, nevertheless bore a look of chagrin and serious disappointment, and he was livid — with rage or fear. The blow, in its very unexpectedness, was hard to bear, and the accused gathered his defenders about him at once in earnest conference.'

The *World's* version of how Hall reacted to Garvey's appearance differed somewhat from that of the *Tribune.* 'The only man in the room,' the *World* reporter wrote, 'who retained his ordinary composure was the defendant himself. Mr. Hall was engaged in writing when Garvey entered; he looked up a moment and then continued his work in hand without being in the least disturbed by the sudden and rather dramatic appearance of the man upon whose testimony counsel for the prosecution were relying for the ultimate triumph of their cause.'

Garvey's manner on the stand, according to the *Tribune* reporter, 'certainly was agitated and his motions nervous and frightened. His voice slightly quivered as he replied, even to servility, as guilty men in such embarrassing positions are apt to be.'

Garvey testified that the signature on the $41,563.42 warrant was his. He was then asked if this was 'a just and honest account.' At this point, Burrill, of defense counsel, objected to the admissibility of the warrant. After much argument, the warrant was admitted in evidence. For the next two days Garvey testified concerning the payment of monies to him for alleged labor and materials for the courthouse. He said he received only 35 per cent of the amount of his bills. In one instance, after calculating the amount he expected to get back for legitimate labor and materials, he added $5,000 'for myself for expenses of the fall — political expenses — my own assessments. . . . I thus anticipated my expenses for the fall campaign.' The contractors were, apparently, expected to make campaign contributions out of their 35 per cent. Garvey solved the problem by anticipating such demands when he calculated how much was 'legitimately' due him for his contracting work.

Garvey said he did $60,000 worth of work for Tweed in Greenwich, Connecticut, and $13,000 at Cos Cob, which sums were, of course, paid for out of the county treasury. Garvey's testimony, however, did not implicate Hall directly.

The following Monday morning, when court opened, it was noted that the foreman of the jury, Matthias Clark, of 525 Greenwich Street, was not present. Judge Daly instructed the clerk to read a communication addressed to the court by Dr. J. W. Wright of 8 Charlton Street. He reported that Clark had been 'suffering from nervous prostration since Friday [and had] suffered from an attack of paralysis about two years ago, and as I find that a continuance of this kind of service may induce a second attack, I would earnestly recommend that he be entirely relieved.' Court was adjourned until the following Friday. Clark died on Tuesday. Hall, with his counsel, Judge Daly, and some members of the prosecution staff attended Clark's funeral.

On Friday, Judge Daly declared a mistrial and the eleven remaining jurors were dismissed.

III

Hall spent most of the summer of 1872 at Valley View. He rode horseback, read, and wrote meditative verses. His family were with him, and it distressed him deeply that his five daughters and son were at an age when children are affected by any public disapproval of their parents. Cara, his oldest child, was twenty-two and a talented painter. She was being courted by a Virginia gentleman named Carol Randolph. Maria Theresa, twenty, was a writer of children's stories, a pianist, and a cartoonist. Alice, eighteen, was a singer. Louise Oakey, fifteen, prided herself on designing ladies' hats. Josephine, thirteen, was slightly crippled with infantile paralysis but showed signs of being a character actress. Herbert Oakey, ten, was following his father's suggestion that he learn printing.

Hall's wife was understandably unhappy about his political difficulties. The Barnes family were so eminently respectable that even the suggestion of dishonor was a matter of great pain to them. Mrs. Hall stood by her husband, but in the end his difficulties destroyed their marriage. Also with Hall was his mother, now in her seventy-fourth year, and his sister Marcia, forty-two.

The city to which Hall and his family returned in the fall was an exciting place. A Presidential campaign was on and one of the candidates was Horace Greeley. President Ulysses S. Grant was scheduled to run for a second term. The Republicans under his leadership had built up a national reputation for Federal corruption. The Democratic party was still badly disorganized as a result of the Civil War. Tammany Hall, which was and is synonymous with the New York Democratic party, was even more disorganized as a result of the Ring scandals. A group of insurgent Republicans had banded together to elect a reform candidate. Their battle cry, best summed up in Greeley's words, 'Turn the rascals out,' was civil service reform. Carl Schurz, Joseph Pulitzer, Charles Francis Adams, Whitelaw Reid, were among their leaders, as was Edward W. Stoughton, a friend of Hall's, one of his legal counsel at his trial, and a Union Club member.

One of Greeley's supporters was Theodore Tilton, the brilliant young editor who was soon to gain notoriety as a result of being cuckolded by the famous preacher, Henry Ward Beecher. Tilton, Whitelaw Reid, and a group of thirty professional politicians had worked so skillfully on the floor of the convention that Greeley had won. Reid, like almost everyone connected with the Liberal Republicans, was surprised to find himself with such a strange candidate. 'Greeley is an interesting curiosity,' Reid wrote his friend John Bigelow, 'which everyone likes to see and to show and in whom we all feel a certain amount of pride, but I do not think anyone can seriously believe in his fitness for any administrative position whatever. If they do, they know as little of him as he knows of himself.' When Stoughton heard the convention announce the nomination of Horace Greeley he was, according to Lyman Tremain, 'like the young man spoken of in the Scripture, and went away sorrowful. He returned to the place from which he came with a large bumble-bee in his bonnet, a wiser, if not a better man.'

The Democrats held their national convention at Cooper Union on 3 June 1872, and gave their approval to Greeley, the Reform Republican candidate. It was thus made politically inadvisable to let up on the prosecution of Hall. Greeley had been charged by both the *Times* and Nast with being easy on Hall. Any letup would be seized on by the Republicans who had renominated Grant. Although Hall and Greeley were both 'characters,' there the similarity ended. Greeley was the homespun intellectual who looked as if he'd slept in his clothes and prided himself on being a hick farmer in a sophisticated city. He actually had a farm just outside New York City. Hall had baited Greeley for years but Greeley was reported to have been more amused than distressed by attacks from the dapper little District Attorney and Mayor. Hall maintained that Greeley used his paper 'to think aloud in at all times of the day and night; in moods bilious, phlegmatic, saturnine, sanguine; before breakfast and after breakfast.'

Although the reformers, whom Greeley had finally joined, appeared to be sweeping all before them, they had failed to undo the most lasting harm the Tweed Ring had done to the city. A new city charter, drawn by the Committee of Seventy, though passed by both houses of the state legislature, had been vetoed by Governor Hoffman. New York continued — and continues — to operate under a charter which facilitates corruption.

Both Grant and Greeley partisans used the Tweed Ring scandals to smear each other. In one of the ugliest cartoons he ever drew, Nast showed Tweed, in prison stripes, and Greeley with a pamphlet, 'What I Know About Swallowing,' swallowing each other. Grant's drinking habits were also an issue. The campaign was so bitter that Greeley remarked that he didn't know whether he was running for the Presidency or the penitentiary.

In the city election, three candidates were running for the office of Mayor. Former Mayor William F. Havemeyer, the sugar merchant, was running with the backing of Peter Cooper and the reformers, as well as the regular Republicans. Tammany Hall had again obtained a 'respectability' to run on its ticket — Abraham R. Lawrence, a member of an old, wealthy, and respected New York family. Tammany's rival, Apollo Hall, was running James O'Brien, the man who had betrayed Tweed and the other Ring members. Hall was not a candidate.

There remained to Hall only a few months in which to get himself tried and — as he confidently believed — acquitted before his term of office expired. This was important to him because of the acute embarrassment of serving as Mayor while an indictment hung over him. He also wished to leave his office, as chief magistrate of the city he loved so much, entirely vindicated.

Some of his feeling for New York he had once put into verse:

> The City is in silence wrapped
>   Its pulse now beateth low
> And solemnly like mourning mutes
>   The hours come and go.
>
> No sounds invade the watching air;
>   And in the street, where late
> A thousand souls were hurried by
>   With quick and restless gait,
>
> The Watchman slowly goes his rounds,
>   Communing with himself,
> And handing thousand mem'ries down
>   From every bosom shelf.

9

THE SECOND TRIAL

I

THE DRIVE TO CONVICT the Ring members was renewed that fall with the reformers asking for and receiving from the Grand Jury of the Court of Oyer and Terminer an indictment against Tweed and Connolly for neglect of duty. This new legal maneuver was known as the 'omnibus' indictment and it cited some fifty vouchers authorizing payment of the city's monies. It was hoped that at least one of them would serve to send the Ring members to jail. Hall was not named, but it was reported that Tilden wanted to get a duplicate set of papers made out against the Mayor.

On a Saturday evening at the Manhattan Club, the headquarters of the more entrenched and wealthy Democrats of the town (both reformed and unreformed), Hall listened to a speech on the coming Presidential and Mayoralty elections by Samuel J. Tilden. Hall had not seen Tilden since the latter had suggested that he resign as Mayor in exchange for immunity from prosecution. As he talked, Hall speculated whether Tilden might listen to an appeal on a human level, even though it was to his political advantage to prosecute him. Perhaps he also remembered an estimate of Tilden which one of his acquaintances had made: 'He treats every man as though he might one day become his enemy.' Nevertheless, Hall wrote Tilden a letter the next morning from his home at 13 West Forty-second Street.

'It was remarked in my hearing,' Hall wrote the reform Democrat, 'last evening, after you so gratified the club and its guests, "Mr. Tilden looks as if he not only had a great head, but also a large heart." I propose to address the latter, if you will graciously pardon the intrusion.

'I learn that Mr. Peckham [one of the reformers' lawyers] intends procuring from the Oyer and Terminer G.J. [Grand Jury] a duplicate charge agst. me for official neglect. It is in your power to advise against and prevent this. I think, sir, I can satisfy you that such advice will be in harmony with that unflinching standard of justice by which you measure all men and all things.

'I have filed an unqualified stipulation that pending charges be removed to the O. and T. The removal order has been entered. . . . There is, therefore, no legal necessity for a duplicate. To press one now is only to wound the feelings of my very interesting family by arousing fresh (and doubtless, at this partisan pitch, cruel) newspaper criticism, and without accomplishing any better oblation to justice (either to me or the people, as the case may prove) than could be attained with existing pleading. And especially when some weeks ago I wrote to Atty.-Genl. Barlow I should always be ready for his convenience.

'I think, sir, that ever since, in Sept., 1871, I became convinced of the monstrous frauds (committed by men whose offenses are condoned, or whose battles are carried on over my shoulders, because I neither skulk nor avoid fight) I have done much to atone for any imputed neglect in my acts as an auditor during the month of terrible mental trial to me which followed the inauguration of the new charter (May to June, 1870), as well as to entitle me to consideration upon a mere question of discretion like this I now ask you to proffer to

Mr. Peckham. I say discretion, because, were it a question in his mind of imperative right towards his affirmative action, I could not insult you, nor him, nor myself by the request to forego it. I shall always be willing to meet the *necessary* exactions of the law without asking favor. It is only against unnecessary applications I respectfully protest. Surely my unassailed administration as Dist. Atty. during 12 years; my bearing and course as Mayor in all save these unfortunate audits or non-audits (as you please to phrase it); the character of my appointments since Nov., 1871; my uniform support of Mr. Green in his trying position; and my surrender of much personal pride to aid even personal enemies in accomplishing public good, ought to entitle me to ask from Mr. Peckham to be spared all unnecessary stigmas.

'Pray pardon *me* for thus annoying you who, at this crisis, must be almost overwhelmed with duties. But when I heard the remark with which I began this note, the suggestion came to me with almost the intuition of a woman, and as if the whisper of a daughter — "appeal to his heart."

'This does not require reply, nor is one expected.

'With great respect and regard,

'Your obt. sert.,

'A. Oakey Hall.'

In asking Tilden not to further 'wound the feelings of my very interesting family,' Hall was probably referring to his three daughters of marriageable age and the two just approaching it. Tilden did nothing to stop the procuring of the new indictment against Hall, which was based on four counts for each of fifty-five vouchers, making a total of 220 counts. Being a bachelor, he was perhaps less sensitive to the delicate domestic matter Hall placed before him. The Mayor must have known he was a hard and unrelenting man, attributes which were to help him hack a political path not only to the governorship of New York State but just short of the White House.

II

There was 'a general excitement' in and around the new courthouse on Wednesday, 24 October, according to a reporter for the *Star*, 'as there always is when the "Ring Trials" so called are supposed to be on the topics in some of their multitudinously bewildering phrases. The court officers flew around like things of very much life, and made every other one fly at a lively rate. Door-keepers, who appeared to be selected for their utter freedom from ordinary courtesy and the little knowledge required by the position, slammed the doors in the faces of many whose business brought them there, after the manner of Federal deputies, and admitted crowds of mere sensation seekers.'

Judge John R. Brady was sitting on the bench. When William Marcy Tweed entered the court 'he was emphatically the observed of all the observers. He was dressed in modest, but faultless style with his well-known white necktie and his better-known bland, friendly, placid smile. He shook his friends and counsel warmly by the hand and returned the courteous salutations tendered to him on all sides. He did not look in the least like a man that considered his liberty in jeopardy.'

Tweed asked that the two indictments against him be quashed. Brady refused, Tweed pleaded not guilty, and bail was fixed at $10,000.

'Just as the decision was rendered in the Tweed case, Mayor Hall entered the courtroom, looking gay and festive as a bridegroom. He removed his well-fitting kids and addressing the court said he appeared there in response to a very courteous invitation from the District Attorney. He added that there were two indictments pending against him and that he was ready to go to trial upon either of them at any moment.'

District Attorney Samuel Garvin asked that the case be postponed, but Hall insisted on pleading not guilty and demanded an immediate trial. He said he would take the first twelve jurors chosen. Judge Brady ordered a jury impaneled. Hall suggested that Alfred A. Baker be excused because he was 'an old attached friend of mine whom it would not be proper to have sit as a juror on my trial.' Hall asked that two other jurors be excused on the grounds that they were older than himself. Garvin still objected to going ahead.

'If the court pleases,' Hall said, 'I have been suffering under these cruel imputations so long that when I see a jury in the box I hail it as the star of my deliverance.'

Court was adjourned until the next morning.

In commenting on Hall's insistence on his being tried, the *Star* said the next day: 'Whatever may have been the wisdom of Mr. Hall's promptness in a legal light, there can be no doubt it will have its effect with the public, who know him, like him, and have faith in him, and will stand by him. It will be quite in order for the *Times* to puff Judge Brady and for the *Tribune* to bully him today. Fortunately, when Jennings was pitching pennies in Whitechapel and Whitelaw Reid was sucking Bourbon at the West, John Brady was playing tag in City Hall Park, and all the imported editors can tell him about Oakey Hall, his duty and his chance for popularity, can be put in one very small corner of his quizzical eye.'

The second day of the trial, the reporter for the *Star* noted, a large crowd waited outside the Court of Oyer and Terminer 'but not being invited to seats inside, they appeared to feel the social and atmospheric coolness and, acting upon the promptings of the inner and outer man, they left in profanely-uttered disgust.' One of the prosecuting attorneys, Lyman Tremain, hurried into court from Albany, 'looking decidedly traveled.' He asked Wheeler Peckham, one of his colleagues in the prosecution, 'how the mischief he allowed Hall to turn his flank on the previous day and to catch him unprepared. Peckham said he thought it was done by a legal change of front or base, wasn't sure which.'

The *Star* continued: 'In the line of visitors the lion was very decidedly Andy J. Garvey, the renowned Ring plasterer, millionaire informer. He stole in quietly and took up a modest position behind the door. No sooner, however, was the important fact of his presence made generally known than there was a rush to see the phenomenon and he sloped to escape the infliction. . . . That high-toned buster and three-decked Reformer, Handy Andy Garvey . . . looked like a lion and on his lyin' the prosecution depend. . . .

'There are 11 mustaches in the jury box, 2 pretty bald heads, several long noses and 12 square men. All the papers sent their best-looking reporters to this trial and consequence is that the press table was noticeable for manly beauty. None of them smoke, drink or chew. . . .

'Mayor Hall always dresses neatly, always appears to the manor born, but is peculiarly at home in court. He has a shelving forehead and the shelf is well packed with what Americans value most — brains.'

The witnesses and the testimony in the second trial were much the same as in the first. Richard Storrs, deputy comptroller, testified again regarding the signing of the vouchers and the 'countersigning' of them by Mayor Hall. He said that about a thousand warrants were drawn a year and that 'thirty, forty, or fifty thousand dollars was not an unusual amount in the year 1870.'

Although a good deal was going on in New York that fall of 1872, the trial received considerable space in the newspapers. The *Star* was supporting Havemeyer for Mayor but also felt that Hall should be vindicated.

'It is fair to assert,' the *Star* said editorially, 'that no resident of New York . . . believes Oakey Hall guilty of wilful neglect of duty, or participation in profits if such there were. . . . We doubt if a more embarrassing case was ever tried. . . . And he is on trial for a technical violation of law, the witnesses against him being confessed thieves, liars, perjurers, and scoundrels who are to be condoned in all their sin if they can swear hard enough to convict a Democratic Mayor and help re-elect the immaculate Grant. . . . "May God speed the right." '

As November approached, the campaigns for President became more intense. Nast was putting his pen to other uses than drawing Hall and the Ring members. One of his cartoons, directed against Greeley, showed the editor being carried home dead in a stretcher. Above him was the masthead of the *Tribune,* decorated with the words, 'The Cheapest Paper In The World.' Mrs. Greeley died on Wednesday, 30 October, and *Harper's Weekly* appeared the same day. Nast was severely criticized for drawing the picture in view of the circumstances. The *Star,* trying to be fair, said: 'It is due Mr. Nast, the draughtsman, to say that the pictures in the current number of *Harper's Weekly* were drawn and printed before the public were aware of the serious illness of Mrs. Greeley.'

III

Hall offered no testimony in rebuttal. On Tuesday, 29 October, his lawyers had, according to the *Sun,* 'a formidable law library' brought into court. Thomas T. C. Buckley, one of the defense attorneys, spoke at length, asking Judge Brady to instruct the jury that none of the acts of the defendant, as stated in the indictment, constituted an offense against common law.

On Wednesday, Tweed made a short appearance in court, but left immediately. A large crowd followed him down the courthouse stairs. Also among the spectators were Tom Nast, Judge Charles Daly and Augustin Daly of the theater, Judge Gunning Bedford, and Recorder Hackett. All except Nast were good friends of Hall's.

E. W. Stoughton began his closing for the defense 'with a characteristically elegant bow to the court and the jury.' The

Star reporter wrote that Stoughton 'alluded feelingly to the high social position of the accused, his brilliant gifts and distinguished accomplishments, as well as upon the faithful and important services he had rendered to his fellow-citizens in the different high offices to which they had elected him. . . . He walked through the shadow of death. Himself more than his family suffered under this terror . . . Two men, whose hands were tainted with the plunder, have testified before you. Wasn't it strange that this man, Garvey, confessing his crimes, in the next breath says, I don't believe, and I never believed, that Mr. Hall was guilty of any participation in them?'

Stoughton chided Tremain for having used the Hall trial and the counts in the indictment in a political speech Tremain had made at Newburgh the previous Friday when 'he introduced them [the indictments] to prove that Mr. Greeley, as the friend of Tammany Hall, should not be elected President of these United States. . . . Anxious as I am for my learned brother's success, should he fail to win this case, it may at least help him to his own election to the position he so earnestly labored, through these charges, to secure for himself.' Stoughton said Tremain's introduction of the Hall case into the campaign reminded him of the Connecticut district attorney who, seeking the conviction of a man against whom he felt he did not have a very strong case, added a count to this effect: 'And whereas the rascal owes me $50, which he wilfully and maliciously refuses to pay, etc.' In general, Stoughton maintained, the whole pattern of Hall's behavior after the Ring fraud exposures indicated he was not guilty of any neglect of duty nor had he committed any fraud.

The *Star* passed judgment on Stoughton's closing the next day as if it were a theatrical performance, saying: 'Mr. Stoughton's admirable argument . . . was calm and impassioned, logical and pathetic, humorous and severe, strong and tender, practical and poetical. In fact, it was blessed with the cunning of an experienced advocate and the ingeniousness of a friend.'

Tremain made the closing address for the prosecution. He began at eleven and talked for four hours. He made a point of denying that he felt any political animosity against Hall. 'The accused,' he said, 'was a man of rare ability, of great genius and high eminence in his profession and one with whom, though they had been opposed in politics, my personal relations were most pleasant. . . . I rejoice for Mr. Hall's sake that his trial has been separated and not complicated [with that of Tweed and Connolly].'

Tremain probably came closest to the truth in connection with the guilt or innocence of Hall when he said: 'The accused [was] a member of that Ring; and the other members of that Ring, having the power to satisfy his honorable ambition, was not that a consideration which might influence the guardian of the treasury and put him to sleep?' He finished at three o'clock and Judge Brady made an innocuous charge to the jury, which retired at three-thirty. At seven, the jury went to dinner and returned to deliberate again. Since it had not reached a decision by half past nine, Judge Brady adjourned court until the next morning. The jury deliberated all night and at one point the debate was reported to be 'very stormy.'

The next morning, at eleven, court convened. According to the *Star,* 'Oakey Hall, in a claret-colored coat, skin-tight gloves, well-polished spectacles, was the central figure. He looked quite buoyant with hope and brimming over with wit and humor of the rarest kind, as he always is. His two law partners, Augustus L. Brown and Aaron J. Vanderpoel, were on either side, both looking as if they felt confident in their friend's exoneration from the charge imputed to him. Then came a crowd of distinguished men, lawyers, generals, aldermen, assemblymen, politicians; loafers, sensation seekers, two women and a clergyman. . . . The crowd was excited, the prosecuting officers were nervous, and the prosecuted officer was at his ease, so were the court officers.' The jury filed in, and the clerk asked if they had reached a verdict. Charles J. Brill, 'the pale and melancholy foreman,' according to the *Star* half-rising, said, 'We have not.'

'There was another low rumbling of the sea of humans. This time it meant utter disappointment and dissatisfaction. The Peckhams both sighed in sympathetic silence. Tremain felt his coat tail for a handkerchief and not finding one prudently refrained from weeping. He relieved himself by scowling upon the dubious jury. Mayor Hall murmured, "This is the greatest disappointment I have met in forty-six years — the worst trial of all."

'Judge Brady did not think well of it either. Looking at the foreman more in sorrow than in anger, he said, "I regret that you have not agreed upon a verdict. Don't you think if you remained inside a little longer you could agree?"

'Foreman — No, sir; I think we would never agree.

'Third Juror — We have taken several ballots and we cannot agree.

'Six Jurors (in chorus) — No, sir; no chance; can't agree.

'Judge (severely) — Am I to understand that discussion of this case in its different aspects is exhausted and that you cannot agree?

'Chorus — That's just it. We cannot agree. No chance.

'Judge (shaking his head) — Then I see nothing that I can do with you but to discharge you (waving his hand). — You are discharged.

'Valentine (the Clerk) — Gentlemen, you may go.

'Count Johannes (Hall's secretary) — Go, go; *only* go.'

The usual talkative juror, found by a reporter for the *Star*, gave this version of what had taken place in the jury room: 'Immediately on going into that narrow little room we cast a ballot. The result was seven for conviction and five for acquittal. We discussed and discussed and balloted again. The result was seven for conviction and five for acquittal. . . . From the beginning there was not one that dreamt of finding a verdict on the common law count — that is corruptly certifying fraudulent bills as correct with the guilty knowledge of the fact. . . . We could trace no evidence of willful neglect and could never, if we were to remain in that 12 by 16 room until doomsday and after. The seven were as obstinate in the opposite conviction. . . .'

The New York *Evening Telegram* stated flatly that 'after the jurymen had discussed the evidence given for the prosecution . . . one of the members said that the case was instituted to make capital for the Republican party and the Committee of Seventy and that Mr. Peckham and Mr. Tremain would be well paid for their services. Another juryman said that Mr. Tremain was trying to make his present efforts in the trial a steppingstone to Congress. This statement was denied by several jurymen — who denounced Mayor Hall as a member of Tammany — and party lines were soon drawn between the jury which was composed of seven Republicans and five Democrats. . . . When the jury came into court, the seven Republicans were in favor of a conviction, and the five Democrats for acquittal.'

'We regret,' the New York *Express* commented, 'because the trial will have to be had over again, that the jury did not come to the conclusion the public have generally come to, that when the statute imposed upon the Mayor of the city the duty of auditing all the accounts, it imposed upon him work he could not possibly do himself — but which he must necessarily intrust to others, and that hence in "neglect" he was only guilty of not doing the impossible.

'In the trial there has been nothing to connect Mr. Hall with conspiracy to rob the treasury, or to collude with those who were robbing it, or to show that he has in any way profited by these robberies — nor was wilful neglect in auditing shown, only neglect, which, if by statute a misdemeanor, is a misdemeanor every bank director in this city is guilty of, or every head of every great firm or manufacturing company — for so vast are many concerns that no one man can "audit" them or keep the run of the details of them.'

'Mayor Hall,' said the *Star* editorially, 'is still, and worthily, the Chief Magistrate of New York, and if he were at the head of Tammany's ticket his name would lend it the strength it needs — the strength which might save it from utter annihilation on Tuesday next. Politics should be kept out of the jury box.'

IV

As Hall's trial drew to its indecisive conclusion the horse plague reached its height. Almost one hundred horses a day were carted to the New York Rendering Company's dock at the foot of West Thirty-eighth Street. Ten dead animals were noted on one day in the Third Avenue Railroad Depot. The most serious danger the plague posed was the damage to the Fire Department horses. Out of 144 horses in the Department only two were reported well, 34 were unfit for use, and four were on the point of death. 'A first class steam fire-engine with a self-propelling attachment' was ordered from the Amoskeag Works at Manchester, New Hampshire. The *Star* noted that 'The horse disease is spreading all over the country. Chicago has it and Boston still wails, and news to the effect that the "epidemic is here" has been received from every important city East and West.'

At the funeral of Mrs. Horace Greeley, the *Star* noted that 'owing to the prevalence of the epidemic among the horses, only ten carriages could be obtained but many private conveyances followed to the cemetery.'

In the election on 5 November, Greeley was defeated, polling 2,800,000 to General Grant's 3,600,000 votes. General John A. Dix, the Union General, was elected Governor of New York State and William F. Havemeyer, the candi-

In the summer of 1871 the country was stricken by a serious horse plague. It provided Nast with another theme with which to caricature Tweed's 'Mare,' as he dubbed him.

date of both the Republicans and Reformers, was elected Mayor of New York City.

Hall continued his duties as Mayor with special emphasis on the ceremonial aspects of the job. On 21 November he asked the common council to pass resolutions of welcome to Henry M. Stanley and arranged for a 'popular welcome in

City Hall' for him. Stanley had arrived the day before and all warring factions in the city seemed willing to unite in doing honor to the young *Herald* journalist, who had found Livingstone in darkest Africa. Whitelaw Reid, who was about to become owner of the *Tribune,* gave a reception for Stanley at the Lotos Club on Irving Place, and Hall, as one of the founders of the club, helped preside.

A week later, distressing news came from Pleasantville, New York, three miles from Greeley's home at Chappaqua. Greeley had been taken there to a private home for mental patients with what the *Tribune* called 'nervous prostration.' John Bigelow wrote in his diary, 'I think he has been crazy for years.' It was reported that Greeley was in a coma and dying. There were also two reports of what he was murmuring in his coma. One quoted him as cursing those who were trying to seize control of his beloved *Tribune*. Whitelaw Reid, who saw him at the end, reported his last words as, 'I know that my Redeemer liveth.'

Greeley died on Friday, 29 November, three weeks after his wife. He left instructions that his burial was to be simple. But the competition to do him honor was so keen that his funeral turned out to be the biggest and most impressive New York had ever seen. His body was brought to New York to lie in state in the Governor's Room on the second floor of City Hall. 'Oakey Hall,' according to the *Star,* 'has outdone himself in earnest striving to secure amplest municipal and public honor to the memory of his deceased antagonist.'

The funeral was held at the Church of the Divine Paternity where Dr. Edwin Hubbell Chapin, Greeley's old Universalist pastor, gave a long, learned eulogy from the pulpit. Henry Ward Beecher also spoke — in a 'musical, low-pitched, moving voice.' Whitelaw Reid and his lieutenant, John Hay, dressed in very correct black attire, were among the mourners. Also present were: the Governors of New York, New Jersey, and Connecticut, Phineas T. Barnum, Charles A. Dana, William Cullen Bryant, George William Curtis of *Harper's Weekly,* Manton Marble of the *World,* and George Jones of the *Times.*

Afterwards, a procession escorted the body from Forty-fifth Street to the Battery, where it was placed aboard a ferryboat to be taken to Greenwood Cemetery in Brooklyn. The first carriage following the family mourners was occupied by General Ulysses S. Grant, President of the United States. 'Down Broadway,' said the lead editorial in Frank Leslie's *New York Illustrated Times,* 'an immense procession slowly bore the dead body and made its way through half a million of people. At the head, far in advance, marched Oakey Hall, Mayor of the city. He looked well, felt better, and thus paid the honors of the metropolis to the memory of one of the great men of the nation."

V

Shortly before noon on New Year's Day, 1873, Hall journeyed downtown to City Hall to turn over his office to the incoming Mayor. The walls had been stripped bare of paintings, engraved portraits, and photographs, the desks and bookcases of personal possessions and mementoes. It was a solemn and affecting moment, but he could not resist a final joke. The calendar on his desk said 'January 11' instead of 'January 1.' 'This must be a mistake,' he remarked, 'unless it means one going out and one coming in.' Just then Mayor Havemeyer walked into the office with John Foley and other distinguished reform leaders. Hall and Havemeyer shook hands and then Hall, with a gesture toward the empty chair at the Mayor's desk, said, 'Mr. Mayor, I desire to restore you to that vacant chair and to give you the keys of your private office and wish you a very Happy New Year.' Havemeyer replied: 'I thank you very much for all your kindness to me.' Colonel Joline, Hall's old factotum, then brought in the mail and handed it to Havemeyer. Hall, noting that the top letter was from the coroner's office, said, 'I think that letter should have been addressed to me for I am the dead Mayor.'

On 4 January, Nast, who had not lampooned Hall for some time, drew a full-page cartoon in *Harper's* showing Hall as a blind man being led away from City Hall by a bulldog attached to a leash. Around Hall's neck hung a sign reading, 'Pity the poor but honest blind man who saw nothing of the Tammany Ring's STEALINGS.' Two signs were posted on City Hall, 'Herculean job to clean this mare's stable,' and '1873 — I wish the citizens a Happy New Year and real REFORM.' A Hercules was shown sweeping 'fraudulent signatures' and other documents from the porch of City Hall. In the background Tweed, Sweeny, Connolly, and others were walking toward a sign reading 'Steamers to all parts of the world.' A huge finger in the sky pointed to Hall. The title of the cartoon was 'THE FINGER OF SCORN shall follow them, if law (sometimes called justice) can not.'

When Hall left the Mayor's office on New Year's Day, 1873, two trials had ended in no verdict against him. Nast labeled this cartoon THE FINGER OF SCORN SHALL FOLLOW THEM IF LAW (SOMETIMES CALLED JUSTICE) CAN NOT. It was an accurate prediction.

10

THE THIRD TRIAL

I

HALL RETURNED TO THE practice of law and the manufacture of wit. He defended a slaughterer charged with killing animals by scalding them. The reporters crowded around him in court hoping to pick up a witticism from his lips. They were not disappointed. The case, he told them, 'involved hogs, the four-legged variety, not the two-legged, and the question was whether they were to die by getting into hot water.' There is, perhaps, a perceptible tinge of bitterness in this piece of humor. Some of his cases concerned city employees. When he appeared in court as counsel for two police commissioners, he returned the reporters' greeting by quoting Shakespeare — 'Once more into the breach, dear friends, once more.'

Most of January, 1873, he spent in bed recovering from a fall he had on a Sunday evening while walking on Sixth Avenue. He was taken to his home on Forty-second Street and Dr. J. E. Carnochan called to treat him. 'Under the surgeon's skilful operation,' the *Herald* said, 'the broken and misplaced bones and parts were adjusted, but the pain was so acute that it was deemed necessary to anaesthetize the patient. It is more than probable that the ex-Mayor will be confined to his residence for a month or six weeks from the effects of the injury.'

'As experience has proved,' the *Star* said, 'the impossibility of keeping our ex-Mayor down, we expect to see him out and at work again before a month. Such men are not to be either put down or kept down physically, politically, or otherwise.'

A letter to a friend at this time shows Hall as irrepressible as ever, with his humor seemingly exhaustless and punning over. 'I thank you for your words of sympathy,' he wrote. 'Sympathy knits friendship — why not bones? . . . If my mind turns to law, I think first of lex talionis; no reference here to Taglioni the dancer. If to practice, I ask how many clients I shall save from Limbo. . . . If to traveling, I think of Cork or Leghorn. . . . If I think of politics, I wonder if I shall be qualified for the position of secretary of legation or legate to the Pope, and if my thoughts turn to gastronomy, I say: "Donnez moi des legumes."

'I am inundated with ball tickets from all parts of the country, two or three being appropriately in aid of hospitals. Circulars also begin to arrive about cork legs, reclining and wheel chairs, bed-rests, crutches, etc. Although I fortunately had a policy in an accident company, prospectuses from other companies are sent, as possible reminders of the future, and one kind friend has sent me a vase of Fall leaves.

'In every way I realize that I am like poor France — disordered — and especially in the Bonepartes.

'I shall be a *Home Journal* for at least a fortnight more. Luckily I am no longer a public man, or my leg would be in everybody's mouth.'

On 3 June 1873, Hall's beloved sister, Marcia A. Hall, died. She was in her forty-fourth year and had been ill with a spinal weakness since she was a child of thirteen. Hall had paid for her support and medical expenses. Never married, she devoted her life to church work and religious writing.

She had also written twenty-nine books for children and a temperance story called 'Walter and His Sleigh.' Hall was so devoted to Marcia that he published a book, shortly after her death, made up of eulogies of her by himself and her friends. At her grave he recited the following poem:

The Death of a Sister

The stars that shine
O'er day's decline
May tell the hour of love,
The balmy whisper in the leaves,
The golden moon above;
But vain the hour
Of softest power;
The moon is dark to thee —
My sister and my faithful one!
And oh! her death to me!

II

On 17 September 1873, the great panic and depression of the 1870's began with the closing of the doors of Jay Cooke & Co., the biggest financial house in the country. More than 23,000 business firms closed their doors in the next three years. By 1876, commercial failures had reached the rate of 9,000 a year. That fall of 1873, another participant in the Ring frauds, State Senator Henry W. Genet, was brought to trial. Hall testified for the prosecution and Genet was convicted. It was said that in exchange for his testimony the District Attorney's office would not prosecute the neglect of duty case against him. New Yorkers were therefore surprised when Hall's case was called for trial on Monday, 22 December, in the Court of Oyer and Terminer before Justice Daniels. Once more, Hall accepted the jurors almost as they were called. Edward W. Stoughton again defended him and

Wheeler Peckham and Lyman Tremain conducted the prosecution. Many of the witnesses who had testified in Hall's previous trials were called. Hall offered no evidence in his own behalf.

Stoughton emphasized that 'Hall was not a suspicious man,' and that besides his duties in connection with the Sinking Fund Commission, the Board of Apportionment, and various trusts such as Sailor's Snug Harbor, the Astor Library, and several hospitals, he had to sign while Mayor some 35,000 warrants a year. Hall's statements in court were described by an observer as 'manly, direct, self-respectful, and judicious.'

In his charge to the jury, Judge Daniels said there was no evidence of any conspiracy between Hall and his associates and 'nothing connected him with the fraudulent bills.'

The jury retired at six o'clock on Christmas Eve. Hall stayed in the courtroom and entertained his friends with stories of other Christmas Eves he had spent in court when he was District Attorney. Once, he said, while awaiting the verdict of a jury in a murder case he had written a short story called 'The Christmas Juryman.' He was, he said, not only a great admirer of Dickens, but had written a number of stories in the tradition of 'A Christmas Carol.'

He was the center of attention; perhaps it sufficed. But the ordeal being undergone by his family at this time is made vividly clear in a letter from one of his kinsmen to Mrs. Oakey Hall. It was written as the jury was considering its verdict and, while breathing confidence, there is just the suspicion of a hint in it for her to be brave in the face of a possible adverse decision.

'My dear Kate,

'You and yours are so constantly in my mind, that I must say a kind word, though I hardly know how to begin.

'I know, as well as you do, that Oakey is in no way morally responsible for acts committed by others, during the time he occupied the Chair of the Chief Magistrate of the City: and this is conceded by every disinterested person with whom I have talked; and this feeling is almost universal with good and true minded men: and no just person can withhold his approval and admiration of the manly and noble way that Oakey has met the case.

'I deeply sympathize with you, Aunt Elsie, and the children in these, your days of anxiety and trouble; and I hope and believe that I can wish you a Merry Christmas, with the joyous, triumphant and honorable acquittal of Oakey; to whom I offer my earnest sympathy of confidence, esteem and love.

'Ever truly Your Friend and Cousin,

'James F. Hall.'

At eight the jury returned and the foreman asked if the defendant could be convicted on 'simple' or only on 'wilful' neglect of duty? Judge Daniels said the neglect must be wilful and it was up to the jury to decide whether the act was wilful. He added that if they did not find a verdict within an hour they would be locked up for the night. They returned at ten-thirty and the foreman said they had found Hall not guilty. The audience cheered and shouted congratulations to Hall. Some of them flung their hats into the air. Hall sat at his counsel's table sobbing into his arms. Judge Daniels made no objection to this courtroom demonstration.

The decision was well received by members of both the bench and the bar. 'It was a long time before [Hall] was released from the concourse,' according to *Leslie's Weekly*, 'and when he reached his carriage, a poor ill-clad Irishman shouted, "God bless ye, Mister Mayor an' a Happy New Year!"'

The good news was despatched to Mrs. Hall by two telegraph messages — one through Western Union and one via the Police Department communications system. Captain

On Christmas Eve, 1873, Hall was finally acquitted in court after his third trial, nearly a year after he left the office of Mayor. *Leslie's Weekly* carried this drawing of the occasion early in 1874. *Harper's Weekly* and Nast ignored it.

John H. McCullagh, Captain of the 29th Precinct, sent a patrolman to her house with the note, 'Just received from Central Office following despatch: Notify Mrs. A. O. Hall 13 W 42nd St. her husband is acquitted, will be home shortly.'

Added to Hall's satisfaction over this vindication and of having his family relieved of the indignity of seeing his honor held open to question were the many expressions of good will he received, in person and in letters. Whitelaw Reid wrote: 'Valueless as it may be, I cannot refrain from sending you my sincere congratulations. I should make it in person but I know you will have a crowded Christmas. Everybody seems pleased. With kind regards to Mrs. Hall and the young ladies.' L. I. Everitt, cashier of the National Broadway Bank, wrote: 'Permit me to offer my congratulations upon the splendid vindication of yourself from the aspersions sought to be cast upon you . . . it conduced much to my enjoyment of the Christmas festival when I read . . . of your acquittal of the base charges, which all who *know* you, always indignantly repudiated.'

There were letters from Peter Cooper, from friends in Albany and other parts of the country. Hall's mother received a letter from a friend, Caroline D. Roberts: 'What a blessed Christmas Gift you have in the acquittal of your son. The *Sun* has just told us and we are more than thankful. I doubt if you had any realizing idea of Oakey's great danger. Only yesterday one of the best lawyers told me he did not see how it was possible that he could escape as things were managed. Oh! Lord I will praise Thee. Let this be our song. Special words of love and cheer to Oakey and his family from Mr. R. and each of us.'

His friend, Morris Phillips, editor of the *Home Journal*, wrote an affectionate letter to Hall: 'My humble voice (expressed in writing) may not be unwelcome nor disdained — and in any event I cannot remain silent under the pleasant and present circumstances. All the inmates of our house watched the case with anxious, eager interest — even my dear old mother, now *near fourscore,* let fall tears of joy when she heard the decision in behalf of her son's esteemed friend and teacher.'

III

Newspapers all over the country published editorials on Hall's acquittal. The *Times* was not pleased and took the view 'the prosecution was rather lamely conducted.' The most interesting editorial was in the *World* and was probably written by Manton Marble. 'Three cheers — unprecedented in a New York courtroom,' the *World* said, 'which greeted the verdict proceeded not altogether from personal friendship for Mr. Hall but also from the feeling that in the vindication of Mr. Hall the respectability of New York had also been vindicated. The classes of New Yorkers who for many years held haughtily aloof from municipal politics were yet concerned to see that the most conspicuous and honorable office in the city government should not be entrusted to a man of low life or stained character. They almost always had their way. It was as a sop to this social Cerberus that the Ring named men to be Mayors who were within the social pale from which the members of the Ring were excluded. . . . If it had been proved that he partook the rascalities and shared the plunder of the Ring which put him in power, the shock to the society of New York would have been greater than that produced by the conviction of twenty Tweeds who were beyond the border and not amenable to the penalties of anybody that deserves to be called society in New York. . . .'

'The Ring,' said the *Weekly National Intelligencer* of Washington, 'shrewd if unscrupulous, knew that they could not afford to utterly defy public opinion so they always kept to the fore enough respectabilities such as Recorder Hackett, Governor Hoffman, Oakey Hall and Judge Bedford, as idols to blind the eyes of the heathen to the debaucheries of the priesthood.'

'We couldn't persuade ourselves,' said the New Orleans *Commercial Bulletin,* 'that this genial and cultivated gentleman well and favorably known here many years ago as the regular correspondent of the Old Commercial Bulletin of this city, could have knowingly become an accomplice with the infamous band that, under forged forms, sapped the vitals of our great metropolitan city. The writer of "The Manhattaner in New Orleans" could not be aught but a gentleman.'

'His bitterest enemies,' said the New York *Evening Telegram,* 'never went so far as to charge that he dishonestly enlarged his bank account to the extent of one dollar by his office as Mayor and member of the Board of Audit. . . . The result is a great personal triumph for Mr. Hall. His acquittal meets with nearly universal favor.'

But there were indications here and there that the finger of scorn which Nast had drawn above Hall in a cartoon the year before was still over his head. The Brooklyn *Union,* for example, said it did not agree with the verdict. Hall immediately despatched a letter of protest to his friend Henry Ward Beecher, Brooklyn's leading preacher-citizen and an editor of the *Union.*

'I was surprised at your note,' Beecher wrote Hall on 5 January, 'and still more on turning to the *Union,* to see the ungracious paragraph. Of course, it had not met my eye before passing on, tho' the man who did it, is a good and honorable man and would not for the world do injustice, and in this case, evidently acted rather under others' influence, but on proper investigation — I will rectify it.

'Indeed, I had it in my heart to write you a note on the rendition of the verdict, congratulating you. You certainly were in a bad crowd, and to have escaped without any personal stain and without other blame than that implied in not sufficiently distrusting the men about you, is no small gain.'

Both Samuel Tilden, soon to become Governor of New York, and Charles O'Conor, the fiery reform lawyer, were to state in later years their belief that Hall had not received any of the Ring plunder. Henry Lauren Clinton, who had tried so hard to convict Hall in his first trial, wrote in his book, *Celebrated Trials:* 'In all the investigations in respect to the proceeds of Ring frauds, none were ever traced to Mr. Hall. There is no evidence that he ever reaped any pecuniary advantages from his political and official relations with those who composed the Ring. Since the termination of his last trial he has stood before the community *vindicated* from the charges made against him when the Ring frauds were exposed.'

11

HALL GOES ON THE STAGE

I

HALL CONTINUED his law practice after his acquittal, but judging from the cases he took into court, it could not have been very lucrative. He now joined Augustin Daly in the management of the Fifth Avenue Theatre. In a note to Hall, Daly asked that 'Mrs. Hall's signature be verified' on a bond, which would indicate that some of her money may have been used to help finance the theater. Daly expressed the hope he would soon see Hall 'occupy your accustomed box at the *new* as at the old Fifth Avenue — which your kindness is helping to materially rebuild.'

'Mr. Oakey Hall's interest in the success of Mr. Daly's theatre,' *Leslie's Weekly* commented, 'has long been familiar to the public and his devotion to Thespis as a source of amusement rather than profit is thoroughly in consonance with the artistic tastes of this public-spirited gentleman. We feel confident that in Mr. Hall's affection for the stage, the actor has found a liberal patron.'

His law experience stood him in good stead in his new venture. One of the most curious cases Hall took to court at this time involved the Theatre License Law of 1872 which, according to Hall's brief on behalf of a group of leading theatrical managers, was 'a scheme to force . . . each theatrical manager to pay five hundred dollars a year license fee for the sole use of the Juvenile Delinquent Society or else expose their places of business to be summarily entered by the police and closed or else shut up by means of an injunction obtainable by the society.' Hall quoted the Supreme Court ruling in Tanner *vs.* Trustees of Albion in which it was stated that 'Playhouses were originally instituted for the laudable design of recommending virtue to the imitation of the people and exposing vice and folly.' 'Yet,' wrote Hall, 'the unconstitutional act of 1872 remains on the statute-book a standing stigma to managers, and an insult to all the cultivated classes who nightly grace the Opera-house or the theatres of the plaintiffs.' The law was repealed. Eventually it was ruled that the $500 tax should be paid into the city treasury.

Hall had long before achieved some recognition as a writer for the stage, and it was, therefore, not surprising when, in the fall of 1875, two years after his acquittal, he wrote a full-length play in four acts about an innocent man sent to prison for stealing. He called on his friends, Chandos Fulton, the director, and William Stuart, the manager, at the Park Theatre on the east side of Broadway at Twenty-second Street. Hall told them that he would like them to produce his play. He added that he proposed to play the lead part himself. Both men assured Hall they were flattered at his having chosen them of all the producers in town to produce his play. He suggested they meet for lunch next day at the Manhattan Club to hear him read it. Hall arranged for Felix, the Manhattan Club chef, to provide an especially excellent lunch. After hearing it read, Fulton and Stuart were not entirely convinced that the play would be a success but, at a later luncheon, attended by the writers William Henry Hurlbert and Dion Boucicault, Fulton and Stuart agreed to produce it. Hurlbert and Boucicault had helped Hall with the writing and were naturally enthusiastic. The final decision, however, was undoubtedly influenced by the tremendous publicity value inherent in a play not only by and about a former Mayor of New York, one who had been a controversial figure for years, but having that former Mayor in the leading role. Hall had marshaled good reasons for playing the chief part himself.

'He contended,' Fulton wrote later, 'that as a jury-lawyer he had been acting all his life; that he would merely be shifting the scene from the forum of the courtroom to the stage; and, a dramatic author or tinkerer of numerous plays we wot of, he certainly knew all about the requirements of the actor's art.'

The name of Hall's play was *The Crucible*. Rehearsals were begun on 3 December. Two days later, William Marcy Tweed escaped from Ludlow Street jail. This reflected favorably on Hall who, unlike the rest of the Ring, refused to budge from New York.

Hall put some of his own money into the production of *The Crucible*. No expense was spared in making the scenery. Thirty-four experienced actors were hired for the supporting roles.

'At the rehearsals,' Fulton later wrote, 'like an experienced actor, one to the manor born, Hall had "walked through his part," merely proving his mastery of the lines and the business, and never assaying to act. . . . The gentle consideration and forebearance that characterize the true gentleman . . . were conspicuously displayed by him, in the role of an actor, in his demeanor and treatment of his associates at rehearsal and in the ordeal of the run of the play when he had indeed vexations sufficient to ruffle his temper and courtesy, but which never did.'

The night before the opening, there was an elaborate dress rehearsal 'with scenery, band and props.' Lester Wallack,

Rose Eytinge, John Gilbert, and John Brougham, theatrical celebrities of the day, were present. 'At this private performance,' wrote Fulton, 'Hall let himself go and acted the character with a naturalness and aplomb, displaying power and mimetic and declamatory ability, pathetic as well as humorous, that excited enthusiasm in us all, and those present whom I have mentioned heartily confirmed our belief that he would make a great hit the next night, especially, as, accustomed as he was to public speaking, there was not the usual apprehension in regard to debutants that his voice would fail him or he would be stricken by stage fright.'

The whole town wished Hall well in his new enterprise. Even the *Times* declared itself editorially on the matter of *The Crucible*. 'As a politician,' said the *Times,* 'it is very well known that we are no admirers of Mr. Hall. But we have fought our battle with him, and have no intention of following him into the domain of the Muses to fight it all over again. We do not now believe — much as appearances at first were against him — that he ever shared in the profits of the old Ring Government. Since its overthrow he has struggled gallantly against a host of circumstances which would long ago have crushed less buoyant and indomitable natures. The sympathies of his friends have never deserted him, and we, who have been among his severest antagonists, have now no worse wishes for him than that he may win both fortune and fame in his new enterprise.'

II

The opening of *The Crucible* took place at the Park Theatre on Saturday evening, 18 December, an extremely cold and windy night. The house was sold out, the receipts reaching 'the unprecedented sum of $1,700.' Some of those who attended the opening were: Mr. and Mrs. Robert Cutting; Louis John Jennings, the *Times* editor, and his family; Siro

Louis and Charles Delmonico; Joaquin Miller, the poet; W. H. Vanderbilt, William Winter, General Chester A. Arthur, Judge Albert Cardozo, Recorder Hackett, Henry Bergh, Commodore Garrison, and according to the *Star,* 'all the critics and the entire membership of the Bald Headed Club.' Augustus L. Brown, one of Hall's law partners, refused to attend the opening because he said he did not wish 'to see Mr. Hall make a fool of himself.' His other partner, Aaron J. Vanderpoel, attended in company with Morris Phillips, editor of the *Home Journal.*

The curtain was late going up. Hall came on stage in the middle of the first act, 'with a characteristically debonair air,' according to Fulton, 'and humming a tune, his natural acting won the house, and in the entr'acte the consensus of opinion in the lobby was that he would score an emphatic success.' A ticket broker named Rullman immediately offered to buy out the house for the ensuing week. When Hall came on stage, according to *The Spirit of the Times,* 'the house, metaphorically speaking, rose and cheered the debutant with genuine heartiness. Of course, Mr. Hall, the object of this ovation, bowed again and again, and, when the storm of applause subsided he began to act, to the surprise of all, with the coolness of an experienced performer, showing not the least perturbation or signs of nervousness.'

'In the first [act] we are introduced,' said *The Spirit of the Times* in a résumé of the plot, 'to the countinghouse of Mr. Pensleigh, a London banker, beneath the table of which sleeps a certain youth, who is deaf and dumb, afflictions which, in his case, considering the astonishing liveliness of his disposition, as illustrated by Miss Marie Louise, are decided advantages, for if he added speech to his other qualifications, Heaven alone knows what would happen. Mr.

Oakey Hall's name appeared twice on the playbill advertising *The Crucible,* the play he wrote to vindicate himself. He was listed twice: as lessee and manager, and in the cast of characters as 'Wilmot Keirton, the man of metal.'

PARK THEATRE

Lessees and Managers.........Messrs. W. STUART & OAKEY HALL
Director....................................Mr. CHANDOS FULTON
Treasurer...........Mr. F. A. SAYER | Stage Manager.........Mr. J. C. PADGETT
Leader of Orchestra. Mr. H. WANNEMACHER | Prompter...........Mr. J. P. COOKE

Every Evening at 8, and Saturday Matinee at 2,

THE COLLABORATED MELO-DRAMA, IN FOUR ACTS.

CRUCIBLE!

Hester Keirton, the woman of love and faith........................Miss Minnie Doyle
(First appearance in New York.)
Clemency Newcombe, the lady of the kitchen cabinet.........Miss Annie Edmondson
Eve Pensleigh, the woman of mystery........................Miss Annie Wakeman
Susan Knowley, the maid of clover and daisies..................Miss Constance Leigh
Peggy Taffey, the woman of tears and fears...................Miss Ivy E. Rodanina
Stevey Newcombe, the boy of poetic pantomime ....Marie Louise
(First appearance in New York)
Silas Craft, the man of usury and law ....John Dillon
(First appearance in New York.)
Lt. Frank Rodney, R. N., the man of love and war. ....Cyril Searle
(First appearance in New York.)
Reuben Pengleigh, the man of avarice..... ....T. J. Hind
Frotty Newcombe, the man of watchfulness............................J. C Padgett
Timothy Taffey, the commatherin confectioner............................M. C. Daly
(First appearance in 6 years.)
John Linkford, the man of duty and heart......................W. J. Ferguson
Count Fabrega,   }
Juror Fogle,   } the man of aliases and disguises, { ....Vining Bowers
Phil, the Scrivener.   }
(First appearance in New York in two years.)
Knoutley, the man for fees and keys ....W. Scallon
Thomas Ricketts, the convict who repented.... ....C. T. Parsloe
(First appearance in New York in three years.)

THE DISAGREEING TWELVE,

Mr. Foreman Taffey.

Blinksop, the juror for gambling.... | Muggins, the skeptical juror ....
           W. Scallon | G. W. Murray
Kickshaw, the spirited juror......... | Pemmican, the juror for Scotch Ban-
           Frank Langley | nocks............... J W. Brutone
Cross, the juror who loved air......... | Smithers, the juror for Matilda Jane,
           W. A. Rouse | C. Rosene
Carpenter, the juror who liked suffoca- | Snagley, the jolly juror from York-
tion....................J. C. Franklin | shire.........C. Parsloe
Mildmay, the juror with a baby. .... | Templeton, the juror for conscience,
           C. Clarence | H. B. Cutler

Fogle, the Talesman.

Adolphus, Q. C. the man for oratory....................................Harry Gwynette
De Gex, the barrister up to snuff..............................C. Parker
Austin, the clerk of wrong balances, ...G. R. Holmes
(First appearance in New York.)
The Q. C.'s clerk, the man for precedence, ...W. Peters
The Barrister's clerk, a man of consequence,.........................M. Wilton
His Lordship's Tipstaff, a man of language,..........................J. A. Wilks
The Court Tipstaff, a man of honour.........................Charles Montrose
Wilmot Keirton, the man of metal.................................Oakey Hall
Judges, clerks, ushers, guards and convicts, etc., etc., etc.

Trotty Newcome, office messenger, and father of this youth, opens the play by drinking off the contents of a mug of ale, which has been drugged in such a manner that he immediately falls asleep, whereupon Mrs. Eva Pensleigh comes in mysteriously. Everything this lady does is mysterious, she being, according to the bill, the woman of mystery. She always enters and goes off the stage to slow music, of a funereal description. After she has besported herself mysteriously, to her heart's content, Mr. Philip, the scrivener, another mysterious character, joins her. Then it becomes evident that she has drugged the messenger with a view of aiding Mr. Philip to steal £3,000 from her husband's safe. This she does, because her distinguished friend, who is known as the Count, has, in bygone years, made the acquaintance of her first husband, who was undergoing involuntary retirement in a penal settlement in his company. This unfortunate gentleman, however, is dead, but upon his body Mr. Philip, the scrivener, alias the Count, discovered certain papers, which contained evidence of his wife's previous ill-conduct. With these in his possession, he endeavors to blackmail her, and finally induces her, in order to free herself of his presence, to drug her husband's employes, and to assist him in robbing that gentleman. Neither, of course, is aware that the deaf boy lies hidden under the table, and whilst they are busily engaged in their robbery, that urchin carefully watches and takes note of the proceedings. As soon as they have made off with the £3,000 he emerges from his place of concealment and endeavors to wake up the stupefied messenger, and explain to him in pantomime what has taken place. This he fails to make intelligible to that venerable person, which, considering the eccentric manner in which he sets to work to do it, is not at all to be wondered at. Then enter the other characters of the play, and with them Mr. Hall, as Wilmot Keirton, the cashier. After a good deal of incidental business, such as opening letters, reading letters,

and moving to and fro, the crime which has just been perpetrated is discovered, and before the act closes Keirton is accused of robbery, and taken off to Bow Street, much to the
agony of the deaf and dumb boy, who by the way can neither
read nor write, but is in a very afflicted state of mind, indeed,
and utterly unable to make anybody understand him.

'The second act introduces us to a villa in the outskirts of
London where dwell Keirton's sister and her betrothed, Lieutenant Frank, R.N. This young couple is presented us, to
put it mildly, as billing and cooing in a remarkably ardent
manner, using language which would throw into the shade
the poetical effusions of that admirer of the eldest Miss Peck-
sniff, and "who figured once a week in poet's corner of a
country weekly." Whilst these excellent and gushing young
people are still in the midst of their lovemaking, Keirton
arrives from London, having been bailed out by a magistrate.
The deaf and dumb boy now once more puts in an appearance, and on beholding the innocent cashier, makes violent
pantomime to no purpose. Detectives also arrive, and, before
the act closes, Keirton's sister and her lover are made wretched
by the revelation of that gentleman's supposed guest. He
protests his innocence. The Lieutenant at first declares he
will not marry the sister of an accused thief, but finally re-
lents, and takes that young lady to his heart, amidst the bless-
ings of all the virtuous characters assembled, and to the ill-
concealed contempt of the wicked.

'In the third act Keirton is tried by jury, and found guilty.

'Act the fourth takes place in Millbank Prison, near London, on a visiting day. It would be difficult, indeed, to give
any account of the hidden motive which induces all the characters in the play to select this special day for paying their
visits to their friends and relations in jail, or describe the
extraordinary manner in which, as soon as one departs, another arrives, much after the fashion of those remarkable in-
habitants of toy boxes, popularly known as "jacks." It would

be also next door to impossible to render any satisfactory account of the astonishing proceedings of the deaf and dumb boy at this stage of affairs, who not only drinks milk like a tomcat, but also seizes upon everybody from behind, and drags them about in an alarming manner, and, after obtaining their attention, goes straightway through a series of pantomimic gestures, which he is unfortunately of opinion will convey to their minds a complete account of the robbery.

'Whilst this young gentleman is thus industriously engaged, Mrs. Pensleigh arrives, as usual, mysteriously veiled. She has come to make complete confession of her crime, but is followed by the rascal who forced her to commit it. This gentlemanly person, who is generally known by the *alias* of The Count, is recognized by the dumb boy, and is finally accused of the robbery, and, being driven, as it were, into a corner, endeavors to throw himself over a parapet. This purpose is frustrated by Lieutenant Frank, who shoots him in the arm, and he is brought back to make a clean breast of it, which he does amidst universal rejoicing. Poor Mr. Keirton is immediately declared innocent, and received back in the arms of his sister.'

According to Fulton, Hall's acting deteriorated as the play progressed. 'As the character developed and acting was required of him, he had so far simply been himself, Hall lost his aplomb' Fulton wrote, 'and went to pieces in his efforts to embody his clearly conceived conception of the role.' In the last act, which took place in prison, Hall wore a striped prisoner's costume. On rehearsal night he had used a prisoner's suit made to fit for him by the costumer, but on opening night he wore one which he had had friends send down from the shop at Sing Sing. The suit, instead of adding to the realism of the scene, as he had hoped, fitted him so badly that he looked ridiculous.

After the first scene in the office on opening night, Hall shaved off his beard. For the prison scene he shaved off his mustache. Also, after the office scene, he did not wear his pince-nez. Thus the familiar beard, mustache, and droopy pince-nez, made so well known by the Nast cartoons, were eliminated. He sensed that this disappointed the audience. Being very nearsighted, he was awkward without his glasses. But worst of all, shaving his mustache affected his speech.

'He presented,' Fulton wrote, 'a pitiable appearance of an utterly demoralized actor, who evidently knew what he wanted to do, but did not know how to do it.'

At the end of the performance, Hall made a curtain speech in which he said that in the future he expected to be considered as an actor and to be impartially criticized as such. The audience again applauded vigorously before filing into the street where, as one critic wrote, 'the wind, like a perfect fiend, armed with innumerable razors, knives and other sharp weapons, rushed along the streets with tornado swiftness.'

III

The drama critics were friendly but expressed reservations. 'We cannot,' said the critic of *The Spirit of the Times*, 'with the best intentions, call it a successful work, for it is not remarkable for its interest or dramatic purpose, and it is of no use asserting the contrary.'

'As an actor,' said the *Star*, 'we can hardly judge him as yet. He was not so much on trial as on exhibition last night. His friends filled the house. The first night gang had possession of the theatre, as speculators had of the rest of the house. His reception was, of course, immense. Ordinarily first nighters don't split their gloves in applauding, but it was the put up thing to give Oakey to understand that he was welcome as a friend and a fellow, even if he were to be damned as an artist. Men clapped, ladies waved, the play was stopped and O.K. bowed. Then it went on, was interrupted and the whole thing was De Capoed over and over again. "The Crucible," though decidedly slow, has the merit of plot and situation, and after revision may secure a lodgement in public favor. Mr. Hall was nervous, but managed himself well — indeed admirably . . . We now leave Oakey ORevoir.'

The following Monday night Hall played to an almost empty house, the receipts being under $200. Fulton launched an advertising campaign which included plastering the pillars of the 'El' and which resulted in himself and Paulding, the bill poster, being taken into court. The play ran for twenty-two performances, closing on Saturday evening, 8 January. At the end of his last performance Hall made another curtain speech in which he thanked his audience 'for the wonderfully generous treatment I have received at your hands.'

'I remarked in the prison scene,' he said, 'one hiss in the dress circle, but this was good as the gentleman probably thought that when he gets his convict clothes he will play his part better than I could. As I observe a number of lawyers and ladies, who look as though they might understand Latin, in the audience, I may say to him, Laudamus ab his. The management have announced that this is the last night of Oakey Hall, but, as a particular friend of his, I hope it is not the last of him. The physicians say I must drop the legal harness, but my friends say I must not, and besiege me at the box office, in the dressing-room, and everywhere. My friends and enemies differ as to whether I can act or not, but they all agree that I was a good advocate; this probably in the same spirit as we admit, when a man is under the turf, that he was endowed with all the virtues from his cradle to his grave. After all, perhaps Macbeth was right when he said: "At least, we'll die with harness on our backs." Before the footlights a man is always egotistical, and I am tempted to keep you just a few minutes longer. But this is Saturday night, the night for meeting of sweethearts and lovers, and as I see a number of them here I shall continue.' Hall then made allusion to report that his play had been a collaboration. 'Gaboriau, Ledoucier, and five novels by George Eliot,' he said, 'and a number of French dramas, have been used to construct this play, and it has lived as long as most original comedies.'

A variety of reasons were advanced for the failure of *The Crucible*. 'I am satisfied,' Fulton wrote, 'that if Hall had acted with the naturalness and intelligence displayed in the office scene in the subsequent acts, he would have achieved the success which had been foreshadowed by his private performance and which we all so confidently anticipated for him before the rise of the curtain. He was confident after the rest and reflection of Sunday that he would come out all right on Monday night. His sanguine temperament was ever one of his most charming characteristics. The drop in the house the second night, however, completely crushed his spirit and he never rallied and was anxious thereafter for us to release him from the engagement.'

'It was a sorry sight,' Morris Phillips later wrote, 'to behold the gentleman and scholar, Mr. Hall, in a striped suit. He was unequal to personating so vile a character, and Mr. Hall's career as an actor came to an end then and there.'

'I . . . really quitted the stage,' Hall wrote fifteen years later, 'because that profession was so distasteful and health-distressing to an aged mother — to whose nurture and care I owed all that was good in my composition — who believed a theatre was a limited section of Sheol.'

Apparently, *The Crucible* was not printed, and no copy of it seems to have survived. But a sixteen-page pamplet called, *Crucible, or Feathering A Mayor's Nest, A Mellow Drama*, is on deposit at the Library of Congress and the New-York Historical Society. It was printed in 1875 by Charles E. Sargent and was, apparently, a farce Hall wrote on his own play. The plot centers around a cashier who is falsely accused of stealing from a savings bank and is sent to the Tombs. A girl named Katie King saves the day for him by holding a huge dumbbell by a hair over the jury as they are asked for their verdict. After the foreman announces 'not guilty,' she drops it on them 'in such a manner as to crush to smithereens the entire twelve. When the Court Constable asks what is to be done with them, Recorder Hackett [his real name was used] says: "Deliver them to Mr. Wheeler Peckham, with my compliments — he's been inquiring for a struck jury, I hear." '

12

THE DISAPPEARANCE OF OAKEY HALL

I

HALL AGAIN RETURNED to his proper profession but resigned from the law firm he had helped to found. Vanderpoel wanted him to stay but Brown, who had come vigorously to Hall's defense during the Ring scandals, disapproved of Hall's excursions into the theater. He, too, probably regarded the theater as 'a limited section of Sheol.' The business manager of the firm, he was distressed by Hall's financial plight. Hall not only was reported to have lost $40,000 in Daly's Fifth Avenue Theatre, but was besieged with suits arising from unpaid bills for stage equipment used in *The Crucible.*

Hall set up his offices in Rooms 38, 39, and 40 of the Tribune Building at 30 Ann Street. He took a three-year lease at $1,750 a year, payable in quarterly installments. The lease, dated 10 January 1876, was handled by Gordon L. Ford, business manager of the *Tribune,* who sent it to Whitelaw Reid for his signature with this cryptic note: 'Is this an unexceptionable tenant?' Reid signed the lease, answering, 'I should think so. W.R.'

Hall used one of the rooms as an office, one as a reception

room, and the third, according to the *Sun*, as 'an elegant bedroom.' He was spending less and less time at home and was reported to have been seen in company with an actress named Ella Morgan Davies.

Hall distributed a card at this time, giving his new address and a description of the type of legal work he was prepared to accept: 'He will hereafter confine himself as ADVOCATE to the following specialties: Cases connected with Criminal Law, Personal Remedies, Libel Defense, Actions against Sheriffs and Marshal, Copyright and Theatrical Law, Surrogate Procedure and Municipal matters. He will also, as COUNSEL, specially take charge of questions affected by Commercial Fraud, Police Investigation, Attempts at Social Extortion, or which require Diplomatic Negotiations.'

The Ring scandal still engaged the attention of the newspapers. On 29 May, word reached New York from Vigo, Spain, that the Spanish authorities had arrested Tweed. They had recognized him from the Nast cartoons which had received world-wide distribution. Until the American consul informed them otherwise, they believed he was a kidnapper of children because one of the cartoons showed Tweed as a giant holding in the air a miniature-sized policeman by the scruff of his neck. A month later, New Yorkers began celebrating their biggest Fourth of July, the 100th anniversary of the Declaration of Independence, with a great parade, fireworks, and much speechmaking.

Hall received some satisfaction in seeing his old adversary and former fellow Tammany Democrat, Samuel J. Tilden, defeated for the Presidency by Rutherford B. Hayes. In the local elections, Smith Ely, a Tammany Democrat, was elected Mayor of New York. Another wave of reform had come and gone, but the Tammany Tiger was immortal.

The work that Hall had outlined for himself — cases having to do with criminal law, copyright law, and the law in relation to the theater — although it was what interested him most, was not remunerative. Besides, the competition of the celebrated law firm of Howe & Hummel was too formidable, and he was unwilling to engage in the techniques, perfected by this colorful pair, of bribing juries, judges, anyone who could help win their cases. A note in one of the New York papers at this time gives a clue to the extent that Howe & Hummel monopolized the field in which Hall was trying to function. 'Managers are tired of having every discharged chorus singer crying out, "We'll go to 'Owe and 'Ummel if you don't pay us," and forcing us to employ Howe and Hummel to beat them.' Apparently Hall was friendly to the firm, because he signed a petition to the Judges of the Supreme Court of New York asking that Abraham H. Hummel, who had been disbarred, be allowed to resume practice. The petition, which told of Hummel's heroic efforts to support his aged mother and younger sister, was granted.

Hall further contributed to his economic insecurity by trying to pursue his writing career. A letter he wrote to Jesse Haney, a magazine publisher of 119 Nassau Street, has a familiar ring to writers: 'Referring to your last note, pardon me for saying that my daughter sails next Tuesday per *Idaho* and if convenient I would like to hand her before Saturday the $150 you mentioned. I shall have a pleasant fiction (pleasant to me) that it represents profits.'

II

On New Year's Day, 1877, one of Hall's valued friends and clients got himself into serious difficulty. He was James Gordon Bennett, the younger, whose father had also been a friend and client of Hall's. In 1871, Hall had watched young Bennett and his sister go off to Europe while the elder Bennett, knowing that he was seriously ill, tried to persuade them to stay in New York. Hall had suggested to young

Bennett at the time that it might be a good idea if he postponed the trip but, as Hall himself said, 'They were full of life and enthusiasm and the prospect of an outing in Europe made them particularly buoyant.' Two weeks later Hall cabled young Bennett that his father was dying, but the brother and sister arrived three days after his death. Hall had knelt at the foot of Bennett's bed as Cardinal McCloskey read the ritual that made possible the old publisher's eleventh-hour reception into the Catholic Church.

The difficulty into which young Bennett had got himself was of a nature which rendered Hall or anyone else incapable of helping him. It was the custom in the New York of the 'seventies for families of means to hold open house on New Year's Day in the afternoon. The young blades of the town went from brownstone to brownstone to wish a Happy New Year to the host and hostess and pass judgment on the quality of the contents of the punch bowl, which was generally eggnog — made to the Yankee formula, the cream well thinned with rum. Young Bennett was a spoiled and arrogant young man, celebrated for his heavy drinking. As he stumbled up the steps leading to the brownstone-front house of Dr. William May at 44 West Ninth Street, he realized he had to go to the bathroom. Dr. and Mrs. May, who had come from Baltimore a few years previously, had a son, Frederick, and a daughter, Caroline, who were in their early twenties. The engagement of young Bennett to Caroline May, it was reported, was shortly to be announced.

The versions of what occurred when Bennett entered the house vary. He was reported to have urinated (1) under a grand piano, (2) into a cannel coal fireplace, (3) into a china umbrella stand, and (4) into 'a blue delft Chinese bowl.' Wherever the offense took place, Bennett was hurriedly removed from the house. On 3 January, Fred May encountered Bennett outside the Union Club, probably intentionally, as

he was not only not a member himself but had in his hand
a cowhide strip with which he proceeded to horsewhip Bennett. The two men clinched and rolled in the snow. Presumably, May had satisfied his code of Southern chivalry.
Bennett, in order to save the last shred of his honor, did the
only thing left for him to do — he challenged May to a duel.
The two men met four days later at Slaughter's Gap in Delaware, where it was possible for one duelist to stand in Mary-
land and shoot at his adversary in Delaware — a geographic
condition which provided endless legal complications in the
event of arrest for murder. Bennett's second was S. Howland
Robbins, a fellow member of the Union Club. May fired at
the sky, while Bennett was so nervous he didn't fire at all.
The honors of the two young New Yorkers were declared
satisfied and the affair was presumably ended. But there was
an aftermath. Bennett wore, whenever he thought there was
a possibility of encountering May, a steel mesh bullet-proof
vest under his jacket. Several years later, while in Paris, he
learned that May had followed him there to shoot him. He
sent an emissary to ascertain May's exact intentions regarding him. May laughed and sent word that he had no designs
whatsoever on Bennett's life. Thereafter, according to a
French mistress of Bennett's, the young publisher dispensed
with his steel vest.

Bennett was not expelled from the Union Club, perhaps
because no member of the May family was then a member.
Nonetheless, Bennett's place in New York society, already
tenuous, was now destroyed. He and Hall were both in the
position of having been 'cast beyond the pale of polite society.' Bennett soon left New York to spend the rest of his
life sailing aimlessly on his yacht and traveling in Europe. It
was reported, at the time of his leaving New York, that Hall
was to become editor of the *Herald*. The report proved untrue, but a few years later Bennett was to send for Hall and
make him his London secretary and American counsel.

III

Six weeks after the Bennett affair which, needless to say, was not printed in the *Herald,* Hall defended a client who had killed a man in a brawl in Washington Market. The two men were laborers who helped unload produce. The defendant was James Rice and he had killed one Hugh McCabe in a fist fight. Judge Brady, an old friend of Hall's, presided. Hall put in a good defense of Rice, but the jury brought in a verdict of murder in the third degree. When the foreman announced the verdict, Hall, who was sitting at counsel's table, put his hands to his face and wept bitterly. He then stood up and told the court that it was his fault the man was not acquitted, that if ever a man deserved to be acquitted Rice did, and that he would never again try a homicide case. His behavior was not particularly remarked at the time, as it seemed reasonably in character with his usual courtroom theatrics. On Wednesday, 21 March 1877, however, the courtroom incident was vividly recalled when newspapers front-paged the story that ex-Mayor Hall was mysteriously missing from New York.

'WHERE IS EX-MAYOR HALL?' the *Sun* asked in a headline to a column-and-a-quarter story on its front page. 'GRAVE APPREHENSIONS THAT AGITATE HIS INTIMATE FRIENDS. Financial Embarrassments that Have Been No Secret — His Unexplained Absence from Court — His Recent Rather Irregular Life.'

The story of Hall's disappearance occupied considerable space in the newspapers for almost three weeks because it had the priceless ingredient of suspense. Hall had last been seen the previous Friday evening at about seven o'clock in his office. He had put on his overcoat, hat, and overshoes and walked out into the chill night. He was reported to have had about $500 in his possession, and to have been buying up some foreign currency. Some of his friends expressed fear that he might have committed suicide. Aaron Vanderpoel assured

reporters that this was impossible. He said that Hall held
no money in trust and that his accounts were written up to
the Friday of his disappearance.

It was reported that Hall was 'living in the slums of
Brooklyn.' When a reporter checked this with the chief of
police in that borough, he was greeted with a retort that became, for a time, the signal for gales of laughter among any
group of Manhattanites when it was quoted. 'There are,' said
the chief, 'no slums in Brooklyn.' It was suggested that Hall
had fled the country to avoid testifying against Peter 'Brains'
Sweeny, who had returned to New York from abroad. This
was disputed on the grounds that Hall certainly had sufficient knowledge of the courts to know that Sweeny's case
would not be tried for many months.

Hall's good friend, Stephen Fiske, manager of the Fifth
Avenue Theatre, told a reporter that 'if the ex-Mayor knew
that any such story (about his running away) were being
circulated about him, he was just the man to keep out of the
way for three or four days and make a sensation of the report.'
At Delmonico's and the Fifth Avenue Hotel, Hall's friends
among the habitués said they had no idea where he could
be but they had known for some time that he was hard up.

A bartender reported that Hall was seen handing a lady
into a carriage. Someone else reported seeing him walking
up and down nervously in front of the Astor House. A cab
driver named Quinn claimed to have driven Hall to the Hart-
ford & New Haven Depot at nine o'clock Friday night. A
reader of the *Tribune* wrote a letter to the editor stating that
Hall had been seen in Boston on 12 March 'assisting a lady
pick out a rosebud at a florist near the Parker House.'

IV

When Hall's client, James Rice, came up for sentencing
on Tuesday, Hall was not present in court. Judge Brady gave

Rice three years in state's prison, less eight months for good behavior. Hall's failure to appear in court confirmed rumors of his disappearance. That afternoon and next morning the story was the talk of New York. On Saturday, 1 April, the *Times* quoted a clerk in the offices of the Warren Line in Boston as saying he had recognized Hall from the Nast caricatures and that he had sailed on the ship *Victoria* for England. Another Bostonian said Hall had attended a performance of *London Assurance* at the Globe Theatre the night before he sailed.

Reporters seem not to have questioned the Hall family about his disappearance, although the *Tribune* quoted a lady who said it was her opinion that his family knew where he was, supporting her assertion with the fact that she had seen one of his daughters attending Dr. Tyng's church and 'her face showed no token of grief.'

The newspapers, which had shown signs of being more friendly to Hall after his acquittal, again turned on him. 'Impoverished by his own spendthrift habits,' the *Tribune* said, 'and the extravagant demands of others, he could not arrange as others of more miserly habits and covetous dispositions had arranged, for peace and security from arrest at the price of dishonor.' The *Times* fairly snorted editorially, saying, 'Oakey Hall is naturally a trifler. His monogram was a pictorial pun.'

The story reached a climax when a *New York Times* correspondent cabled that Hall had landed in Southampton on the *Victoria* on 5 April. He reported that Hall was traveling under the name of W. E. Sutliffe. 'He has about a fortnight's beard,' the report stated, 'and side whiskers and was dressed in dark clothes — a dark blue shirt, red scarf, small common cap and spectacles instead of the customary eyeglasses.' A *Tribune* reporter who had known Hall in New York sent word that he had identified Hall but that Hall had insisted his name was Sutliffe. Passengers reported that Hall had been a jolly traveling companion and had made puns all the way across the Atlantic.

The *New York Times* man followed Hall to London and reported that he was living in the quarters of a woman who, he thought, had come on ahead to make arrangements. 'She is about 38 years old,' the *Times* man wrote, 'about five foot five in height, with a good figure, dark brown hair, clear complexion, large eyes, large mouth. She has a wart about two inches below her left ear.' Hall was also using the name Corbell, according to the reporter.

Tom Nast, on 21 April, capped the story by drawing another cartoon of Hall, whom he had neglected for several years. It consisted solely of Hall's droopy pince-nez hanging on a spike. The caption was 'H'all That's Left.'

The Hall mystery slowly died out. His clerk went to work for Brown & Vanderpoel. On 14 May, Ford, the business manager of the *Tribune,* officially canceled Hall's lease.

V

Had Hall been in New York a few months later he might have had good reason to flee. William Marcy Tweed, brought from a Spanish prison the year before, was now ready to talk. The Tammany tycoon who had once flashed diamond studs and a gold-plated smile was sick, and what must have been worse, virtually penniless. No distinguished counsel rushed to his side — grandiose fees were neither flaunted nor forthcoming. One lawyer — John D. Townsend — was willing to take his case for an over-all price of $10,000, but Tweed even had difficulty raising this sum, which in his days of opulence and power would have been something to generate his contempt. He gave part cash, the rest in securities. But he had something else to draw on, if not a bank account — his knowledge of the Ring. He was ready to co-operate — to testify for the city, which had instituted a num-

When Hall was reported as mysteriously missing from New York, only to turn up later in England, Nast drew one of his last cartoons lampooning him. The caption was H'ALL THAT'S LEFT.

ber of suits to regain the stolen monies. He was optimistic; after all, what he had to tell would be from the Tiger's mouth. Through John Kelly, the new Tammany leader, he made his arrangements, assisted by Townsend. All he asked in return was his freedom. But Governor Lucius Robinson and Attorney General Charles S. Fairchild knew political suicide when they saw it. They said no. The city had obtained judgments in the sum of some $20,000,000 against Tweed, and they decided to let the law take its course.

Townsend, according to Henry Lauren Clinton, discharged his professional duties faithfully 'even though his fee remained fixed regardless of the time or expenses he incurred.' Townsend's principal try at springing Tweed was a good one even though it didn't work. He arranged for Tweed to make a full confession of his misdeeds, had it typed up in legal language, and forwarded it, without Tweed's signature, to the Attorney General sometime around December, 1876. Fairchild sent it back on the grounds that no new indictments could be obtained as a result of the information in it, and calling attention to the fact that it contained no corroborating testimony. The *Herald* obtained a copy of the confession and published it exclusively on 10 October 1877.

According to the *Herald* version, Tweed began by saying the Ring members met 'in the keeper's room of City Hall and there swore fidelity and devotion to each other.' The first mention of Hall carried with it a certain flavor of vindictiveness. 'A. Oakey Hall came when notified,' according to Tweed, 'and remained as long as he was required.' But worse was to follow: 'Mr. Hall was a general adviser and counsellor in all legislative and other matters requiring legal skill and ingenuity.' Regarding the disappearance of the vouchers at City Hall, it was stated that 'Mr. Tweed said in a conversation with A. Oakey Hall, then Mayor, relative to the examination of vouchers by the subcommittee associated with the committee of citizens of which William A. Gould was chairman, that Mr. Hall informed Mr. Tweed that if the vouchers were not examined it would tend to and would probably break down the prosecution against the Ring. Mr. Tweed thereupon counselled with Mr. N. H. Cook who was then attached to the Department of Public Works and the head of the bureau therein as to the possibilities of obtaining access to and destroying said vouchers. Mr. Cook examined the Comptroller's office and reported to Mr. Tweed that he believed the vouchers could be obtained and destroyed and told Mr. Tweed to leave the matter in his hands and he would attend to it.'

Tweed went on to say of the division of the spoils that he, 'Sweeny, Hall and Connolly . . . each should receive ten per cent of the gross amount' collected from pocketing 50 per cent of the amounts of bills paid to the contractors. Later, the crooked contractors were ordered to pay back 65 per cent of the amount of their bills. 'After payment of a few bills,' Tweed said, 'Hall was notified that it had required so much money to pass the [city] charter and for other legislation that the different members would have to be content with five per cent each.' The actual divvy or boodle, as graft was referred to, was 25 per cent for Tweed, 20 per cent for Connolly, 10 per cent for Sweeny, and 5 per cent for Hall.

Tweed thus put into the record the fact that Hall was not only a swindler but had been swindled by other swindlers.

VI

Less than a month after publication of the Tweed confession, a reporter for the *Telegram* was startled to see at seven o'clock in the morning of 2 November a man who appeared to be A. Oakey Hall walking uptown toward Washington Square. He chatted with Hall only long enough to make sure it was the ex-Mayor, then raced to his office to get the news on Hall's return into the first edition of his paper. Hall was walking to the home of his old friend and law partner, Aaron J. Vanderpoel, at 1 West Sixteenth Street. Vanderpoel entertained Hall at breakfast and the two men talked for three hours. At ten-thirty, Hall went uptown to his home at 13 West Forty-second Street to see his family, just arrived from Valley View, the Hall summer home.

Vanderpoel, later in the day, told a *Tribune* reporter that Hall's appearance was that of a well but not a strong man. 'His eyes are bright,' the *Tribune* man wrote, 'and his voice pleasant and resonant, but there is a strange paleness of the complexion not to be expected after the winds and sunshine of an ocean voyage.' Vanderpoel told the *Tribune* man that Hall had left New York 'in consequence of mental derangement resulting from overwork and anxiety.' Vanderpoel stressed to the reporter that he considered Hall completely restored in mind. The *Tribune* story indicated doubt that Hall had just returned from England; the reporter had interviewed the purser of the *City of Montreal,* which had arrived in the harbor the previous night. The purser said he knew Hall and that he had not been among the passengers, either cabin or steerage.

When Hall appeared at the door of his house, his family was greatly astonished, according to the *Tribune,* but he remained calm and self-possessed. His first inquiries were in regard to his wife, mother, and five children. Reporters who came to interview him were turned away with word that he had said nothing about his trip and had only discussed family matters. He took a nap before dinner and retired early. Apparently, he did see a reporter for the *Evening Express* because the next day one of its columns carried an interview depicting 'the genial ex-Mayor . . . seated in his luxurious parlor, surrounded by objects of art and vertu. He looked remarkably well, his grizzled-gray mustache being the only hirsute adornment to his face, while his bright clear eye scintillates as of yore. He had gained something in flesh, and his sojourn abroad has made him a much younger man in appearance and manner than when the writer last met him — about three weeks before his departure.'

The reporter began by asking him to clear up the mystery of how he had arrived in New York. 'Well, my dear fellow,'

Hall replied, 'some of the papers say it was the *Netherlands* that arrived at Philadelphia the other day; but if the public do not believe that tell them that I came back upon a raft.'

Although the reporter noted in his story that he had made 'no allusion to the mysterious lady with the wart under the left ear,' he did not hesitate to ask Hall if 'the Ring frauds have anything to do with your departure?'

'Not in the least,' Hall said, 'for if they had why should I have returned? My status in that regard is not altered in the least from what it was six months ago. The simple truth of the matter is I was worn out, needed rest, and obtained it after a manner of my own choosing; and why a private gentleman going abroad and returning to his family should be made the subject of so much newspaper notoriety I cannot imagine. . . . The interviews printed in the morning papers were purely imagination but well worked up, under the circumstances. . . . It isn't the way I should run a paper, you know (laughing). And right here let me say that from this time forth I shall endeavor to sink personality. I have been the food for insatiate newspaper men long enough and hereafter I shall live a quiet, retired life, neither seeking nor asking for any mention, even in the humblest sheet.'

The reporter reminded Hall that 'the accusation the late Boss has made, implicating you as a *particeps criminis,* has led many persons to suppose that your return was to place yourself before that committee [investigating Tweed] and deny such charges.' Hall replied by asking the reporter if he recollected what Napoleon said when he was asked if he would fight a certain battle in a certain place? According to Hall, Napoleon said, 'If my army goes there and we meet the enemy there may be a fight.' (The *Tribune* that morning had quoted Wheeler H. Peckham — a Ring prosecutor — to the effect that there were no civil suits by the People against Hall and, so far as he knew, none was contemplated. As for criminal suits, Peckham was not sure whether or not all had been discontinued but added that all the indictments were found before Hall's acquittal. The District Attorney's office stated that there were no indictments on which Mr. Hall could be tried.)

Hall told the reporter for the *Telegram* that he had stayed in London at the house of a medical friend under whose care he was. He said he 'liked London as a residence . . . there is not an alley, lane, street, or spot in or around London, or its suburbs, that I do not know. I went among the people, studied their habits, life and customs, and they are measurably better off than Americans suppose.' He said he had spent only six weeks on the Continent. He commented on a variety of subjects. English newspapers: 'Very peculiar.' New York politics: 'Tammany will win! The men she has nominated are the best.' His future writing career: 'Nothing, beyond writing for one or two English newspapers with which he had made arrangements before he had left for home.'

Hall and the reporter left the Forty-second Street house together, 'he to visit a relative and the scribe to tell the public what the mysterious man, who was reported to have visited all the foreign localities excepting Kamtschatka and Timbuctoo, had really being doing.'

According to Hall's descendants, it was generally believed in the family that his going to London was the result of 'a nervous breakdown.' Certainly the difficulties he had encountered during the preceding five years were more than adequate to create in him what psychiatrists call 'a situational depression following a severe feeling of panic.' If so, he probably did just the right thing to cure himself as he removed himself entirely from immediate pressures and rested for six months — the usual time span for clearing up this type of mental illness.

There is also the suggestion, in something he told a friend, that his going off to London may have taken place during a loss of memory, or amnesia. A year or two after his return from London, Hall worked on the *World* in the same office with Julian Ralph, a fellow writer. The two men got to know each other very well. According to Ralph, who did not publish the information until twenty years later, Hall 'woke up one morning in a hall bedroom in Mayfair, in the heart of London, and as he lay in bed looking with wonder at his surroundings a woman knocked and entered the room. She asked him if he would have his usual breakfast. He inquired what his usual breakfast was, and she, astonished in her turn, told him that he always had a pennyworth of tea, a penny roll, a penny pot of butter, and an egg which cost a penny.

'He asked her to sit down, and then, by cross-examining her, he found that he had lived a whole season in that house under a name he never knew, that he appeared to be "a City man" (English for a man in business), that he went out every morning, came back every evening, went very frequently to the theater, and was the quietest, most irreproachable of all her lodgers. "In a word," Hall said, "I had lived the life of another man for months, unconscious of my own identity, unrecognized by anyone, and fulfilling the well-rounded half of a dual existence." '

13

OAKEY HALL IN LONDON

I

HAD HALL BEEN EITHER WISE or well, or his family more understanding, he would have been spared the strenuous roles which he was now to assume, and which were to lead him to another flight from reality or nightmare. The first was thrust upon him. Three days after his return from London, an old friend, Commodore Tooker, who worked in the offices of Jarrett & Palmer, managers of the Booth Theatre, was sitting at his desk 'when all of a sudden I happened to think what an enormous amount of gratuitous advertising Hall had managed to get and what a remarkable interest all classes of people took in his movements, so I jumped up and I hollered at Harry Palmer, "I have it — Oakey Hall is the cure for us. If we can get him to lecture for six months there is a fortune in it." '

Tooker wrote to Hall and asked if he would be amenable to the idea of a lecture tour. Hall answered in a few days saying he liked the idea immensely and had worked out a skeleton of the lecture he would give. Tooker, Jarrett, and Palmer went to Hall's house with contracts, and after signing them, Hall read his lecture. It was called 'What Will

Their Verdict Be? A Dramatic, Historic and Imaginary Cause Célèbre.' It was planned, at Hall's request, that he lecture first in Boston, then in Philadelphia, last in New York. When Hall was asked if he planned to make any allusion to Tweed or the Ring in his lecture, he said: 'Great heavens! no. Solomon once casually remarked: "There is a place for everything" and Boston people don't care anything about the Ring. What's Hecuba to Boston or Boston to Hecuba?'

Hall's Boston lecture was scheduled for Monday evening, 26 March 1887, at the Music Hall. He took the Fall River boat on Friday evening and checked into Tremont House on Saturday morning.

About 1,200 people attended Hall's lecture, which was priced at seventy-five cents for reserved seats and fifty for general admission. Few women attended because the weather turned out to be bad. The reporter for the Boston *Globe* wrote that the gathering was not at all a representative Boston audience and observed that the New Yorkers present 'were easily distinguishable by an "indescribable air." ' The audience was seated at 7:30 but Hall did not appear until 8:15. Naturally, this gave rise to remarks that 'perhaps Hall has disappeared again.' When he came on the platform, he was 'in the conventional dress suit and wore a plain black tie. . . . Perfectly self-possessed, and easily familiar with his theme, the lecturer proceeded to speak without notes. . . . The lecture was enlivened two or three times by bright and witty passages such as one might expect from the great New York punster. . . . He avoided gestures almost entirely and occupied his right hand by twirling the famous eyeglasses that the pencil of Nast has made so familiar to the public, while his left hand hung by the thumb to his waistcoat pocket.'

His lecture was a one-man historical pageant with Hall acting all the parts. The setting was the Pantheon of History with Fame acting as judges of all the American Presidents.

Eighteen centuries made up the jury. Hall's talk was full
of classical allusions, well-known lines of poetry, and many
puns. When he said that Cupid would act as the court inter-
preter he remarked that 'Cupid usually begins with a court
and is quite apt to end his business in a court.' After waiting
for the laughter to die down he added that Cupid made
clear the origin of the word cupidity, for the God of Love
was more interested in a purse than a person. William Cullen Bryant was called as the deciding witness because he was
writing a history of the Presidents, all of whom he had
known except Washington. In the end, the jury voted half
in favor of Washington and half in favor of Lincoln.

'Your noble John A. Andrew,' Hall said in closing, 'and
Charles Sumner were the forerunners and disciples of that
freedom in which Lincoln baptized a race. If your allegiance
falters and divides between the Father of his Country and
the Father of his Race, remember that one of them was a
Joshua to whom it was permitted to enter into the Promised
Land, and that the other was the Moses, who, by the in-
scrutable decree of Providence, was compelled to close his
eyes on the mere confines of freedom.'

Both New York and Boston papers agreed that Hall had
held the interest of his audience, but noted its disappointment at hearing nothing about the Ring. 'His lecture,' the
Globe said, 'has many faults: it needs to be cleared from
much over-refinement of verbiage and a tendency to pedantry; but this done, it will be no unworthy production . . .
before any audience of cultivated people in the land.' A
reporter for the Boston *Sunday Herald* wrote an extensive
interview with the 'Hon. A. Oakey Hall, best known as
having been Mayor of New York, ex-District Attorney, lawyer, advocate, journalist, actor, and now lecturer — a gentleman of the most versatile attainments and capacity.

'Mr. Hall,' the *Herald* man wrote, 'is a man of apparently
about 55 years of age [Hall was 51], a little above medium

height, well built but not stout or fleshy, with a mobile, in-
telligent face, surmounted by a good head of gray hair, which
he parts nearly in the middle. His features are regular, with
the nose inclining to the Roman style and expressive at once
of good nature and determination. His eyes are gray and,
seen through the glasses he habitually wears, keen and searching. He wears a good-sized, though not heavy gray mustache,
but otherwise his face is close-shaved. To see him even in
a crowd, one would at once be led to place him as a man of
more than ordinary ability, and a more intimate association
with him would easily confirm this. . . . He has the ease
and bonhomie of the man of the world, with all the breadth
and brightness of the journalist.'

Hall endeared himself to this reporter by talking of Harvard University 'with feeling and respect. He spoke of his
college at Harvard, and said that he was one of three H's
who at one time studied in its law school, the others being
now distinguished men — President Hayes, and Judge Hoadley of Ohio. "Hayes wasn't very much in sympathy with us.
He was rather a swell, and I wasn't. He always had plenty
of money. I think all the Birchard family were well to do,
for that matter." '

The reporter tactfully broached the subject of Hall's trip
to London by observing that it had occasioned some surprise.
'I have very little remembrance,' Hall said, 'of leaving this
country. My going away was utterly motiveless. There wasn't
the slightest reason for it. There is no question about it; it
was simply an insane impulse. I was utterly worn out. Nature
had sustained a burden beyond her ability to bear. I had
been twenty years in public life without a holiday, never
having been out of New York five days at a time. I knew
I was going away from New York. I had a dim, indistinct
feeling that it was all right and necessary for me to go. The
idea never occurred to me that I was doing anything out of
the way.' The reporter asked his opinion about the Tweed

confession and Hall said he read about it the morning before he sailed from England 'or I might not have come so soon.' Asked if he considered that Tweed's revelations had been made to obtain mercy from the courts, Hall replied: 'It is claimed that he is making desperate efforts to get himself clear. These Ring matters are very much like an ordinary political football.'

The reporter digressed a moment to ask if Hall thought the May duel was what was keeping young Bennett in Europe. 'I suppose the marriage is broken off,' Hall said, 'but I have no doubt that in remaining in Europe he simply consults his own inclinations.'

One of the most interesting things Hall said in the interview, in the light of his later actions, was his mention of the fact that he had known Judah P. Benjamin in New Orleans. Benjamin, Secretary of State under the Confederacy, had been the center of a Union Club rift that had eventually resulted in the formation of the Union League Club, by members who advocated his expulsion, and the Manhattan Club, by members who defended him against expulsion.

'I drifted upon him in London last summer,' Hall said. 'I would like well to do what he has managed to do. Do you know he has joined the English bar? He has the very cream of English law practice. He stepped right into it. He is a strangely able man. . . . He was a British subject already, as I am myself. That is, according to the English natural law, the grandson of a British-born subject can, if he likes, claim a subject's rights and privileges, but this claim does not extend beyond the third generation.'

Asked about his future plans, Hall said, 'I shall probably take charge of a New York daily paper as managing editor. I may say that I like the exhilaration arising from the consciousness of the power that a man possesses who is in a position to lay out plans for the operations of an able staff of writers for a public journal, and to watch the effect of his policy upon public opinion, and I mean to try it. My friends are averse to my going back to the law, so that I shall probably settle down permanently to the life of a journalist — a life that, more than any other, has always had a fascination for me.'

Hall lectured in other cities that winter of 1877–78, and long interviews with him were printed in the local papers. But the attendance was poor, and the tour was finally abandoned.

In the spring of 1878, on 12 April, a good deal of the interest in the Ring scandal ended with the death of William Marcy Tweed in Ludlow Street jail, in the warden's apartment. Considerable attention was paid to his last words because it was recalled that, at his sentencing, when his 'pedigree' was taken he had replied, when asked his religion, 'None.' (He had also said, when asked his occupation, 'Statesman.') Like so many Tammany officials, Tweed sought solace in religion as he neared his end. To Mary Fitzsimmons, daughter of his jailor, Tweed said: 'Mary, I have tried to do good by everyone; if I have not, it is not my fault. I am ready to die, and I know God will receive me.' He also said, 'I guess Tilden and Fairchild have killed me at last. I hope they will be satisfied now.' Tweed died while the bell of the Essex Market clock tolled the noon hour.

II

The year 1878 brought Hall to another phase of his career. He became an editor of the *World*. Hall had been practicing law since his lecture tour, but had not enjoyed his cases as 'it put too much pressure on his brain and wearied him.' Rather than find himself in the whirl of excitement, as a friend of Hall's said, 'and bewilderment, such as overcame him a year before, he resolutely resolved to change his profession.' Hall took over the city editor's desk at the *World* on the morning of 18 November, according to the Associated Press, which sent out the news on its national wire. As with any story concerning Hall, puns were in order. 'A. Oakey Hall is like Atlas,' the Detroit *Free Press* said, 'he supports the *World*, at least its local columns.'

'A. Oakey Hall is getting on in the world,' said the Baltimore *Gazette*. 'A few years ago he was the brilliant and witty Mayor of the city of New York. Now he is the honored and respected City Editor of the New York *World*. The reporter who "gets left" on an item will consider it a great honor to be jawed when he comes down in the morning.' The Toledo *Commercial* observed that 'This is pretty well for an ex-Mayor of New York.' Getting the job must have given Hall considerable satisfaction, for he had announced, shortly after his election as chief magistrate of the city, that he'd rather be the city editor of a great New York paper than Mayor.

Hall directed coverage of a big story his first day on the job — the reported finding of the body of A. T. Stewart, the department store owner, whose remains had been stolen by thieves on 7 November from St. Mark's churchyard.

The publisher of the *World* was Tom Scott who, shortly after Hall went to work for the paper, sold it to Jay Gould. Both men, Hall was to write later, 'sought to control it for their Wall Street purposes.' It was said that Gould was so obvious in his slanting of the financial news that New Yorkers caught on to what he was doing only two or three days after the paper came into his hands. The editor of the *World* at this time was William Henry Hurlbert, who had had a hand in Hall's play. Once a Unitarian minister, an unhappy love affair had made him renounce the pulpit and dedicate himself to a life of bachelorhood. Apparently, his bachelorhood did not include celibacy, for Hurlbert achieved quite a reputation as a gallant. One of his affairs was to end as a notorious court case. A reporter whom Hall used to recall later as a striking character was 'the Crichtonian James B. Townsend, who on the *World* first invented the word "dude." '

By 1881, Hall appears to have become the active editorial director of the paper. Hurlbert had virtually barricaded himself in a bachelor apartment located at the corner of Waverly Place and University. 'The building is dreary,' one newspaperman wrote, 'and his doors are boarded up jealously. One might knock at the outer door for a week, and unless he had an appointment no result would be visible. His castle is his own. But when once the door is opened the scene is one of extravagant luxury. Statuary, rugs, bric-a-brac, the costly contributions of every age and every clime, seem to be thrown together in chaotic disregard of the laws of order. The result is brilliant in the extreme. Here the witty, handsome editor entertains a small circle of masculine guests and a still choicer circle of the other sex.' It was further reported that Jay Gould was helping to make Hurlbert independently rich by letting him take advantage of his Wall Street manipulations. Hall's friends hoped that Gould would favor Hall similarly, but he never did.

In fact, it would appear that in 1881 Hall was very hard up. Bangs & Co. sold Hall's library during the week beginning Monday, 21 January. It was a magnificent collection of books containing rare and first editions in the fields of drama, crime and legal literature, poetry, Americana, fiction, and biography. There were 'original editions of Miss Edgeworth, James, Dickens, Thackeray, Bulwer and Hawthorne; some of them with autographs inserted.' There was a full set of *Valentine's Manuals,* an unexpurgated *Tom Brown,* volumes of Cruikshankiana, the transcripts of the trials of Charles I and Louis XVI, rare books relating to Shakespeare, two sets of Shakespeare especially illustrated, Shakespeare in outline drawings, the music of Shakespeare's plays, bound

volumes of Greeley's *New Yorker,* called the germ of the
Tribune, and about 2,500 other equally interesting books.
The sale realized $6,812.26 and was attended by leading book
collectors, actors, managers, *litterateurs* (as one paper put it),
and distinguished members of the bar. Giving up his library
must have been a blow to Hall. 'It shows,' one paper said,
'the fluctuations of fortune here. He was once rich, with a
good practice, but now is an attache of one of the morning papers.'

The job Hall did on the *World* won the admiration of his
newspaper colleagues. 'He gives no sign of tiring,' a commentator, who signed himself Rapidan, wrote. 'On the contrary he seems to have gone on the *World* to stay. Not a man
in the office is more regular at his post, or more earnest
with the work he has to do. Oakey always was a man of the
world and that's reason enough why he should be satisfied
with the *World,* and do all he can for it. He is doing all he
can, and more than that, he feels that the position is as honorable as any he ever held.'

'His knowledge of [New York City] is perhaps too recon-
dite,' another newspaper colleague observed. This reporter
recalled, as an example, an occasion when Hall and a group
of reporters were looking over the passenger list of a ship
about to sail for Europe. They came across the name of a
Captain Constantenos. The group naturally turned to Hall
to identify the man.

'Constantenos, Constantenos,' Hall said, according to the
reporter. 'Um — ah — now let me see. Didn't a daughter
of Hamilton Fish marry a son of the Greek envoy here some-
where back in the 'fifties? No! It must have been one of the
Evartses. You know they lived up on Second Avenue near
Stuyvesant Park and had a grape arbor at the back of the
house. I used to play there when I was a boy. But of course
that's not Constantenos! No! The name is familiar, very
familiar and I know he is connected with some family here,

but I can't really say which. Constantenos! Now let me see.'
At this point one of the reporters asked if Captain Constantenos wasn't the name of Barnum's tatooed man? It was.
The reporter who recounted the anecdote said the best
description of Hall was one Hall himself had used in describing another old New Yorker: 'Oh, that gentleman is always
giving us personal reminiscences of the city as it was under
the reign of William and Mary.'

In the middle of March, 1883, Gould realized that he
was losing between $3,000 and $5,000 a week publishing
the *World*. Finally, just before sailing for Europe, he told
Hurlbert he was going to sell the paper. Hurlbert begged
Gould, it was reported, to let him put the paper on a paying
basis, and Gould gave him the chance. Hurlbert began the
traditional way — he fired the music and the drama critics,
five night editors, sixteen reporters, the city editor, the
assistant city editor, and eight compositors on a day's notice.
'One of the meanest things about the move,' a newspaperman
wrote, 'was the sudden discharge of ex-Mayor A. Oakey Hall,
who was the principal editorial writer, and by far the most
valuable man on the paper. He was not even allowed a
chance to resign but was shipped in the same summary
manner as were the other unfortunate scribes on the paper.'
Hurlbert added a final indignity to his reorganization of the
World by arranging to get his city news from a 'local press
agent.'

Hall must have foreseen what was coming because he
purchased almost immediately, with the help of friends, a
penny newspaper called *Truth* which had been owned and
operated by Josh Hart, a former theatrical manager. The
purchase price was reported to be $100,000 for four-fifths
of the stock, with $10,000 as a down payment, the rest to be
paid in three months. It had been said that Joseph Pulitzer
had planned to purchase *Truth*, but the deal had fallen
through. The motto of the new *Truth* was to be, Hall an-

nounced, Lincoln's great phrase, 'With malice toward none and charity for all.' Writers were the first beneficiaries of this benevolent editorial policy, as Hall raised the space rates of *Truth* from three to five dollars a column. Again news of Hall received national attention. 'Truth needs over Halling,' said the Philadelphia *Times*. The Salem (Ohio) *Buckeye's* editor observed that 'The chief editor of the New York daily *Truth* is A. Oakey Hall. We hope *Truth* sticks to truth.' 'Oakey Hall is to manage *Truth*,' the Philadelphia *Record* said, 'under a new dispensation. Would it not have been a better arrangement to let Truth manage Oakey Hall?'

Hall edited *Truth* for a little more than eight months. He gave up on 5 December 1883, as a result, apparently, of serious disagreement with Hart, for he later wrote, 'I became editor of the *Daily Truth,* owned by a speculative gentleman named Hart who had made a fortune as a theatrical manager; but when I discovered that he was using the paper for his personal private uses I resigned.'

By 1884, Hall and his family had moved uptown to 1008 Madison Avenue. The neighborhood of their old home on Forty-second Street between Fifth and Sixth was becoming more and more commercial. On 8 January 1884, Hall's third oldest daughter, Alice d'Assignie Hall, now thirty, was married to Charles Rossire, the son of a wealthy and socially distinguished New York family. The Rossires and Halls had been friends since before the Civil War when the two families had occupied nearby summer places on the banks of the Hudson near Weehawken. Although the invitations to the wedding went out under the name of Mr. and Mrs. A. Oakey Hall, Hall himself apparently was not present to give his daughter away because a newspaper dispatch he sent to New York indicated he was in London as early as 2 January.

His departure this time was accompanied by considerable

fanfare. A number of large banquets and smaller dinner parties were tendered him. The most significant was a sumptuous dinner given to him at Delmonico's by the leading lawyers and judges in New York. Their tribute to him was no mere formality, as they were later to express their approval of him in a more tangible form.

Whitelaw Reid, now celebrated as the publisher of Greeley's old *Tribune*, presided over a farewell dinner to Hall given by the Lotos Club. The New York Press Club, which Hall had helped found, also gave him a dinner.

III

Hall's second departure for England gave rise to considerable conjecture. It is possible that his presence was not desired at the marriage of his daughter; he was a sentimental man, and much as he would have liked to be a central figure at this ceremony, he deferred to the feelings of his wife and daughter, particularly the latter. The signs, in any case, are clear that he was not getting along with his wife. In the genealogical records of the Hall family there is the following note: 'AOH practically deserted his family in 1884 and never lived with his wife again.' But this is both truth and a gloss. Hall was a sick man, and it may legitimately be supposed that had he been a member of a different family, his peculiar behavior would have tended to bring forth, not a widening of the breach, but loving care.

Hall's state of mind is apparent in an interview he gave before sailing: 'Yes, it is true. I leave journalism, by your leave. Not on compulsion, my dear boy' — he was still scattering Shakespearean tags — 'though there were reasons for leaving quite as plenty as blackberries. But I leave. I depart, in fact. I shall sail for England, where I shall engage with a firm of London solicitors. I have been making preparations for the change for some time past. I could

stay. I have invitations enough. But I do not feel like sub-
mitting to the buffets of misfortune here.'

It must have been particularly galling for him — and his
family — to read, in the paper to which he had given such
devoted service, the following squib which the *World,*
without reason and without taste, published at this time:
'Oakey says he has bidden farewell to America forever. In
London he lives and in London he hopes to die. Ta-ta
Oakey. Sorry you have gone back on your nativity — but
we'll try to get along without you. Take our advice in this:
don't go on the stage. The stage has been more than one
man's Waterloo.'

In later years, when Hall wrote about his 1884 trip to
London, he said that he went on a cabled invitation from
James Gordon Bennett, the younger, to become his London
legal representative and sub-head of the *Herald's* London
bureau. Apparently, he was sufficiently aware of young Bennett's administrative vagaries not to put his entire London
future in one editorial basket. On 8 January, the day his
daughter was married, he began writing a series of London
letters for the Sunday edition of the Brooklyn *Daily Eagle.*
The first, two and a half columns long, was entitled: 'LONDON
GOSSIP; Mr. A. Oakey Hall Retails Some Of, For The *Eagle.*'
The piece was written on a Sunday and reveals that he had
been in London the previous Sunday. It was mostly about
preachers and churches. Hall noted, for example, 'one thing
commendatory in the worship of the rich here — they do not
use carriage service to rubric service as freely as in America.
Thereby they imitate the Hebrews in strict remembrance of
the Sabbatarian commandment. I have remarked the almost
total absence of carriages in front of the Fifth Avenue
Synagogue of a Saturday while in front of St. Bartholomew's
and of the Brick Church hard by, on the next day, the
streets thereabout were cluttered with coaches. Perhaps the
Briton is not particular, while giving his own coachman a

rest, about the cabmen and the drivers and guards of the railways, who are employed by somebody else.' Hall thought it 'curious' to see the notices of announcements of church services and hunting appointments side by side in the church and state papers. 'To pray is constitutional and to hunt equally so,' he wrote. 'A devil's hunt on Sunday and a devil of a hunt on Monday.'

The Brooklyn *Eagle* made Hall's London Letter a Sunday feature for the next six months. Two of the lead paragraphs of letters he wrote that winter, and in the spring, give an idea of some of the things that interested Hall about the London of his day.

'State and church are having hard tussles in the matter of the Cairns-Garmoyle-Fortescue scandal,' he wrote on 13 February, 'and last Sunday one or two conservative parsons covertly referred to the impossibility of pious parents countenancing the affiliations of their children with the stage. Some humor exists in the fact that when Lord Garmoyle presented his expected bride to his mother the latter gave her a Bible, doubtless supposing that an actress was a heathen. The fact is that Lord and Lady Cairns are north-of-Ireland fanatics who are even worse in their zeal for a faith than a Mussulman. Already a religious friend of Lord Cairns (who, by the way, is notable for his opinion during the Confederate war that it was lawful and no breach of neutrality for Englishmen to advertise in London for loans to aid the Confederacy) has introduced a bill to prevent suits for breaches of promise of marriage, as if Parliament could choose between contracts and say that one of them shall be suable and another non-suable or otherwise alter or remedy than by declaring how a contract to marry shall be made — whether with a kiss in the presence of witnesses, in writing or by an Oriental method of betrothal.'

'It is Sunday morning,' he wrote on 11 May. 'I am standing at the gate of Danes Inn. I have just taken an after-breakfast walk around it in the gardens of Clement's and New Inns, that are bounded by slums on the north — the Globe and Comique theaters on the south — the law courts on the east and quaint old Newcastle street on the west. Foliage, verdure and flowers, with hopping sparrows and singing birds, in these gardens have combined to make a curious *rus in urbe*. As I stand in the grateful sunshine the busy Strand of yesterday seems comatose. A few cabs crawl by and the omnibuses are decorously driven. Opposite to me a few loungers are gazing into the empictured windows of the *Graphic* and *Illustrated News* buildings, that amicably rival each other almost side by side. . . . The solemn stillness which Gray described as coming over Stoke Poges is all around this usually deafening part of London. Fifty feet at my right, in Wych street, is an old Elizabethan house, propped up by scaffolding. I am partially leaning against the wall of the Kings Head Inn, immortalized by Dickens in "Household Words," and two hundred years old. Seventy-five feet at my left is the Church of St. Clement Danes. On its spire sits a pigeon — recalling N. P. Willis's sweet poem to the pigeon on the belfry of the old South Church in Boston.' And so forth. His material was sent by mail; by cable, it would have been prohibitive.

That spring, what was probably Hall's strongest tie with New York City was finally severed. A cable arrived telling him of the death of his mother, Elsie Lansing Hall. She was eighty-five. The papers noted that she had been one of the first Sunday school teachers in the United States and had established the first boardinghouse for self-supporting women ever opened in New York.

IV

Hall was not long in adjusting to the London political climate. In the middle of April Londoners were weighing the advantages and disadvantages of combining the city of London with outlying communities into one huge municipality. Hall took the popular view, which was against it. In the traditional manner — a letter to the London *Times* — he outlined his reasons why the bill, advocated by the Home Secretary, should not be passed. Briefly mentioning his 'connection during the last quarter of a century with the government of New York City,' he went on to say that 'Down to about the year 1850 the former City [of New York] was governed substantially under Royal charters granted to it in the 17th and 18th centuries. Under these the various wards of the city proper severally elected common councilmen and various officials. Watchful supervision was not only possible but thoroughly existed; extravagant taxation was prevented, aggregated jobbery was unknown, and individual emulation advantageously excited. About 1850 a political party controlling the State supervisory Legislature practically abolished those Royal charters, together with the distributive voice of localities in the municipal government, and began to centre this in a largely increased Legislature. Seven years later (intervening years witnessing annual and unsuccessful legislative experiments instituted with the view of rectifying increasing mischiefs) the same party developed a scheme for uniting New York, Brooklyn, and three adjacent counties — an area together of 30 square miles — into a mammoth municipal government for purposes of police and sanitation, to be controlled by commissioners selected from each of the localities thus aggregated. The intention was avowed, if this succeeded, of next consolidating all the powers of government connected with these localities into one huge municipality. The primary changes, however proved to be so cumbersome, confusing, corrupting, and unpopular, that in a short time, by the common consent of all parties, New York, Brooklyn, and all the suburban localities wholly returned to their old local forms of government.

'Boston, again, like London, includes under its name many neighborhoods and separate towns, forming a metropolitan area of great extent, wealth, and commercial importance. Within this area there are a dozen municipalities with mayors and separate councils, some large and some smaller, but all generous and emulating rivals of each other in good government. Only a few agitators have ever proposed to create over this great Boston area a consolidation of all these municipal governments, but so far ineffectually. It is recognized in and around Boston that those living in the centre and those in the extremities of this area possess few interests in common, and that each is best acquainted with the life and needs of his own locality, while in a measure ignorant of those of others; lastly, that among them exists no real community either of municipal citizenship or of social life. They prefer, therefore, to deal *locally* with local affairs rather than submit to the government of a mammoth caucus.

'I am, Sir, your obedient servant,

'A. Oakey Hall, ex-Mayor of New York

'3, Dane's Inn, April 20, 1884.'

Three days later, on Wednesday, 23 April, Hall was a guest of honor at a dinner of the City Lands Committee held at the London Guildhall Tavern. The London *City Press* noted that 'dinner was admirably served' and went on to report that 'Mr. Oakey Hall, ex-Mayor of New York, responded in a speech of remarkable power and humor. It was strange that Americans, with their experience of democratic government [Hall said], were trying to get as near the liberty of a monarchy as they could and yet the tone of many English people lay in that direction. He looked with distrust upon a measure which threatened annihilation to the traditions of the greatest City in the civilized world. (Cheers.) It would be nothing but creating a mammoth caucus which would prey upon the taxpayers.'

The London papers commented favorably on Hall's volunteering of his views on the centralization issue and referred to his Tweed Ring background only fleetingly. 'What he does not know,' one paper said, 'about the ways of municipal jobbery and corruption can hardly be worth knowing.' Another London paper commented that 'Mr. Oakey Hall well remembers the gigantic frauds of Tweed and his gang and he has known judges exercising criminal jurisdiction who were the patrons if not the accomplices of thieves.' The dignified Whitehall *Review* observed that, 'Mr. Hall has at least the merit of being an impartial judge. He is hardly likely to yield to this faction or to that; and although he intends to reside in this country permanently, he cannot in the nature of things be affected by the association or traditions of the form of government under which London has hitherto existed.' On 12 May, Hall gave a lecture on 'American Experiences of Centralized Municipalities' at Prince's Hall, Piccadilly. He was also appointed to the General Council of the London Metropolitan Ratepayers' Protection Association, an organization of leading citizens presided over by Lord George Hamilton, the Earl of Clarendon, the Earl of Egmont, and Viscount Pollinton. A writer for a New York newspaper, noting Hall's progress in seeking new cities to conquer, penned a short squib entitled, 'From Gotham to Gog.' 'As proof that a City Hall politician,' he said, 'takes to political water anywhere after the fashion of ducks, lame or otherwise, may be taken the case of Ex-Mayor A. Oakey Hall. Recent London papers show him swimming gayly in the tide of London municipal politics, making speeches and writing letters on the new scheme to consolidate all the local boards of that city into a huge municipality. He seemed as much at home as if Gog and Magog were his uncles.'

Hall had settled himself comfortably in an apartment in 'one of a series of picturesque buildings just off the Strand' — 3 Dane's Inn. Besides his newspaper writing, he was serving as London legal representative for Bennett and others, and was acting as representative for A. M. Palmer, the New York theatrical manager, in 'the purchase of plays and engagement of actors in London.' He was given guest privileges at the Savage Club and spent a good deal of his time there. He began to meet the leading London literary figures, one New York paper noting that he 'has been received graciously by Lord Coleridge.'

'He has found much favour in literary circles,' a London paper noted, 'and is a frequent guest at houses where Bohemia and Mayfair dine together. Mr. Hall is a most fluent and interesting talker and has a number of amusing stories to tell of his municipal and other experiences.'

In his wish to emulate Judah P. Benjamin and practice law before the English bar, Hall began to make considerable headway. Leading members of the New York bench and bar signed a petition to the Joint Council of the Inns of Court in London asking that Hall be allowed to practice law in England. This document, which has recently come to light, was signed by an imposing list of judges and distinguished lawyers, including Noah Davis, presiding justice of the Supreme Court of New York State; Edwards Pierrepont, former United States Attorney General and former Envoy Extraordinary and Minister Plenipotentiary to the Court of St. James's; Clarence A. Seward, former Secretary of State for the United States; Elliot F. Shepard, President of the New York State Bar Association; Aaron Vanderpoel, Hall's former law partner and now President of the Law Department of New York University; Francis C. Barlow, Attorney General of the State of New York, who had once prosecuted him; Roscoe Conkling; and Elihu Root.

Hall was admitted to the Inns of Court. Young Bennett was

his principal client, and Hall also served as his London Secretary, later becoming head of the *Herald's* London bureau. In 1888, when General Benjamin Harrison was elected twenty-third President of the United States, Hall handled the transmission of the news to England so well that one London paper said, 'More newspaper enterprise! The "cute" London representative of the New York *Herald*, Mr. Oakey Hall, deserves our thanks for being the first in the field with the news that General Harrison has been elected as the new President.' He came to be regarded with such affection in London that when Hall's old paper, *Truth*, published an article on the Tweed Ring in which it was stated that 'Hall lost position, and finally became a newspaper reporter,' a London paper took issue with *Truth* and said, 'Mr. Oakey Hall came to London a little over five years ago and soon established himself in the good opinions of everybody. While going through the somewhat slow process of "eating his dinners," he came to the rescue of the New York *Herald* by taking the very responsible position of its London editor. Mr. Hall has done his work well and occupied the London editorial chair ever since and I think I am not mistaken in stating that he has held this position for the longest time on record. This feat will be appreciated by all those who happen to know anything of the periodical epochs of eccentricity indulged in by Mr. James Gordon Bennett, the proprietor.'

V

Early in the winter of 1888, Hall began setting up plans for a London edition of the *Herald*. Bennett, it was said, was anxious to establish the paper to further his European social ambitions. A building in the Strand, opposite Burleigh Street, was rented to house the new paper, and early in January, 1889, signs were hung from its windows announcing the forthcoming publication of the London *Herald* 'to be published every day including Sunday.' A reporter for the Pall Mall *Gazette* called on Hall at his chambers in Dane's Inn 'in search of information as to this journalistic invasion.' Hall charmed the reporter into writing an interview that amounted to a compelling come-on for the new paper, concerning which he said, 'In all departments the idea will be even to excel the direct, crisp, and attractive style for which the Pall Mall *Gazette* has become noted.'

'This London edition,' Hall said, reaching heights of the copywriter's eloquence, 'will be the first English daily newspaper to recognize that the world's events do not respect Sundays and holidays; for it will appear without interruption every morning of the year, and its Sunday issue will aim to be particularly attractive in gossipy, piquant, literary, theatrical, artistic, and chatty features. These, however, will also receive attention on business days.' Financial news from all over the world, he said, would be published on week days and special attention given to securities on the New York Stock Market due to the new importance the English were according what they called 'Americans.'

'It will also give,' Hall continued, 'daily important social and fashionable occurrences; and it will aim to be exhaustive in its intelligence and independent comments about all sporting events in racing, hunting, yachting, coursing, archery, and cricket circles. These will become leading features not only as regards England, but France, America, the Riviera, &c. Interviews in all parts of the world will receive special attention. Endeavours will be made to eschew heavy or perfunctory or baldly stated accounts of events. These will come from the pens of detailed reporters in graphic and not perfunctory style. All the cable and telegraphic machinery in the hands of special news gatherers which for many years the New York *Herald* has established and used will be at the service of the London edition. The politics of every country

will be considered from the standpoint of impartial observa-
tion excluding all symptoms of an "organ." Members of
Parliament will be practically on the staff. . . . Although
the proprietor and many of the writers will be American,
the tone of the paper will be cosmopolitan and as attractive
to John Bull as to Jonathan.'

The actual staff of the London *Herald*, Hall said, would
be headed by John Russell Young, 'the gentleman who was
General Grant's compagnon du voyage around the world and
also United States Minister to China.' Aubrey Stanhope
would be business manager and William C. Reick chief of
the news department. 'A lady prominent in Society,' Hall
said, 'will report upon its functions; also W. E. Rawlings, a
picturesque reporter from New York, but au fait with
England, will be a writer. Victor Gingold would supervise
details of the Capelcourt and other markets of London.'

Bennett's London *Herald* had a Roman candle existence.
The erratic and unpredictable Bennett hired and fired several
staffs before the paper came to an end, just as the New York
Herald was to do a few years later. Even Hall, an old friend
of both father and son, had differences with young Bennett
which resulted in his leaving the publisher's employ. But
Hall, in his many reminiscences, made no complaint about
young Bennett.

The passing of the London *Herald* was still another change
in his fortunes which Hall took in his stride. But his work
on the paper had gained him a new friend, one who had
been publicly his most bitter enemy. Toward the end of the
Herald's days, Hall wrote editorials for and made up the
editorial page of the paper. Assisting him in this work was
Louis John Jennings, former editor of the *New York Times*
who, during the exposures of the Tweed Ring scandal, had
established an all-time high for invective and abuse of a
Mayor of New York City.

14

THE SUIT AGAINST BRYCE

I

As the 1880's drew to a close, Hall settled down to a contented life in London. Club life was flourishing again as it had in the Georgian age, and Hall was welcome in the city's artistic and theatrical circles. He was often to be found of an evening at the Greenroom Club, or with fashionable Victorian gentlemen at the Brook or Savage clubs. 'His acquaintance here,' a London newspaperman wrote, 'is very large, for he is a most companionable man — a typical bon vivant.'

Unknown to him, however, the comparative serenity of his life in London as a barrister, journalist, and clubman was about to be threatened from a most unexpected quarter. For more than a decade a serious and scholarly Oxford University professor had been at work on an enormous project which was now nearing completion. He was James Bryce, who had recently become a member of the House of Parliament and maintained quarters at 54 Portland Place, a block away from Hall's quarters at Dane's Inn. But the two men had not met. Bryce had read hundreds of books, studied documents, and interviewed hundreds of people including many distinguished Americans when he visited the United States. At the Rochester Democratic Convention he had watched Tweed in action. His *American Commonwealth* was published by Macmillan in England and the Century Company in the United States on 12 December 1888. For the next year it was reviewed, discussed, and written about both in the United States and Europe. 'It was the largest, most complete, and most painstaking study of American institutions,' the New York *World* was to say, 'which has been written by a foreigner. Upon its publication it easily took first rank and superseded De Tocqueville's *Democracy* which had been the standard up to that time.

'*The American Commonwealth* attracted almost more attention abroad that it did in the United States. It was everywhere recognized as the product of a master mind upon one of the highest subjects which can engage the human intellect, and it placed Prof. Bryce in the very front rank among modern historians and commentators.'

Chapter 88 of *The American Commonwealth* was not written by Professor Bryce but by a professor of history at Columbia — Frank Johnson Goodnow. 'This part,' an introduction to the chapter explained, 'contains some illustrations drawn from American history of the workings of political institutions and public opinion.' It told the story of the Tweed Ring. In describing its various members, Goodnow wrote that 'Hall was of better birth than the rest and had considerable literary ability, of which he was inordinately proud. Under an appearance of artless simplicity he concealed a great ambition. Though generally supposed to occupy a somewhat higher moral plane than his associates, he was never considered remarkable for the severity of his principles.' Regarding Hall's election to the Mayor's office, Goodnow said that 'a threatened defection of Roman Catholic votes was checked by the hint that subventions given by the Ring to Catholic charitable institutions would be withdrawn if Catholic votes should be cast for the opposing candidates.' He cited the numerous sins of the Ring without mentioning Hall specifically and told details of the Court House frauds, commenting, 'Here the operations of the Ring can with difficulty be distinguished from ordinary theft.' The *New York Times,* he said, 'boldly denounced the members of the Ring as *thieves* and *swindlers* and defied them to sue the paper for libel.' At the end of the chapter Goodnow noted that 'Hall was tried and obtained a favorable verdict, but he has chosen to live out of America.'

Hall was, understandably enough, extremely bitter about the way he had come off in *The American Commonwealth.* Not long after the publication of the book, his youngest daughter, Louise Oakey Hall, came to London to marry her fiancé, George Carl Bratanahl, a young American businessman who was working as manager of the London office of the Ansonia Clock Co. Hall helped arrange the marriage ceremony and gave his daughter in marriage to Bratanahl on 28 August 1889. What should have been a happy occasion, the renewing of ties with his daughter, was completely marred.

II

Hall was particularly disturbed by the vehicle which contained this new attack on his probity. He shared the universal respect for Bryce as an historian and student of political science. His resentment was directed against Professor Goodnow. Hall wrote to the *World:* 'And for what did he concoct these libels and publish them fifteen years after my acquittal of impeachment; aye, publish them not in an evanescent newspaper form so that apology and retraction might follow, but in an ably written historical volume, indorsed by the eminent and scholarly member of the Parliament for Aberdeen University, and that goes for permanency into all the libraries of the world for all time? He wrote these libels for a literary fee and to obtain for his employer [Bryce] the value of an American copyright.

'I owe this man no courtesy, and I do not hesitate to say that as a professor he is morally unfit to be classed in the history of Columbia College along with such teachers in it as Seth Low, Barnard, King, Duer, Anthon, Renwick, Davies, Lieber.' By the summer of 1889, Hall had determined to sue Bryce for libel. He asked for damages of ten thousand pounds and costs, alleging eighteen specific charges of libel. He later outlined them, in a letter to the *World,* as follows:

'1. That when I became Mayor I was "phenomenally dishonest," and that "my career constitutes the greatest reproach that has ever been cast upon popular government."

'2. That I was "never considered remarkable for the severity of my principles."

'3. That I "enlarged the city pay-roll to create new places."

'4. That I placed upon the Bench "corrupt Judges on whom I could rely."

'5. That my "official hands were unclean and grasping."

'6. That I aided "in unduly expending an enormous amount to procure the charter of 1870."

'7. That I "devised schemes for plundering the city."

'8. That I aided in legislative bribery.

'9. That I "checked a threatened defection of Roman Catholic votes by hinting officially that if the Catholic vote should be cast for my opponent as Mayor subventions to Catholic charitable institutions would be withdrawn by me."

'10. That I assisted in "the open bribery of a Republican member of the Legislature."

'11. That I inaugurated a "campaign of plunder."

'12. That I engaged in "methods to fill my pockets" and that my "methods were of different degrees of immorality," and "ran along the gamut of public dishonesty from abuse of official position for the advancement of private ends to transactions difficult to be distinguished from actual theft."

'13. That I purchased property on the line of street openings; packed Commissioners of Estimate for damages, so as to give me large profits.

'14. That as Mayor I aided in reducing "damages accruing to the city from $454,398 to the paltry sum of $45."

'15. That I aided in "transforming the Board of Street Openings" — which, by the way, was never organized during my Mayorality — "into a means for enriching myself."

'16. That in the "building of the new Court House for the county" I took some of the "difference between original and raised bills."

'17. That as "a leading actor in this disgraceful drama I did not fail to pay, in some measure, the penalty of my deeds."

'18. That I then chose to live out of America, meaning — as George Lewis's innuendo in the statement of claim less emphatically phrased it — thereby that I suffered the penalty of my misdeeds by being compelled to flee my country and live in exile.'

As the *World* was to point out, 'The suit came upon [Bryce] as unexpectedly as a clap of thunder out of a clear sky . . . at the very moment when the literary world was ringing with the praises of the new work.' Many of Bryce's friends were particularly upset that he should have been burdened with the suit before embarking on his honeymoon — he had just married.

Hall was represented by a London solicitor named George Lewis, a personal friend. It was reported that he took the case 'on shares,' the British manner of saying on a contingency basis. Bryce immediately retained Sir Charles Russell, the brother of Bertrand Russell, and noted for his courtroom exposure of the Pigott forgeries. He had also defended the Prince of Wales' friends — one of whom had been charged with cheating — in the recent baccarat scandal.

A reporter for the *World* interviewed Professor Goodnow, who said that he failed to see that 'any of the statements made by me in the article . . . are libelous . . . Mr. Hall, in my opinion, has a poor show to get any damages.'

Hall replied to Goodnow in a letter written in London on 19 October and published in the *World* on 1 November.

'This Professor,' he wrote, 'I am told, occupies the chair in Columbia College of Political Science — one branch of which science, in the slang of the day, whether in England or the States, is to misrepresent your opponent. . . . I only hope that he will not have the additional cowardice of remaining away from the London trial — leaving Prof. Bryce in the lurch — but will allow me to meet him in the witness box, face to face, just as all New Yorkers know I freely and frankly met my accusers sixteen years ago. And perhaps after the event he will deserve from the Aberdeen University a degree of L.L.D. — that some of my humorous friends may say signifies Doctor of Libellous Lies.'

Goodnow, meanwhile, spent the summer looking up material which would substantiate the charges he had made. He wrote Bryce, on 10 October, that he had checked the circumstances of the Tweed Ring's plan to widen Broadway and that 'it was always regarded as a great fraud.' The opening of college, he said, had prevented his devoting as much time as he needed 'to looking up details.' He added: 'I feel as I did that if it is decided that Chapter 88 is libellous we can find evidence which if not sufficient to convict Hall criminally will certainly be enough to allow us to justify whatever libel there is. People here, for the most part, seem to regard Hall's acquittal as altogether insufficient proof of his innocence and many, indeed most, of those with whom I have spoken think his chance of getting any damages is so small as to be of no account.'

III

By May of 1890, Bryce had had his first encounter with Hall, probably at a pre-trial examination, and wrote Professor Goodnow about it. 'I am very sorry to learn,' Goodnow replied, 'that he is really pushing the case. I had hoped that he had dropped it. Not having heard from him for so long a time, and having seen in the papers that Jennings was occupying with Mr. Bennett the position that Hall had, I had felt that Hall felt that he had vindicated himself sufficiently by bringing the suit and would let the matter rest. His lack of funds I supposed would prevent him from doing any more. I cannot think that any one here is helping him though the Tammany of today have been making desperate efforts lately to win public confidence.' Frederick Sheldon, an American friend of Bryce's, wrote that he had found cuttings relating to the case and that 'a democratic office-holding friend of mine suggested that "Jimmie O'Brien" might be a good witness for you against Hall. I do not know him except by reputation.'

Bryce visited the United States in the summer of 1890 and on his return to England received a letter from Poultney Bigelow, who was Minister to the Court of Saint James's, telling him that he had learned that Hall's solicitor 'is carrying on the suit ags't you as his own account & nominally for Oakey Hall. On the 1st of October Hall wrote a piteous note for an advance of a pound or so, stating that he was hard pressed. My friend has seen this letter; knows the party to whom it was written; & the services on behalf of which the advance was asked. The *Herald* & J. G. Bennett are, it would seem, quite out of it.'

Bryce now made arrangements to have testimony taken in New York before the British consul. Meanwhile, John Notman of Butler, Stillman & Hubbard was taking depositions from witnesses in New York. Hall decided to return to New York to be present at the taking of testimony. He arrived at Hoboken on 18 May 1891, on the North German Lloyd steamship *Aller*. The reporters found him waiting to have his luggage checked by the customs officials under the H sign. Their main quarry on the ship was William Henry Hurlbert, the former *World* editor, who had just undergone a lawsuit in London as a result of a breach of promise suit by

Gladys Evelyn, a well-known actress. Mrs. Hurlbert was standing near her husband as the questioning took place and one reporter noted that she was 'a stately, portly woman with brown hair and eyes, was attired in a black cloth walking gown, and wore a jet beaded wrap, and a velvet and jet hat. In her hand she carried a tortoise shell lorgnette which she constantly used in watching the Custom House officers as they examined her personal luggage.'

When the reporters got around to interviewing Hall they found him very distracted, but he pulled himself together sufficiently to tell them he had come to the United States on private business, and that the trip with Hurlbert was not prearranged. The *World* reporter wrote that Hall 'had not changed much since he went away to become an English barrister. A foreign correspondent, a teller of strange tales abroad and from abroad, an international dispenser of bon-mots, so to speak, A. Oakey Hall has the same aggressive gray mustache, the same eyeglasses [actually, they were not the old pince-nez], the same quizzing looks coming through them.' Hall said he would be at 'my wife's home at Short Hills, N.J., and in the city a great deal with headquarters at the Lotos Club. In the early Winter I shall go back to stay — yes, to stay permanently. There I can work. Here I am only a visitor.'

Hall had been met at the dock by his only son, Herbert Oakey Hall, now twenty-nine, who was wearing a mourning band on his arm. He told his father that his sister, Maria Theresa, who had married a young lawyer named William Bigelow Crosby, had died and been buried while Hall was at sea. Hall, falling upon a wicker trunk among his baggage, sobbed like a child while customs officers whispered who he was and why he was overcome with grief. Soon his son, with words of consolation, led his father away. Nothing is known of the meeting between Hall and the other members of his family.

Hall's friends made his return the occasion for celebrations. Besides private receptions, banquets were given by the New York Press Club, the Manhattan Club, the Lotos Club, and others. Stephen Fiske, now editor of the *Spirit of the Times* and dean of the New York Drama Club, arranged the first small dinner party. It was held at the Lotos Club and the table was set in front of Hall's portrait, which was decorated with evergreens. Morris Phillips, editor of the *Home Journal*, and Judge Gunning Bedford were also present. A red rose was hung over the table to indicate, according to the *Home Journal*, that everything said was 'sub rosa.' The editors of several publications were present and, as a result, several full accounts of the dinner were published, 'sub rosa' notwithstanding.

IV

In the late fall of 1891, before the British consul, the taking of testimony in the Hall vs. Bryce libel suit began. The *World* noted that most of those who were questioned were 'reluctant witnesses.' Andrew H. Green, former comptroller for the reformers, and George Jones, publisher of the *New York Times,* were among them. Green, the *Times* said, 'was by no means eager or valuable.'

It became clear, as the questioning continued, what Bryce's defense would be. It was fourfold. The first line was, the *World* said, 'a novel one and in support of it Prof. Bryce's lawyers have put upon the stand many well-known literary men in this city. It is in effect that Prof. Bryce, as a historian, was justified by the facts and by literary precedent in publishing what he did, that it is the just province of such a commentator to review historical events like the existence of the Tweed Ring, and that such expositions are demanded by the truth of history. In this it is contended that the historian must be guided by the records, whether the events treated took place twenty years ago or 100 years ago, and that he cannot be expected to personally verify every fact, but must be governed by the written record. This record, it is contended, was consulted by Prof. Bryce, through Prof. Goodnow, and that newspaper files, public documents and court records all tell the same story as the chapter on the Tweed Ring, which was founded upon them.

'The second line of defense pursued by Prof. Bryce's lawyers here has been that there was no malice behind the alleged libellous publication. Prof. Goodnow on this point has testified that he did not know Mr. Hall, and had no personal interest in the doings of the Tweed Ring beyond that of any other citizen. Prof. Bryce, when the case is called in the English court, will also testify that he did not know Mr. Hall, and could have no personal interest in the matter one way or the other beyond that of an impartial historian.

'The third defense to the libel suit is that A. Oakey Hall . . . cannot show what lawyers call "actual damages."

'The fourth defense is based upon the merits of the case, and this is the one which has given the defendant and his lawyers so much trouble. This defense is that all the statements made in the book in reference to Oakey Hall are true and that, consequently, there was no libel. In order to substantiate this the whole history of the Tweed Ring has been gone into. In case the three other objections are overruled and the case comes to a trial on the merits of the alleged libel, then the High Court of Justice will have to investigate the history of the Tweed Ring.

'For this purpose there will be laid before the court in London all the records on the subject which are on file in this city, vouchers for payments of millions of dollars from the Comptroller's office, records of courts where Tweed Ring cases were tried, the records of the Aldermanic Board for the time, reports of legislative investigating committees more or less relative to the subject and newspaper articles of the time. Was or was not A. Oakey Hall one of the Tweed Ring? is the question which the British court must answer in so far "The American Commonwealth" alleges him to have been a member.'

The hearings continued through the latter part of February, 1892. In the course of them, Prof. Goodnow was again interviewed by a *World* reporter. He repeated what he said before, that he was surprised, that he didn't think Hall could collect damages, and that 'I could only write upon information and belief. I was only ten or twelve years of age when the exposures of the Tweed Ring took place, and what I wrote for Prof. Bryce was based on the records of the time. . . . It never occurred to me that I was writing libellous matter and it would not have to anybody else.'

Hall again wrote a vigorous letter to the *World,* outlining how he had been libelled and pointing out that Goodnow's statements 'were *good now* until the other side is properly heard.'

But now Hall received a blast in the public prints from an ancient enemy — Tom Nast. Hall took it gracefully and sent Nast a photograph of himself labeled 'Exhibit 32 for Identification. Mr. Hall's compliments to Mr. Nast. Since the latter has again deemed it necessary to bring the former into pictorial prominence, he begs to enclose the last photograph showing a change of appearance rendered necessary by a pending event.' Nast replied, according to Albert Bigelow Paine, his biographer, that a change in appearance made no difference but 'a change of principles' would. Nast gave the letter to Bryce who put it in evidence, according to Paine, to show Hall 'courted publicity.'

Paine could not find out what the 'pending event' was, but there is an indication of it from something Hall wrote on 20 April 1892. On that date, he handed to Ballard Smith, an editor of the *World,* his obituary in which he said: 'I shall pass from this to the other life with only one regret — that of leaving to follow me one who is all the world to me.' He was

probably not referring to his wife, but to Mrs. John Clifton-
Clifton whom he afterwards reportedly married. This lady,
who lived in Scranton, Pennsylvania, was to tell a reporter
for the New York *Herald* that her husband, Captain John
Clifton-Clifton (of the British army) had been a 'warm
friend' of Hall's and that Hall 'stood with me at his grave
when he died in 1889.'

Meanwhile, John Notman, Bryce's American counsel, reported to the historian on the testimony being taken in New
York. 'I confess,' he wrote in the winter of 1892, 'that it is
difficult to see why Mr. Hall was not convicted on his trial,
which was upon an indictment for dereliction of duty. I have
not been able to find that the stenographer's minutes of the
testimony of the witnesses on the trial were ever written out,
but my impression is, from what I can ascertain, that the real
issue was lost sight of, and that the case went off in the minds
of the jury as though it were to prove that Hall shared in
the plunder, and that such had not been proven. That, however, was not the point of the indictment.'

V

Hall returned to London in the winter of 1892. In November, the month that Hall sailed, Bryce was in correspondence with his London solicitor, Cecil Coward, concerning
the matter of his restoring the Tweed Ring chapter, which
he had withdrawn, to *The American Commonwealth,* pending the outcome of the suit; leaving it in would have been
compounding the libel. 'I can conceive,' Coward wrote on
17 November, 'it possible that the article might be repub-
lished in such a form as to rouse him [Hall] once more to
action. At the same time it seems to me hardly possible to
doubt that the phraseology of the article might be so modi-
fied as to prevent the possibility of criticism, whilst leaving
the article itself unimpaired. As a practical measure I should

carry out the view you suggest and get the Professor [Good-now] to revise the article in his own way, and submit it to you before publication. You will thus readily ascertain whether adverse criticism could be brought to bear upon it, by consulting someone in the position of Sir Charles Russell.'

An idea of the financial burden Bryce was carrying as a result of the suit is contained in the last paragraph of Coward's letter. 'With regard to the costs already incurred,' Coward said, 'I regret to say that the amount you handed me some-time ago was not nearly sufficient to cover the actual sums we have paid out of pocket in respect of printers' charges, counsels' fees etc., but it will quite suffice if you will kindly send us a further cheque at or about Christmas.'

Although Hall had returned to England, the suit remained on the docket with neither side moving for any action. In May, 1895, Bryce wrote Coward that he would like to do something but had been advised 'to let sleeping dogs lie.' He said he was contemplating a new article on the Tweed Ring himself and wanted counsel on the advisability of publishing it in the third edition of his book, and whether to move for dismissal of the case.

'If the new issue,' Coward wrote, 'were to contain the article in its old form, there can be no doubt, I should think, of the necessity for getting the action disposed of before publication took place, because, if we were to republish it & it were decided that you were wrong, you might be mulcted in substantial damage. . . . If, on the other hand, the new article is one to which exception cannot properly be taken, then it seems to me clear that there is no reason why we should move in the present action.

'Obviously you are never likely to be better off than you are now, for if you force the case on, and get it dismissed for want of prosecution, you will never get a penny of costs out of Hall. On the other hand if he were, for spite or otherwise, to force you on to trial, you would be put to further grievous expense so that, upon the whole, it is advantageous to leave things where they are.'

Three years later, in January, 1898, Bryce wrote Coward a letter in which he proposed to issue a public statement blasting Hall and his solicitors who, it appears, had approached him for a settlement. The time had come, Bryce felt, to move to have the suit dismissed for lack of prosecution in order to pave the way for publication of the omitted chapter. Coward didn't agree with Bryce's proposals. He wrote that Hall's failing to prosecute the case actively did not necessarily indicate 'the truth of the charges made against him. At the same time there might of course have been other reasons to compel him to do as he had done — such as want of means, which if stated, would tend at any rate to take the sting out of your retort.

'As to whether it is morally right or otherwise advisable to make use of, in a public manner, of proposals made during the course of a litigation with a view to a settlement, I confess that I hold the strongest opinion to the contrary. Many a proposal is made with a view to peace, or upon some other ground, without reference to strict rights.'

As to blasting Hall's solicitors, Coward figuratively threw up his hands in horror. 'It seems to me,' he wrote, 'that your proposition would subject you to an action for libel at this instance. The action was brought by them. You say you thought it had been so brought only to induce you to buy it off — in other words, it was a blackmailing action which they had instituted. I consider to refer to the solicitors at all is not only erroneous as a matter of principle but highly dangerous.'

On 4 February 1898, Bryce's counsellor appeared before the Queen's Bench of Her Majesty's High Court of Justice in London and moved that the Hall versus Bryce suit be dismissed 'for want of prosecution.' Hall had again left England and returned to New York for good. The motion was granted.

Four days later Bryce wrote the London *Times* that he had inserted a chapter on the Tweed Ring written by himself in the third edition of *The American Commonwealth* — 'not because I doubted either the excellence of or the truth of the statements in Mr. Goodnow's chapter, but I had by 1894 procured in New York (necessarily at great expense) the evidence of many witnesses of the origins, the power and the exploits of Tammany Hall in a form which might be more easily followed by European readers.'

The chapter Bryce wrote on the Tweed Ring fitted better into the character of his book than did the original chapter written by Goodnow. Bryce's comments on Hall's part in the municipal scandals were carefully phrased and he devoted fewer words to Hall than had Goodnow. Bryce's account remained in all subsequent editions of *The American Commonwealth*.

15

THE LONG DECLINE

I

SIX YEARS BEFORE DISMISSAL of the suit against Bryce, Hall had sailed from Bremen on the steamship *Lahn*. He arrived in New York 30 December 1892, to the surprise of his friends. One reason for his unexpected return was probably his friendship with Mrs. Clifton-Clifton. There may have been another reason: his love for New York. A writer for the *Dramatic Mirror* asked him why he had given up a lucrative law practice in London to return. Hall replied: 'Because New York is the finest city on earth. Nowhere in the world is there such an urban vista as greets your eye looking up Fifth Avenue from the corner of Forty-second Street. The cathedral towers, the splendid variety and profusion of architecture are matchless. And where, either in Paris or London, can be found the equal of Madison Square at eight or nine o'clock in the evening? The well-dressed, animated crowds, the brilliant light, the shop windows! My dear fellow, New York is good enough for me to spend the rest of my days in.'

He had made a complete turnabout.

Apparently Hall decided to spend the rest of his days practicing law, because he set up offices in the new Vanderbilt

Building at the corner of Nassau and Beekman Streets in partnership with Bernard J. Douras and August G. Beyer under the firm name of Oakey Hall, Douras & Beyer. But his effort was not successful. The few cases he received were assigned to him by judges who liked him and wanted to help him out. Cases assigned by courts sometimes carry no fee, and when they do, it is apt to be small. One of the cases to which Hall was assigned was that of Antonio Blanco, on trial for murder. As he began his address to the jury, Assistant District Attorney O'Hara invited him to come inside the rail where the prosecutor sits. It was a gracious gesture to a former District Attorney. Hall accepted the invitation and deposited his books and papers on the desk beside the assistant D.A.

'Suddenly,' according to the New York *Journal*, 'he threw his head in the air and left the courtroom. He returned after a few moments and took his old place outside the rail where advocates ordinarily speak for their clients. Mr. O'Hara whispered to him and told him that he was welcome to speak from the District Attorney's place, but Mr. Hall shook his head and said, "Oh, no. I have changed my mind. I thank you for your courtesy, but that place in there is full of ghosts." '

Another client whom he was assigned to defend was Emma Goldman, the anarchist.

Hall's wife now lived at Millburn, New Jersey, with their only unmarried daughter, Josephine Barnes Hall. He apparently visited there, but his own residence was in New York. Josephine kept in touch with him. She was not only extremely devoted to him but used every opportunity to proclaim her father's innocence. A letter he wrote to her after he had taken up his law practice in New York tells something of their relationship, and of his own state of mind:

'My darling Joe. I am when in the office always in mood to be "bothered" (your word) and anywhere to hear from you or the Mama on affairs. I have long ago become used to *exigencies.* . . . I am busied night and day trying to push law things; and sometimes am tempted to be discouraged but then come up "smiling in the next round." I did not however give up too soon the worry and wear and tear of coming up and going down and keeping tally of trains. I am sorry too I was so ill at Millburn for it has left nasty memories. I get nothing as yet from law. All from newspapers and am at the recorder often of nights . . . Kisses to the Mama and self.

> 'Lovingly,
> 'The Dad.'

Hall was at work 'often of nights' writing the same piece over and over again. He could always sell the story of when he was Mayor to a newspaper, or personal recollections of this or that in New York's history. The Sunday *World* ran a five-column piece by him entitled 'My Mayoralty. Boss Tweed and His Methods Compared with the More Absolute Autocracy of the Present Tammany Hall Boss — Interesting Inside History of the Days of the old Tweed Ring.' The Bok Syndicate sent out a piece entitled, 'When I Was Mayor of New York City. A. Oakey Hall Relates His Experiences.' In them, he protested his complete innocence. For the *Green Bag,* a serious semi-literary magazine of interest to members of the bar, he wrote a detailed article called 'The English and American Bar in Contrast.'

Besides his newspaper and magazine articles, Hall was completing, during the mid-'nineties, two very ambitious projects. One was a volume called *Courts and Judges of New York City,* to be published by the firm of Moses King at 346 Broadway. A prospectus for the book noted that Hall was writing the 'individual sketches of judges, lawyers and court clerks,' and that he was one of the 'few men who could personally recall and characterize so many of the judges of the past half century.' The other project was a history of the Tweed Ring which was completed in 1898 but never published. Its whereabouts today are unknown. Hall told a reporter for the *Herald* that when the volume was published he would be 'fully vindicated.'

Despite his journalistic activities, Hall was rapidly fading into obscurity. If he did not know it himself, he received a reminder. 'Oakey Hall looks well,' a writer for the *Post* said. 'I saw him yesterday in a Fourth Avenue car, comfortably wrapped in a hospitable ulster, and I thought as man after man entered the car, none of whom apparently recognized him, How soon we are forgotten.'

Hall's appearance had changed considerably. Pale, with dark eyes accentuating his paleness, his hair was now white, as were his beard and bushy mustache. He still dressed impeccably; a photograph taken of him in 1898 shows him wearing a wing collar with a flowing back bow tie with thin white stripes. His jacket was buttoned high on his chest and the lapels were edged with silk.

On 9 March 1897, his wife, Katherine Louise Barnes Hall, died in New York City. Her death, the New York *Mercury* said, 'recalls a lively period in the history of New York when A. Oakey Hall was Mayor and ran things in his own breezy fashion. Mrs. Hall was a beautiful woman when the ex-Mayor married her years ago, was very prominent during her husband's administration of municipal affairs, and was at the head of many charitable institutions and always ready to extend a helping hand to the poor and needy. Mrs. Hall was quite wealthy in her own right and came of the well-known New York family of Barnes. Both her father, Joseph Barnes, and her grandfather, James S. Barnes, were prominent in New York's financial world.'

II

According to newspaper accounts, Hall married a second time. His bride was Mrs. John Clifton-Clifton, who told a reporter she and Hall were married in New Jersey. But one of Hall's descendants, who made a study of the Hall genealogy, searched in vain for a record of their marriage.

Not long after his marriage, if such it was, Hall was attending a meeting of the Salvation Army at its headquarters, 126 West Fourteenth Street, presided over by Commander Frederick de Latour Booth-Tucker. On the complaint of one Phineas Smith who lived at 131 West Thirteenth Street, almost directly in back of the Army's headquarters, the commander was charged with 'maintaining an ill-governed and disorderly house' where two hundred men and women 'assembled in the night time there to be and to remain singing and playing on musical instruments, making a great noise and otherwise misbehaving themselves, whereby the comfort and repose of the people residing in the neighborhood were disturbed to the common nuisance of the people of the State of New York.' Hall immediately volunteered to defend the commander and appeared in the Court of General Sessions the next day to plead his client not guilty. According to the *Evening Journal,* he addressed the court 'in a sarcastic tone of voice,' saying that his client was charged with the 'heinous crime of holding an all-night prayer meeting.' He then pressed for an immediate trial. The charge was eventually dismissed. Hall's attendance at the Salvation Army meeting as a worshipper was an outward sign of an inner spiritual transition which was to culminate nine months later in conversion to the Catholic Church.

At this time, Hall and his bride were occupying, according to the *Times,* 'a cozy suite of apartments on West Tenth Street.' He told friends that although he was going on seventy-two he felt as young as when he was thirty. There were still times when he felt compelled to protest his innocence of any wrongdoing. In July, 1897, a story in the Troy *Press* stated that he had shared Tweed's plunder and was now living out his life thoroughly discredited. Hall wrote the editor:

'If your New York correspondent makes usually as many mistakes as he has made therein, his reliability (which my life-long friend, Charley Dana, makes the summum bonum of a correspondent) needs constant watching.

'In the first place, I was never charged with sharing Tweed's plunder, but only for the misdemeanor of neglect of duty as Mayor in not detecting frauds — which the jury found were so ingenious as to baffle suspicion until some of the fradulent gang confessed.'

Hall went on to suggest that it was he who had set in motion the reform movement of 1871. 'A message,' he wrote, 'for investigation that I sent to the board of supervisors led to the citizens' Committee of Seventy with whom I entirely cooperated, for my accusation was not of it but of the Republican organization as a political move. I did succeed in removing Tweed, and myself appointed in his place an incumbent recommended by the reform committee.'

Three months after the Troy *Press* incident, Hall received extremely friendly treatment from his old Nemesis, the *New York Times*. The occasion was the fall Mayoralty campaign in which Seth Low was running for the office as the Citizens' Union candidate. T. A. Masterson, a writer for the *Times Illustrated Magazine,* wrote an article on the eight former mayors who were still living. The article included an excellent studio photograph of Hall and a friendly description of him in which there was no mention of the Ring scandals. Hall was quoted at length on the past and future of New York City:

'I came to this city when very young, and knew it well before I was old enough to go to college. The ferryboats then were about the size of our present steam tugs, but the street stages were immense affairs. The biggest of them was the

Lady Washington. It ran from the Castle Garden to Bond Street, which was then the north of the city, and the fare was a shilling. The New York of my boyhood above Bond Street was a country of farms and gardens, with a house, or perhaps a little cluster of houses, standing here and there, as we see now fifty miles from the city. As late as 1857 the present Central Park, below the reservoir, was a district of rocks and ravines. The earth to fill the ravines was carted there at great expense. The big ranges of oaks, elms, and maples now along the Mall never germinated there. They were carted in from Westchester County when good-sized trees, and I saw them transplanted.'

'Judging from the past growth of the metropolis,' Masterson concluded, 'Mr. Hall thinks that within thirty years it will contain 10,000,000 people. On the north he predicts that it will take in everything up to and including White Plains, and on the south, the greater portion of Long Island.'

That same fall, his daughter Josephine began clearing out Valley View in order to sell the property. She wrote her father to ask what he wanted done with the books, papers, and other belongings he still had there. He sent her a letter authorizing her to keep, sell, or give away his things, as he had no place for his books. He said he was using the Astor and Mercantile libraries. He suggested that she sell his collection of coins and keep the funds.

'I enclose a note to hand Caddie [another of his daughters],' he wrote. 'Say to her that I got her sweet note and if, or when, she comes to the Murray Hill Hotel I shall be glad to take note. Just now I am in Anti-Tammany politics and *perhaps* in the coming political shuffle I may turn up an ace. But I fear my bad luck still reigns. Lovingly, The Dad.'

His bad luck apparently continued to reign, for five months later, when Bryce's attorneys in London asked that Hall's suit be dismissed 'for want of prosecution,' the motion, which was granted, was accompanied by a court order directing him to pay the costs of the suit.

A letter Hall wrote to the son of an old friend indicates that Bryce had obtained a judgment against him in New York. The letter, on Lotos Club stationery, was addressed to A. H. Joline, Esq. 'Dear Adrian,' Hall wrote. 'In my old age (but with head and heart as young as ever) I have fallen upon ill financial times and am threatened with a judgment debtor examination of an Americanized London judgment and the consequent parading of my name and circumstances in yellow journalism and a picture and other impertinences, for I have been too prominent to escape slaughter. Under the circumstances of my Shylock having suggested a minimum compromise some of the old students at suggestion of dear old Jim Bookstaver, Woodford, Edelstein, McCook, etc., have chipped in sums between 15 and 25 so that very little remains to save my pride. I therefore venture to ask that you also join them to the extent of your ability.'

There was no consolation in this world. On 25 March 1898, he and his wife were baptized and received into the Roman Catholic Church at the Church of St. Paul the Apostle, Fifty-ninth Street and Columbus Circle, by Father George M. Searle, CSP, a member of the Paulist Order. His sponsors were Peter B. Sweeny and Sweeny's sister, Mrs. Mary L. Bradley. In speaking of his conversion to a reporter, Hall explained that both he and his second wife had had 'leanings' toward Catholicism 'all our lives and have awaited a favorable opportunity of making up our minds.' He had been attracted to Father Searle by a book the priest had written called *Plain Facts for Fair Minds*. Following his conversion, Hall wrote articles for Catholic magazines on Catholic doctrine. Through the spring, summer, and early fall of 1898, Hall completed his book on courts and judges of New York City and delivered the manuscript to the publisher. 'I am getting ready to die,' he wrote a friend; 'my peace is made with God, but not with this hard world.' He had moved from West Tenth Street and was living with his bride in an apartment at 68 Washington Square South.

On Friday morning, 7 October 1898, he awoke shortly before ten o'clock in great pain. His physician, Dr. Antonio Fanoni, was called and he recognized that Hall's heart was failing rapidly. His wife, who was at his bedside, sent for his son, Herbert Oakey Hall, and his four daughters. Toward evening Hall said, 'I think this will be my last illness.' Shortly after 8:30 his wife asked him if he wanted a glass of water and he replied, 'No, thanks, the water is too warm.' At 8:45 he died.

III

Hall's death, in a way, achieved the public vindication for which he had struggled for more than a quarter of a century. The New York *World* devoted half of its front page to it. This was largely the result of Hall's having left with Ballard Smith, of the *World* staff, an obituary notice he had written himself, 'to be used for the *World* and upon his decease; and to be honorably filed in its obituary archives without opening until that event; be it soon or later. Easter season, 1892.'

'I was often in life twitted with eccentricity,' he wrote. 'It is the trait of the Oakey family. . . . And doubtless the fact that I write my own obituary notice will be regarded as the crowning eccentricity of an eccentric career.' He then sketched briefly and lightly his life as District Attorney, Mayor, journalist, and actor. In 1876, he wrote, he had been severely threatened with symptoms of paresis and 'medically

---

Hall left his 'autobiographic' obituary with an editor of the *World* six years and six months before his death. When he died the *World* printed this endorsement which Hall had written on the envelope containing the text of the obituary.

Obituary notice
for
Mr Oakey Hall
to be used
for the World —
upon his decease:
& to be honorably
filed in its
Obituary archives
never without
opening until
that event: be
it soon or later

Easter Season
1892

It is autobiographic

ordered to adopt the only reliable remedy adapted to that insidious disorder — change of employment. I, at first, became an actor but really quitted the stage because that profession was distasteful and health-distressing to an aged mother — to whose nurture and care I owed all that was good in my composition. . . .

'I claim that my episode as District Attorney during so many years entitles me to claim that (notwithstanding my many mistakes in other respects) I deserve metropolitan remembrance.

'I, as prosecutor was never persecutor. I never convicted an innocent accused. I perhaps made mercy too elastic. I never placed victory above justice. And I quitted office without even political aspersion upon any of my official acts. . . .'

The *New York Times* noted that Hall 'left on record his own regrets that he should have been tempted by the offer of a destiny irrelevant to his faculties and acquirements. . . .

'It was their [the Ring members'] game that he played and it was they who pocketed the winnings. His official salaries and his normal earnings at all times comprised his estate. . . .

'His lack of any sense of personal dignity was perhaps the chief defect of a character which had many kindly and attractive faults. . . . He lacked the fitness of things . . . conducting a sort of vaudeville newspaper and personally contributing to it the most atrocious and trivial jokes.

'It is not seemly for an ex-Mayor to make his appearance as an actor in a play of his own composition even if the play and the acting had been good instead of very bad. Perhaps the episode may be taken to denote an actual mental unsoundness from which at one time Mr. Hall suffered, according to his own subsequent confession. But the eccentricities which did not go the length of insanity, nevertheless went far enough greatly to injure the eccentric with sober men.

The curse of Reuben was the curse of Oakey Hall. "Unstable as water, thou shalt not excel." It was the want of stability and the want of dignity which made one of the most kindly and really innocent of human beings a tool of public plunderers and prevented him from becoming and remaining one of the most honored citizens of New York.'

Hall had asked that his funeral be simple and private. There were no pallbearers but, according to the *Times,* 'many persons prominent in the political, social and business life of New York were present' at the requiem mass at St. Leo's Church on Twenty-eighth between Fifth and Madison avenues. 'Nearly all' the state Supreme Court judges were present. The Lotos Club delegation was headed by General Daniel E. Sickles, the Civil War hero, and the Press Club delegation by Joseph Howard, Jr. Also present were Peter 'Brains' Sweeny, who had persuaded Hall to run for Mayor; George A. Story, son of the great Harvard jurist; Aaron H. Vanderpoel, son of Hall's old law partner; Judge Charles P. Daly, who had presided at one of Hall's trials; and former Sheriff James O'Brien, who had betrayed the Ring conspiracy to the *Times.*

O'Brien had been helping Hall financially in recent years and when questioned about it, told a reporter: 'Of the kindliness of Mr. Hall there could be no better illustration than his relations toward me. In my fight against the Tweed Ring I assailed him again and again, and justly, but without shaking his confidence in the members of the Ring, whose willing accomplice he seemed to be. He learned later that I was right. But I never saw the man lose his temper, and after the trouble was over we became the greatest of friends. He bore me no ill will for the unpleasant task I was compelled to undertake.'

Father Thomas J. Ducey said the Mass, assisted by Father Searle, who had baptized Hall. Father Ducey, in delivering a funeral eulogy, said he had known Hall from his boyhood and that 'he had maintained his independence and his self-respect even in his adversity.

'Oakey Hall was an honest man,' Father Ducey continued. 'It was his misfortune to hold the high office of Mayor of New York at a time when control of this party was in the hands of men without integrity and without honor. He left the office poor. What better testimonial could there be to his honesty! Let it be said that those who in the day of his power bent the cringing suppliant knee in the hope that position and preferment might follow shunned him and avoided him in his hour of adversity and poverty.'

Hall's body was placed beside that of his first wife in the Hall family vault at Trinity Cemetery at 155th Street near the Hudson River. Just how poor he was when he died was revealed two months later, on 18 December 1898, in a carefully worded story in the *New York Times* which said: 'A few days after the death of A. Oakey Hall an old friend of the ex-Mayor, prompted by the remembrance of many kindly acts, called at his late home. After much persuasion Mrs. Hall reluctantly acknowledged that her husband's sudden death had left her not only without funds but seriously embarrassed with many debts for household necessities. It was intimated that Mr. H. had many friends who would gladly come to her relief did they know her condition. A. Oakey Hall's second wife was the widow of Captain Clifton, an English Army officer. She is a proud, refined woman and shrank from assistance through the medium of subscribing friends saying, "That in time she would secure a situation and work off Mr. Hall's debts." Finally she permitted the matter to be presented to a few of the oldest friends of the late ex-Mayor.

'Only two made response, Charles P. Daly and Fred R. Coudert. A subscription list was then started, these two each contributing $100. It was then handed to Oswald Ottendorfer and John D. Crimmins who cooperated in the work. Henry Clews consented to act as Treasurer of the fund. On October 10 Mr. Clews handed to Mrs. Hall $2,335, the amount received from 74 subscribers.'

Mrs. Hall went to London to live but returned to New York in November, 1901, to play the role of a bishop's wife in a play by Clyde Fitch called *The Way of the World*, starring Elsie De Wolfe. The *Herald* noted that 'Those of her friends who were present were glad to see that she acquitted herself very well in what she had to do, and bore herself with distinction in the crowd of guests in the drawing room. She is of fine appearance, graceful and dignified in bearing and, to employ a much misused term, has the manners of a lady.'

Mrs. Hall was interviewed by several reporters and she told them that she planned to make the stage her profession and that she hoped, in her next part, to do something more than 'walk across the room.' The *World* carried a large photograph of her which showed her to be a handsome Victorian *grande dame* which, she said, Fitch had told her was the kind of part she ought always to play.

All of Hall's children are dead, and there are descendants of only one of them — Alice d'Assignie Hall, who married Charles Rossire. Shortly before her death in 1931, Josephine Hall presented to the New York Public Library a collection of nearly 3,000 books, pamphlets, documents, scrapbooks, and miscellaneous clippings relating to her father's life. She had zealously guarded and defended his memory through the years. She was probably responsible for a retraction concerning Oakey Hall which appeared in the *New York Times* as late as 1923, following a feature story on his life and career which, in places, seemed to reflect upon him. The feature story was published on 26 August; on 12 September the *Times* made a generous disavowal of any intent to vilify the dead Mayor. Hall, it said, had 'waited long for his vindication, but it came full enough and sweeping enough to satisfy him for the long years of humiliation under the false charge.' Then the *Times* declared:

'At a dinner given to the jurors ex-Judge Noah Davis [who presided at the Tweed Ring trials] made a speech which astonished every one who heard it. In it the Judge said that he had been connected with the trials and exposure of Tweed, and he wished to say that Mr. Hall was innocent of the charge under which he had rested for years. He knew, said the Judge, of his own personal knowledge, the utter baselessness of the charge. This view has since been the accepted one as to the part that Mr. Hall played in that era of crime and defalcation.'

ACKNOWLEDGMENTS AND BIBLIOGRAPHY

First of all, I want to thank William Shawn, editor of *The New Yorker,* for assigning me to do a Profile of A. Oakey Hall. Why he didn't draw and quarter me when I turned up twenty-seven months later with close to 100,000 words, I can only attribute to his Schweitzer-like nature. He understood when I explained I had found the subject so engrossing that I was unable to have done with it until I had exhausted it.

Three of Hall's grandchildren were living when I embarked on my research, Colonel Charles C. Rossire, Mr. Louis D. Rossire, and Mrs. Katherine Rossire Hamilton, all of Hyannis, Massachusetts. I missed meeting Colonel Rossire by six hours. He died of a heart attack while I was en route to Cape Cod to confer with him and his brother and sister. He served with distinction in World War I, was a leader in his community, and, to borrow one of his grandfather's phrases, raised 'a very interesting family.' At his death, the flag at New York's City Hall was lowered to half-staff in his honor. After the funeral, Mr. Rossire and Mrs. Hamilton very graciously received me and turned over to me a large number of books and pamphlets, unpublished Hall letters, papers, and manuscripts, and memorabilia relating to his career. They have in-

structed me to turn this collection over to the New York Public Library as a gift to perpetuate the memory of Colonel
Charles C. Rossire. I am also grateful to Miss Gladys Thatcher
Oakey of Newburgh, New York, who is related to Oakey Hall.
Mrs. Blanche F. Whitaker of Orange County, New York,
wrote extremely interesting letters about visiting the Hall
family when she was a little girl.

Doris and Ross Marvin of Irvington-on-Hudson were helpful neighbors literally and spiritually. Carl Carmer of Octa-
gon House, Irvington-on-Hudson, lent me source books and
gave me encouragement. Others who helped are Richard
Rovere, Dwight Macdonald, Hobart G. Weekes, Geoffrey
Hellman, the late Gustave S. Lobrano, and Ebba Jonsson, all
of *The New Yorker,* and Henley Hill, of New York. Samuel
Hopkins Adams of Wide Waters, Auburn, New York, and the
late John A. Hennessey of Brooklyn, New York, veterans of
yesterday's City Hall beat, recalled the atmosphere of old Park
Row for me.

Paul Crowell, who covers City Hall today for the *New York
Times,* was extremely helpful. I am also indebted to Peter
Sedgwick of the British Foreign Service, a grandson of that
great and vitriolic *New York Times* editor and contemporary
of Hall's, Louis John Jennings; Meyer Berger, reporter number one, of New York; Edwin P. Kilroe of New York, a leading authority on and collector of Tammanyana; Francis
Brown of New York and Amherst, Mass., author of a biography
of another of Hall's contemporaries, Henry Jarvis Raymond,
also a *New York Times* editor; M. R. Werner of New York,
author of the best book on Tammany Hall ever written and a
friend who went far beyond the usual bounds of friendship to
help and encourage me; Milton Halsey Thomas of Columbia
University, scholar and authority on New York City history,
who didn't laugh when he caught some frightful errors in my
manuscript; Victor Jones of the *Boston Globe;* Frank Hogan,

District Attorney of New York County; Carmine de Sapio, today's leader of Tammany Hall, with whom I've had many interesting discussions which changed neither of our minds.

To Carroll Bowen and Leona Capeless of the Oxford University Press I am especially grateful for getting the manuscript into shape for publication.

Reginald Townsend of New York very graciously helped me to an understanding of the Union Club aspect of Hall's life, lent me the excellent history of the club he wrote, and arranged for me to use the club's library.

John G. Bowen, while a scholar at Oxford University, went through the James Bryce papers which are currently being catalogued. With the help of Dr. R. W. Hunt, who bears the title of Keeper of Western Manuscripts, and Charles Batey, Printer to the University, I received photostats of pertinent material relating to Hall's lawsuit against the author of *The American Commonwealth.*

Charles Norman, poet, novelist, raconteur, wit, editor de luxe, and friend, undertook the job of reducing the verbiage to printable length. His judgment in what to cut and his critical view of Hall's poetry were especially useful.

To my wife, Marjory Luce Hill Bowen, who is also a professional librarian, goes my deepest sympathy for nursing me through the ordeal of writing this book. I am also indebted to her for preparing the index.

That great powerhouse of historical research, the New York Public Library, provided invaluable research and was my headquarters. I am particularly indebted to Robert W. Hill, Director of the Manuscript Division, and to Miss Elizabeth Roth of the Print Room.

Judge Edward J. McCullen of the Court of General Sessions arranged for me to see the sanctum sanctorum of the Tammany Society. What's left of it turns out to be a small upstairs room at the National Democratic Club located at Madison Avenue and 37th Street. Some of the books and Indian ceremonial relics of 'the old days' are there.

The Edwin P. Kilroe Tammany Collection at the Columbia University Library was very useful and contains the original typescript of Tweed's confession.

The New-York Historical Society's Wilmer Leech and Wayne Andrews provided help and research materials. The Morgan Library was also helpful. Other librarians to whom I am indebted are David C. Mearns, Chief, Manuscripts Division of The Library of Congress; John R. Russell, University Librarian of The University of Rochester Library; Miss Selma Smith of the Municipal Reference Library of New York.

For the kind of material I wanted on Hall, I leaned heavily on the newspapers of his day. A large number of the more interesting items I would never have found had they not been clipped and preserved by his daughter, Josephine. Some of the New York papers I quoted were the *Times, The Leader,* the *Tribune,* the *Sun,* the *Herald,* the *World,* the *Post,* and the *Telegram.* I also quoted the Pittsburgh *Chronicle* and the Albany *Argus.* Among the magazines I found useful were *Every Saturday, Spirit of the Times, The Mirror, New York Illustrated News, Harper's Weekly, Frank Leslie's Weekly,* the *Home Journal,* and the *North American Review.*

Among the papers of A. Oakey Hall, I found a note in his handwriting which said: 'My Writings worth preserving, Reminiscences of Story, the U.S. Justice, Vol 5 of International magazine 175 & page 503 of the 2nd vol of his Life by his son; "August Reverie" Vol 4 Inter. Magazine page 477 Questions from a worn out lorgnette Ibid page 187. The Ambitious Booklet International Magazine Vol 2 page 477.'

It is interesting that he did not mention the piece he wrote called 'Dinner at the Mayor's.' It was regarded as good when he was alive and I think it remains a graceful and excellent piece of reporting.

Here are other published works by Hall:

The Manhattaner in New Orleans, or Phases of 'Crescent City' Life. New York, 1851.

Grand Juror's Guide. New York, 1855.

Old Whitey's Christmas Trot: A Story for the Holidays. New York, 1857.

Horace Greeley Decently Dissected (in a letter on Horace Greeley addressed by A. Oakey Hall to Joseph Hoxie, Esq.). New York, 1862.

Address delivered before Tammany Society 4 July 1864. Pamphlet.

The People of the State of New York *vs.* John A. Dix, and five others. Outline of Argument of District Attorney Hall for Prosecution. New York, 1864.

The Congressman's Christmas Dreams and the Lobby Member's Happy New Year: A Holiday Sketch. New York, 1870–71.

My Sister's Well-Rounded Life. A Memorial Epistle. New York [1873].

Syllabus of Mr. Hall's Argument against the Theatre License Law. New York, 1873 (?).

American Legislation for the Inebriate. London, 1884.

In the bibliography which follows I have set down the books that I found most useful.

Asbury, Herbert. *The French Quarter.* New York, 1936.

Bigelow, John. *Life of Samuel J. Tilden.* New York, 1895.

Breen, Matthew P. *Thirty Years of New York Politics.* New York, 1899.

Bryce, James. *The American Commonwealth,* first edition. New York, 1888.

Clinton, Henry Lauren. *Celebrated Trials.* New York, 1897.

Every Saturday. Boston, 21 October 1871.

Hall, Abraham Oakey. Catalogue of the Library of A. O. Hall to be sold at auction January 17, 1881 and following days by Bangs & Co. New York, 1881.

Hall, A. Oakey. Scrapbooks of newspaper clippings relating to A. Oakey Hall. Fourteen volumes. New York Public Library Collections.

Headley, J. T. *The Great Riots of New York*. New York, 1873.

Kilroe, Edwin P. Collection of Papers regarding Tammany Hall. Library of Columbia University, New York.

Lynch, Denis Tilden. *The Wild Seventies*. New York, 1941.

Morris, Lloyd. *Incredible New York*. New York, 1951.

Myers, Gustavus. *History of Tammany Hall*. New York, 1924.

New York County Grand Jury. Evidence before the Grand Jury in the Case of A. Oakey Hall. New York, 1871.

New York Times. Obituary page, 8 October 1898.

Riordon, William L. *Plunkitt of Tammany Hall*. Introduction by Roy V. Peel. New York, 1948. (This was first published in 1905 and is subtitled *A Series of very plain Talks on Very Practical politics, delivered by Ex-Senator George Washington Plunkitt, the Tammany Philosopher, from his rostrum—the New York County Court-House Bootblack Stand—and recorded by William L. Riordon*.)

Rovere, Richard H. *Howe & Hummel*. New York, 1947.

Seitz, Don Carlos. *The James Gordon Bennetts*. Indianapolis, 1928.

Steffens, Lincoln. *Autobiography*. New York, 1931.

Stokes, Isaac Newton Phelps. *Iconography of Manhattan Island, 1498, 1909*. New York, 1915–28.

Tanner, Edwin Platt. *Modern Party Battles*, vol. VII of *The History of the State of New York*, edited by Alexander C. Flick. New York, 1935. Esp. chapter V, 'Postwar Problems and Political Reformers.'

Thomas, Milton Halsey. *The Diaries of George Templeton Strong*. New York, 1954.

Werner, M. R. *Tammany Hall*. New York, 1928.

Wilson, J. G. *Memorial History of the City of New York*, vol. III. New York, 1893.

Wingate, Charles F. 'An Episode in Municipal Government, The Tweed Ring,' *North American Review*, vol. CXIX, p. 359 and vol. CXXI, p. 113.

INDEX

Adams, Charles Francis, 168
American Commonwealth, 250ff.
Americus Club, 73, 75
Anderson, Mrs. Elizabeth Ann, 15
Apollo Hall, 169
Appleton, William H., 138
Arthur, Chester A., 202
Astor, John Jacob, 79

Baker, Alfred A., 175
Bancroft, George, 56
Barlow, Frances C., 157ff., 245
Barnard, George Gray, 112
Barnes, James S., 156, 267
Barnes, Joseph Nye, 29, 267
Barnum, Phineas T., 184
Baxter, Edward W., 131
Bedford, Gunning, 155, 177, 257
Beecher, Henry Ward, 58, 153,
    168, 184
Bell, Isaac, 138
Belmont, August, 46ff., 63, 138
Benjamin, Judah P., 26, 46, 231
Bennett, James Gordon, 45, 54,
    246
Bennett, James Gordon, Jr., 46,
    213, 231, 239
Bergh, Henry, 202

Beyer, August G., 265
Bigelow, John, 168
Bigelow, Poultney, 255
Bill, Edward, 130
Blanco, Antio, 265
Blossom Club, 75
Blunt, Nathaniel Bowditch, 31, 33
Bookstover, Jim, 271
Booth-Tucker, Frederick de La-
    tour, 268
Boucicault, Dion, 199
Bradley, John, 40
Bradley, Mrs. Mary L., 271
Brady, John R., 174, 175, 216
Bratanahl, George Carl, 251
Breen, Matthew P., 38, 76
Brennan, Matthew T., 75
Brill, Charles J., 179
Brook Club, 45
Brougham, John, 201
Brown, Augustus L., 31, 83, 129,
    152, 179, 202, 211
Brown, E. D., 79
Bryant, William Cullen, 48, 99,
    185
Bryce, James, 249ff.
Buckley, Thomas C., 158, 177
Burdell murder case, 5ff.

Burrill, John E., 158

Cailicot, Theophilus C., 30
Calumet Club, 46
Cardozo, Albert, 202
Cardozo, Gus D., 66
Carnochan, Dr. J. E., 188
Carter, Timothy Jarvis, 22, 32
Chapin, Edwin Hubbell, 184
Choate, Joseph H., 109ff.
Clapp, Henry, Jr., 54
Clark, Aaron, 20
Clark, Matthias, 166
Clemenceau, Georges, 68
Clendenin, James W., 138
Clews, Henry, 277
Clifton-Clifton, Mrs. John, 260, 264, 267, 277
Clinton, George, 60
Clinton, Henry Lauren, 5, 7, 158, 162, 169, 197, 221
Committee of Seventy, 110, 151
Comstock, Anthony, 153
Comstock, Lucius S., 153, 155
Conkling, Col. F. A., 50
Conkling, Roscoe, 245
Connolly, Richard B., 40, 63, 84, 112ff., 131, 164, 171, 222
Cook, N. H., 221
Cooper, Peter, 169, 194
Copeland, William S., 82, 119
Coudert, Fred R., 276
Coward, Cecil, 260
Crimmins, John D., 277
Crosby, William Bigelow, 256
Cunningham, Mrs. Emma Augusta, 6ff., 162
Curtis, George William, 185
Cutting, Robert, 201
Cutting, William, 138

Daly, Augustin, 177, 198
Daly, Charles P., 158, 177, 275ff.
Dana, Charles A., 185, 269
Daniels, Judge, 190ff.
Davies, Ella Morgan, 212

Davies, Henry E., 7
Davis, Noah, 245, 278
de la Montaignie, John, 14, 22
De Wolfe, Elsie, 277
Delmonico, Charles, 202
Democratic Convention, 1872, 168
Depression of 1873, 190
Dix, John A., 58, 182
Donohue, Mary, 5
Douglas National Committee, 47
Douras, Bernard J., 265
Draft Riots, 1863, 40
Draper, J. H., 156
Ducey, Father Thomas J., 275

Eckel, John J., 6
Edelstein, William, 152
Edwards, Charles, 13
Ely, Smith, 212
Euterpean Society, 30
Evelyn, Gladys, 256
Everitt, L. I., 194
Eytinge, Rose, 201

Fairchild, Charles S., 220
Fanoni, Dr. Antonio, 272
Farragut, David G., 58
Fearing, Henry S., 138
Field, David Dudley, 152
Fisk, James, Jr., 80, 94, 151
Fiske, Stephen, 53, 217
Fitch, Clyde, 277
Fithian, Joel A., 158
Florence, Billy, 75
Foley, John, 112, 185
Foord, John, 85
Ford, Gordon L., 211
Forrest, George J., 129
Fulton, Chandos, 199

Garrison, Commodore, 202
Garvey, Andrew J., 78, 164, 176
Garvey, Mrs. Andrew J., 134
Garvin, Samuel, 174
Genet, Henry W., 60, 190
Gilbert, John, 201

Gingold, Victor, 248
Godwin, Parke, 48
Goldman, Emma, 265
Goodnow, Frank Johnson, 250, 258ff.
Gould, Jay, 31, 233ff.
Gould, William A., 221
Graham, John, 152, 155
Grant, Ulysses S., 182, 185
Gray, George Griswold, 138
Greeley, Horace, 54, 58, 60, 106ff., 134, 153, 167, 182, 184
Green, Andrew H., 114, 118, 257
Greenleaf, Simon, 23
Grinnell, Moses H., 138
Griswold, Rufus W., 29

Hackett, John K., 177, 196, 202
Hall, Abraham Oakey: ancestry, 4, 17; appearance, 4, 52; birth, 17; Assistant District Attorney, 34; children, 35; death, 272; education, 21ff.; elections, District Attorney, 5, 34, 37; Mayor, 51, 57, 58, 80, 132; expulsion from Union Club, 137ff.; Grand Jury hearings, 118ff., 153, 156, 173; humorist, 52ff.; law practice, 26, 28, 31ff., 245; lectures, 43, 248; letter from Tweed, 61; marriage, 5, 29, 32, 267; newspaper work, 65, 72, 232, 236, 239; trials, 158ff., 174ff., 190ff.; writings, 15, 21, 26ff., 29ff., 42ff., 55, 57, 71, 170, 190, 199ff., 209, 266
Hall, Alice d'Assignie (Mrs. Charles Rossire), 35, 167, 277
Hall, Augustus Oakey Vanderpoel, 35
Hall, Cara de la Montaignie, 16, 33, 167
Hall, Elsie Lansing, 167, 241
Hall, Herbert Oakey, 36, 167, 256
Hall, James F., 192
Hall, Josephine Barnes, 35, 167, 270, 277

Hall, Katherine Louise Barnes, 5, 29, 137, 167, 191, 265, 267
Hall, Louise Oakey (Mrs. George Carl Bratanahl), 35, 167, 251
Hall, Marcia d'Assignie, 19, 167, 189
Hall, Maria Theresa (Mrs. William Bigelow Crosby), 16, 35, 167, 256
Hall, Morgan James, 17
Hall, William, 17
Haney, Jesse, 213
Harper, Fletcher, Jr., 81, 153
Harper's Weekly, 58, 81, 95ff.
Harrison, Benjamin, 246
Hart, Josh, 236
Havemeyer, William F., 109, 122, 176, 182, 185
Hay, John, 184
Hayes, Rutherford Birchard, 24, 212, 230
Henderson, Isaac, 48
Hennessy, John A., 76
Henriques, Madeleine, 101
The *Herald*, 65, 98
Hoadley, George, 24, 230
Hoffman, John T., 41, 80, 91, 169
Hone, Philip, 31, 45
Hone, Robert S., 46
Horse plague, 182
Howard, Joseph, Jr., 275
Howe & Hummel, 213
Hows, George W., 164
Hurlbert, William Henry, 199, 233, 255

Irving, James, 148
Irving, Washington, 56

Jennings, Louis John, 84, 100, 175, 201, 248
Joline, Adrian H., 149, 185, 271
Jones, George, 84, 103, 118, 126, 185, 257

Kelly, John, 220
Kelso, James J., 90

King, John A., 46
Knickerbocker Club, 45

Lawrence, Abraham R., 37, 169
Lewis, George, 253
Lincoln, Abraham, 26
London Herald, 246ff.
Lotos Club, 74, 164, 184, 238, 256ff., 275
Louis, Siro, 202
Low, Seth, 269
Lukomski, Romaine A., 160

McCabe, Hugh, 216
McClellan, George Brinton, 114ff.
McClosky, Archbishop, 91
McCullagh, John H., 194
MacGuiness, Peter J., 50
MacLean, George W., 59
Maginnis, Arthur Ambrose, 83
Manhattan Club, 46, 75, 171, 231, 257
Mansfield, Josie, 151
Marble, Manton, 152, 185
Marvin, Uriah, 6
Mason, James M., 26
Masterson, John H., 125
May, Caroline, 214
May, Frederick, 214
May, William, 214
Miller, Joaquin, 202
Montgomery, H. E., 35
Moore, George H., 23
Morgan, J. P., 46
Morgan, Mary, 17
Morris, George Pope, 29, 59
Mount, Richard, 59
Mozart Hall, 37ff.

Nast, Thomas, 56, 63ff., 73ff., 78ff., 96ff., 104ff., 115ff., 131ff., 150ff., 177, 186, 196, 219, 259
New England Society, 69
New York Press Club, 238, 257
New York Printing Company, 81

New York *Sun*, 64
New York *Times*, 58, 97ff., 103
Notman, John, 255, 260

Oakey, Abraham, 17
Oakey, Alicia d'Assignie, 17
Oakey, Elsie Lansing, 17
Oakey, Samuel, 18, 25
O'Brien, James, 82, 84, 169, 255, 275
O'Conor, Charles, 46, 110, 197
Ogden, J. de Peyster, 45
Oliver, Isaac J., 127
Orange Societies, 87ff.
Ottendorfer, Oswald, 277

Paine, Albert Bigelow, 116, 259
Palmer, Robert B., 130
Parlor Conventions, 37
Peckham, Wheeler, 158, 172, 175, 181, 191
People's Union, 37
Perry, Caroline Slidell, 47
Perry, Matthew Calbraith, 47, 56
Phillips, Morris, 194, 202, 209, 257
Pierrepont, Edwards, 245
Plummer, Mary, 68
Plunkitt, George Washington, 148
Post, Edwin A., 138
Price, Joseph H., 83
Pulitzer, Joseph, 168, 236

Randolph, Carol, 167
Rawlings, W. E., 248
Raymond, Henry Jarvis, 58
Red Flag, 44
Reed, Horatio, 160
Reick, William C., 46, 248
Reid, Whitelaw, 68, 175, 184, 194, 211, 238
Rice, James, 216
Robbins, S. Howland, 215
Roberts, Caroline D., 194
Roberts, Marshall O., 79

Robertson, Anthony Lispenard, 46
Robinson, Beverly, 45
Robinson, Lucius, 220
Root, Elihu, 152, 245
Rossa, Jeremiah O'Donovan, ,Bishop, 91
Rossire, Charles, 277
Rothschild family, 47
Russell, Charles, 253, 261
Russell, Henry, 59

St. Nicholas Society, 59
Sanford, Charles W., 25
Schell, Edward, 79
Schurz, Carl, 168
Schuyler, Philip, 138
Scott, Tom, 233
Scott, Winfield, 56
Searle, George M., 271, 275
Seward, Clarence A., 245
Seward, William H., 26, 32
Seymour, Horatio, 34, 41, 49, 56, 79
Shafer, Ira S., 158
Shaler, General, 92
Sheldon, Frederick, 255
Shepard, Elliot F., 245
Sickles, Daniel E., 275
Simpson, Edward, 22
Sistane, George K., 79
Slidell, John, 25ff., 47
Smith, Ballard, 272
Smith, James M., 158
Snodgrass, George V., 6
Social Register ('The List'), 5, 137
Spaulding, Henry F., 119
Stanhope, Aubrey, 248
Stanley, Henry M., 183
Stebbins, Henry G., 123, 151
Stephens, John Lloyd, 31
Stewart, A. T., 58, 233
Stokes, Edward S., 151
Storrs, Richard A., 123, 176
Story, George A., 275

Story, Joseph, 22, 25
Stoughton, E. W., 158, 168, 177, 190
Strong, George Templeton, 80, 112, 136
Stuart, William, 199
Sweeny, Peter B., 40ff., 60ff., 131, 222, 271, 275

Tammany Hall, 1, 39, 167
Taylor, Moses, 79
Tilden, Samuel J., 7, 31, 50, 80, 110, 123, 151, 171ff., 197, 212
Tilton, Theodore, 39, 168
Tooker, Commissioner, 227
Townsend, James B., 234
Townsend, John D., 219
Townsend, Reginald, 137
Tremain, Lyman, 158, 168, 175, 178, 181, 191
Trent Affair, 26
Tweed, Mary Amelia, 83
Tweed, William Marcy, 38, 60, 63, 80, 131, 133, 151, 171, 177, 200, 212, 219, 232
Tweed Charter, 60
Tweed Ring, 56, 108
Tyng, Stephen, 137, 218

Uhl, David, 14
Ullmann, Daniel, 6
Union Club, 26, 41, 45, 75, 137, 152, 158, 168, 214, 231
Union League Club, 45, 231

Van Buren, John, 56
Van Buren, Martin, 56
Vanderbilt, W. H., 202
Vanderpoel, Aaron H., 275
Vanderpoel, Aaron J., 22, 31, 152, 158, 179, 202, 211, 222, 245
Varian, General, 94

Walker, James J., 4

Walloch, Lester, 200
Ward, Artemus, 54
Waterbury, Nelson J., 37
Weed, Thurlow, 32
Werner, M. R., 61

Wheeler, Andrew C., 164
Wilde, Oscar, 53
Winter, William, 202
Wood, Fernando, 34, 37ff., 56
Wright, J. W., 166